COMPUTER
BOOK SERIES
FROM IDG

Quattro Pro for DOS For Dummies

Cheat Sheet

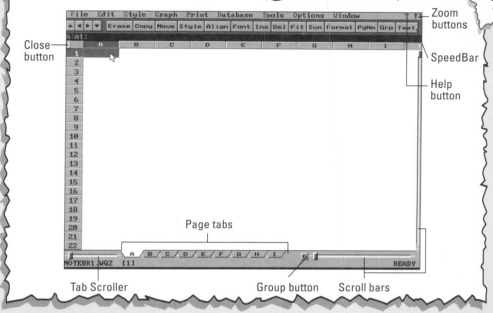

Close button

Zoom buttons

SpeedBar

Help button

Page tabs

Tab Scroller

Group button

Scroll bars

Shortcut Keys

Press This:	To Do This:
Ctrl-A	Align labels or values in a cell
Ctrl-C	Start the process of copying a cell or block
Ctrl-D	Put a date into a cell
Ctrl-E	Erase a cell or block
Ctrl-F	Change the numerical format of a cell or block
Ctrl-G	Create a quick graph
Ctrl-I	Insert one or more new rows or columns
Ctrl-M	Move a cell or block somewhere else
Ctrl-N	Repeat a forward search
Ctrl-P	Repeat a backward search
Ctrl-R	Move or resize a worksheet window
Ctrl-S	Save the worksheet you're working on
Ctrl-T	Arrange all worksheet windows like floor tiles
Ctrl-W	Adjust a column's width
Ctrl-X	Exit Quattro Pro
Alt-0	Activate a different worksheet in memory

Quattro Pro Mouse Tools

Tool	What It Does
SpeedBar	Activates commands, accesses dialog boxes, or changes modes when you click on the appropriate button
Scroll bars	Scrolls through the worksheet when you click or drag the scroll button
Page Tabs	Activates another worksheet page
Tab Scroller	Displays additional page tabs
Group Button	Turns Group mode on or off
Close Button	Closes a worksheet window
Zoom Buttons	Zooms or unzooms a worksheet window
? (Help)	Gets on-line help

. . . For Dummies: #1 Computer Book Series for Beginners

FOR DUMMIES™

COMPUTER BOOK SERIES FROM IDG

Quattro Pro for DOS For Dummies

Cheat Sheet

The EDIT Mode Speed Bar

WYSIWYG Mode	Text Mode	What It Does
▲ ◄ ► ▼	End ▲ ◄ ► ▼	Clicking on the up or down arrow moves the cell pointer to the top or bottom edge (or row) of a block of data (like pressing End, up arrow or End, down arrow); not really very useful when you're editing a cell.
		Clicking on the left or right arrow moves the insertion point one character to the left or right in the input line.
Name	NAM	Shows list of named blocks
Abs	ABS	Toggles cell reference between absolute and relative
Calc	CAL	Calculates the formula on the input line and turns it into a value
Macro	MAC	Displays menu-equivalent macro categories
@	@	Shows a list of @functions
+	+	Enters a plus sign
–	–	Enters a minus sign
N/A	BAR	Shows the other part of the SpeedBar in Text mode
*	*	Enters an asterisk (mulitplication sign)
/	/	Enters a slash (division sign)
(	(	Enters an opening parenthesis
,	,	Enters a comma
)	)	Enters a closing parenthesis

SpeedBars

Note: Using the SpeedBar requires a mouse.

The READY Mode SpeedBar

WYSIWYG Mode	Text Mode	What It Does
▲ ◄ ► ▼	End ▲ ◄ ► ▼	Moves the cell pointer from one edge of a block of data to another (just as if you press the End key followed by an arrow key)
Erase	ERS	Issues the **E**dit ⇨ **E**rase Block command
Copy	CPY	Issues the **E**dit ⇨ **C**opy command
Move	MOV	Issues the **E**dit ⇨ **M**ove command
Style	STY	Issues the **S**tyle ⇨ **U**se Style command
Align	ALN	Issues the **S**tyle ⇨ **A**lignment command
Font	FNT	Issues the **S**tyle ⇨ **F**ont command
Ins	INS	Issues the **E**dit ⇨ **I**nsert command
Del	DEL	Issues the **E**dit ⇨ **D**elete command
Fit	FIT	Issues the **S**tyle ⇨ **B**lock Size ⇨ **A**uto Width command
Sum	SUM	Inserts an @SUM formula
Format	FMT	Issues the **S**tyle ⇨ **N**umeric Format command
PgNm	PAG	Issues the **E**dit ⇨ **P**age ⇨ **N**ame command
Text	N/A	Changes to Text mode
Grp	GRP	Toggles in and out of Group mode
N/A	WYS	Changes to WYSIWYG mode
N/A	BAR	Displays more SpeedBar buttons

When you edit a cell, Quattro Pro displays [Enter] and [Esc] in the input line. You can click on these to simulate pressing Enter or Esc on the keyboard.

. . . For Dummies: #1 Computer Book Series for Beginners

QUATTRO PRO FOR DOS FOR DUMMIES™

by John Walkenbach

Foreword by Stephen Kahn
Senior Vice President
Desktop Software Division
Borland International

IDG BOOKS

IDG Books Worldwide, Inc.
An International Data Group Company

San Mateo, California ◆ Indianapolis, Indiana ◆ Boston, Massachusetts

Quattro Pro for DOS For Dummies

Published by
IDG Books Worldwide, Inc.
An International Data Group Company
155 Bovet Road, Suite 310
San Mateo, CA 94402

Library of Congress Catalog Card No.: 93-79844

ISBN: 1-56884-023-3

Printed in the United States of America

10 9 8 7 6 5 4 3 2 1

Distributed in the United States by IDG Books Worldwide, Inc.

Distributed in Canada by Macmillan of Canada, a Division of Canada Publishing Corporation; by Computer and Technical Books in Miami, Florida for South America and the Aaribbean; by Longman Singapore in Singapore, Malaysia, Thailand and Korea; by Toppan Co. Ltd in Japan; by Asia Computerworld in Hong Kong; by Woodslane Pty. Ltd. in Australia and New Zealand; and by Trahsworld Publishers Ltd in the U.K. and Europe.

For information on where to purchase IDG Books outside of the U.S., please call Christian Turner at 415-312-0633.

For information on translations and availability in other countries, contact Marc Jeffrey Mikulich, Foreign Rights Manager, at IDG Books Worldwide. Fax: 415-358-1260.

For sales inquiries and special prices for bulk quantities, write to the address above or call IDG Books Worldwide at 415-312-0650.

About the Author

John Walkenbach holds a Ph.D. in experimental psychology from the University of Montana and has worked as an instructor, programmer, consultant, and market research manager for a major savings and loan.

He is also a veteran PC whiz who has used virtually every PC spreadsheet that's ever seen the light of day — and several others that were left in the dark. He's a contributing editor for *PC World* and *InfoWorld,* and has published more than 250 articles and reviews in a variety of magazines and technical journals. In addition, he has authored or coauthored several other spreadsheet books for IDG.

When he's not writing about computers, he can probably be found in his MIDI studio entangled in wires and cables — or dodging his neighbors' complaints about the weird, synthetic noises emanating from his house.

About IDG Books Worldwide

Welcome to the world of IDG Books Worldwide.

IDG Books Worldwide, Inc., is a division of International Data Group, the world's largest publisher of computer-related information and the leading global provider of information services on information technology. IDG publishes over 194 computer publications in 62 countries. Forty million people read one or more IDG publications each month.

If you use personal computers, IDG Books is committed to publishing quality books that meet your needs. We rely on our extensive network of publications, including such leading periodicals as *Macworld*, *InfoWorld*, *PC World*, *Computerworld*, *Publish*, *Network World*, and *SunWorld*, to help us make informed and timely decisions in creating useful computer books that meet your needs.

Every IDG book strives to bring extra value and skill-building instruction to the reader. Our books are written by experts, with the backing of IDG periodicals, and with careful thought devoted to issues such as audience, interior design, use of icons, and illustrations. Our editorial staff is a careful mix of high-tech journalists and experienced book people. Our close contact with the makers of computer products helps ensure accuracy and thorough coverage. Our heavy use of personal computers at every step in production means we can deliver books in the most timely manner.

We are delivering books of high quality at competitive prices on topics customers want. At IDG, we believe in quality, and we have been delivering quality for over 25 years. You'll find no better book on a subject than an IDG book.

John Kilcullen
President and C.E.O.
IDG Books Worldwide, Inc.

IDG Books Worldwide, Inc. is a division of International Data Group. The officers are Patrick J. McGovern, Founder and Board Chairman; Walter Boyd, President. International Data Group's publications include: **ARGENTINA's** Computerworld Argentina, InfoWorld Argentina; **ASIA's** Computerworld Hong Kong, PC World Hong Kong, Computerworld Southeast Asia, PC World Singapore, Computerworld Malaysia, PC World Malaysia; **AUSTRALIA's** Computerworld Australia, Australian PC World, Australian Macworld, Network World, Reseller, IDG Sources; **AUSTRIA's** Computerwelt Oesterreich, PC Test; **BRAZIL's** Computerworld, Mundo IBM, Mundo Unix, PC World, Publish; **BULGARIA's** Computerworld Bulgaria, Ediworld, PC & Mac World Bulgaria; **CANADA's** Direct Access, Graduate Computerworld, InfoCanada, Network World Canada; **CHILE's** Computerworld, Informatica; **COLUMBIA's** Computerworld Columbia; **CZECH REPUBLIC's** Computerworld, Elektronika, PC World; **DENMARK's** CAD/CAM WORLD, Communications World, Computerworld Danmark, LOTUS World, Macintosh Produktkatalog, Macworld Danmark, PC World Danmark, PC World Produktguide, Windows World; **EQUADOR's** PC World; **EGYPT's** Computerworld (CW) Middle East, PC World Middle East; **FINLAND's** MikroPC, Tietoviikko, Tietoverkko; **FRANCE's** Distributique, GOLDEN MAC, InfoPC, Languages & Systems, Le Guide du Monde Informatique, Le Monde Informatique, Telecoms & Reseaux; **GERMANY's** Computerwoche, Computerwoche Focus, Computerwoche Extra, Computerwoche Karriere, Information Management, Macwelt, Netzwelt, PC Welt, PC Woche, Publish, Unit; **HUNGARY's** Alaplap, Computerworld SZT, PC World, ; **INDIA's** Computers & Communications; **ISRAEL's** Computerworld Israel, PC World Israel; **ITALY's** Computerworld Italia, Lotus Magazine, Macworld Italia, Networking Italia; **JAPAN's** Computerworld Japan, Macworld Japan, SunWorld Japan, Windows World; **KENYA's** East African Computer News; **KOREA's** Computerworld Korea, Macworld Korea, PC World Korea; **MEXICO's** Compu Edicion, Compu Manufactura, Computacion/Punto de Venta, Computerworld Mexico, MacWorld, Mundo Unix, PC World, Windows; **THE NETHERLAND'S** Computer! Totaal, LAN Magazine, MacWorld; **NEW ZEALAND's** Computer Listings, Computerworld New Zealand, New Zealand PC World; **NIGERIA's** PC World Africa; **NORWAY's** Computerworld Norge, C/World, Lotusworld Norge, Macworld Norge, Networld, PC World Ekspress, PC World Norge, PC World's Product Guide, Publish World, Student Data, Unix World, Windowsworld, IDG Direct Response; **PANAMA's** PC World; **PERU's** Computerworld Peru, PC World; **PEOPLES REPUBLIC OF CHINA's** China Computerworld, PC World China, Electronics International, China Network World; **IDG HIGH TECH BEIJING's** New Product World; **IDG SHENZHEN's** Computer News Digest; **PHILLIPPINES'** Computerworld, PC World; **POLAND's** Computerworld Poland, PC World/Komputer; **PORTUGAL's** Cerebro/PC World, Correio Informatico/Computerworld, MacIn; **ROMANIA's** PC World; **RUSSIA's** Computerworld-Moscow, Mir-PC, Sety; **SLOVENIA's** Monitor Magazine; **SOUTH AFRICA's** Computing S.A.; **SPAIN's** Amiga World, Computerworld Espana, Communicaciones World, Macworld Espana, NeXTWORLD, PC World Espana, Publish, Sunworld; **SWEDEN's** Attack, ComputerSweden, Corporate Computing, Lokala Natverk/LAN, Lotus World, MAC&PC, Macworld, Mikrodatorn, PC World, Publishing & Design (CAP), Datalngenjoren, Maxi Data, Windows World; **SWITZERLAND's** Computerworld Schweiz, Macworld Schweiz, PC & Workstation; **TAIWAN's** Computerworld Taiwan, Global Computer Express, PC World Taiwan; **THAILAND's** Thai Computerworld; **TURKEY's** Computerworld Monitor, Macworld Turkiye, PC World Turkiye; **UNITED KINGDOM's** Lotus Magazine, Macworld, Sunworld; **UNITED STATES'** AmigaWorld, Cable in the Classroom, CD Review, CIO, Computerworld, Desktop Video World, DOS Resource Guide, Electronic News, Federal Computer Week, Federal Integrator, GamePro, IDG Books, InfoWorld, InfoWorld Direct, Laser Event, Macworld, Multimedia World, Network World, NeXTWORLD, PC Games, PC Letter, PC World Publish, Sumeria, SunWorld, SWATPro, Video Event; **VENEZUELA's** Computerworld Venezuela, MicroComputerworld Venezuela; **VIETNAM's** PC World Vietnam

 The text in this book is printed on recycled paper.

Dedication

This one's for Lori...

Credits

Publisher
David Solomon

Acquisitions Editor
Janna Custer

Managing Editor
Mary Bednarek

Project Editor
Tracy L. Barr

Technical Reviewer
Dave Maguiness

Editorial Assistant
Patricia R. Reynolds

Proofreader
Charles A. Hutchinson

Production Manager
Beth J. Baker

Production Coordinator
Cindy L. Phipps

Indexer
Sherry Massey

Book Production
Hunt Graphics Inc.

Acknowledgments

Writing a book like this turned out to be more fun than work. There's a lot to be said for all the talented people behind the scenes who took the bytes I sent in and converted them to even better bytes, using technology and sheer talent. Thanks to all the folks at IDG Books for letting me express myself in ways that were never quite appropriate for other books. Special thanks to Janna Custer, Acquisition Editor, for choosing me to write this one over a great dinner at Jakes in Del Mar. Special thanks to my project editor, Tracy Barr. Besides being a great editor, she's also good at making my PG-rated limericks suitable for the entire family. I'm also indebted to Dave Maguiness for a thorough technical review. And I can't forget about Borland — one great software house that continues to pump out super products. Finally, I gratefully acknowledge the dozens of "dummies" I've worked with over the years (who shall remain nameless). They taught me a lot.

John Walkenbach
La Jolla, California

(The publisher would like to give special thanks to Patrick J. McGovern, without whom this book would not have been possible.)

Say What You Think!

Listen up, all you readers of IDG's international bestsellers: the one — the only — absolutely world famous ...*For Dummies* books! It's time for you to take advantage of a new, direct pipeline to the authors and editors of IDG Books Worldwide. In between putting the finishing touches on the next round of ...*For Dummies* books, the authors and editors of IDG Books Worldwide like to sit around and mull over what their readers have to say. And we know that you readers always say what you think. So here's your chance. We'd really like your input for future printings and editions of this book — and ideas for future ...*For Dummies* titles as well. Tell us what you liked (and didn't like) about this book. How about the chapters you found most useful — or most funny? And since we know you're not a bit shy, what about the chapters you think can be improved?

Just to show you how much we appreciate your input, we'll add you to our Dummies Database/Fan Club and keep you up to date on the latest ...*For Dummies* books, news, cartoons, calendars, and more! Please send your name, address, and phone number, as well as your comments, questions, and suggestions, to our very own ...For Dummies coordinator at the following address:

...For Dummies Coordinator
IDG Books Worldwide
3250 North Post Road, Suite 140
Indianapolis, IN 46226

(Yes, Virginia, there really is a ...*For Dummies* coordinator. We are not making this up.)

Please mention the name of this book in your comments.

Thanks for your input!

IDG BOOKS

Contents at a Glance

Cartoons at a Glance

By Rich Tennant

page 171

page 182

page 11

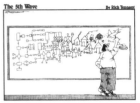

page 279

page 305

page 225

page 132

page 51

page 47

page xxiv

Table of Contents

· ·

Foreword

First a warning: If you lack a sense of humor, you've chosen the wrong book.

Learning to use a spreadsheet has never been more fun, thanks to *Quattro Pro for DOSFor Dummies*. It's a great way to learn what you need to know and not be bothered with lots of technical details that those 700-page books are famous for. It provides all the essential information necessary to do meaningful work and builds a foundation for learning even more if you're so inclined.

IDG Books couldn't have picked a more appropriate author for this book. I've known John Walkenbach for several years. We've had some lively discussions over some delicious dinners while drinking some outstanding red wines. The conversation always seems to turn to spreadsheets. And, like the wine, it's far more colorful than you might imagine (believe it or not, spreadsheet talk can get quite hilarious). John certainly knows spreadsheets, and this book demonstrates that he also knows what's important to beginning users. Better yet, he has a knack for keeping you entertained during the learning process.

We at Borland are proud of Quattro Pro 5.0, and we always welcome third-party enhancements to our products. I think *Quattro Pro for DOS For Dummies* is one of the best spreadsheet enhancements a beginning user can have.

Enjoy.

> Stephen Kahn
> Senior Vice President, Desktop Software Division
> Borland International
> Scotts Valley, California

"KEVIN HERE HEADS UP OUR SOFTWARE DEVELOPMENT TEAM. RIGHT NOW HE'S WORKING ON A SPREADSHEET PROGRAM THAT'S SORT OF A COMBINATION QUATTRO PRO-DONKEY KONG."

Introduction
If Ya Really Gotta Use a Spreadsheet...

I know of a fellow, Magruder,
Who wanted to use a computer.
He picked up this book
And gave it a look
And discovered a fun, cheap tutor.

Here's the deal: You need to learn Quattro Pro, but you don't want to get bogged down with every minute detail. In other words, you're a bottom-line kind of person who likes to cut to the quick. If that's true, you've come to the right place.

Welcome to *Quattro Pro for DOS For Dummies* — your admittedly incomplete guide to one of the most popular spreadsheet programs available. The adjective "incomplete" in the preceding sentence is meant to be a feature. After all, you don't really want to know *everything* about Quattro Pro, now do you? Please be warned that owning this book doesn't necessarily make you a dummy (that's a reputation you must earn on your own).

I'm glad you bought this book. If you're standing in a bookstore trying to make up your mind about it, take my word for it: You'll like it. Here's a sneak preview of what you'll find here:

- ✔ Practical information about Quattro Pro that will get you up to speed quickly

- ✔ Informative examples that demonstrate things you may want to do (or things that someone *else* wants you to do)

- ✔ Very few extraneous details about things that you really don't care about anyway

- ✔ Lively, entertaining, and easy-to-read text, with subtle humor sprinkled liberally throughout its pages (I just love describing my own writing.)

- ✔ Lots of things you can say and do to make you seem smarter than you really are

- ✔ Side-splitting cartoons by Rich Tennant

> ✔ An original limerick at the beginning of every chapter (I did this so I can tell people that my poetry has been published by a major publishing house.)

This is not an advanced reference book. So if the office computer geek needs to look up all the gory details on macro command arguments, you won't find *this* book missing from your desk.

Why'd Ya Do It, Walkenbach?

Why does anybody write a book? Obviously, I hoped millions of people would buy it so that I could retire and live my remaining years in seclusion as a bee keeper. But that wasn't my primary reason (sure, sure...).

Actually, I spend a lot of time helping others solve computer problems (especially spreadsheet problems). Somewhere along the line, I acquired a knack for explaining things in simple terms. I also discovered that there's an important difference between giving someone the solution to his problem and explaining things sufficiently so he doesn't call me the next time a slightly different problem occurs. That's the approach I take in this book. And besides, I like to write about spreadsheets. So there, I *didn't* do it just for the money.

Follow the Yellow Brick Road

My intention is not that you read this book from cover to cover. Frankly, the plot stinks, and the character development leaves much to be desired. If you're about to be exiled to a desert island and you can bring only one book along, I wouldn't feel bad if you chose John Fowles' *The Magus* over *Quattro Pro for DOS For Dummies*.

Although the chapters *do* move along in a quasi-logical progression, they also pretty much stand on their own. Once you learn the basics, you can safely put the book aside until you need to move on to the next challenge. When that time comes, follow these simple steps:

1. Refer to the table of contents for a general topic. If you're in a real hurry, go straight for the index. If your problem is "How do I get rid of the decimal points in this mess?" look under Decimal points, not Mess.

2. Turn to the page that discusses the topic.

3. Read the text that introduces the topic.

4. If you need more information, take a look at any examples provided and work your way through them.

5. If you still can't figure it out, call me (hey, just kidding!).

Unless the task you're trying to do is fairly sophisticated, this book will almost certainly shed some light on it. Even if an example doesn't seem anything like what you're trying to do, you may find that working through it step-by-step provides insights that can help you figure out the task on your own.

The Game Plan

Topics covered in this book usually start with introductory comments and often include one or more examples and step-by-step instructions. Once you locate a chapter that's of interest, you can usually skim through the text to see if the material is going to be helpful.

If you're just starting out with Quattro Pro, I recommend reading some of the initial chapters in their entirety — or at least until the subject matter gets more complex than you need. If you're trying to learn how to do something new with Quattro Pro, you might also benefit from some straight-through reading (as opposed to the skim-through method). For example, if you've never printed anything before, it would be helpful to read Chapter 10 first. Doing so will give you enough background so that you'll be fairly confident when you issue the command to print your work.

Some topics have additional information for those overachievers who want to know even more about the task at hand. In such cases, this superfluous techni-cal dribble is flagged with an icon in the margin. If you don't fall into this overachiever category, make a mental note: *See the Technical Stuff icon, skip the section.*

As long as you have your mental notepad out, here's another one for you: *See the Warning icon, read the section.* You should pay particular attention to these Warning icons. They signal something that can mess you up or cause problems if you're not careful. More about icons later on.

Which of These Things Is Not Like the Other?

Because companies have a hard time selling software that doesn't keep up with the times, software manufacturers adapt to changing needs by releasing new versions of their programs. Quattro Pro is now in Version 5. (If you already have Version 5, skip this section and go directly to the Blatant Plug.)

Note: This book does not cover Quattro Pro for Windows 5. Although it has a similar name, the Windows version of Quattro Pro is a completely different animal. If you have the Windows version of Quattro Pro, this book will only cause you to be more confused than you already are.

This book covers both Version 4 and Version 5 of Quattro Pro for DOS. If you're using Version 4, you may find discussions about a few features that aren't available in your version (specifically, the feature that lets you work with different notebook pages). Features that I talk about that are found *only* in Version 5 are marked with a Version 5 icon. Also, the screen shots used in this book were taken from Version 5, so Version 4 users can simply ignore the notebook tabs at the bottom of the screen shots.

By the way, you might want to consider upgrading to Version 5 (especially if the company you work for is paying for it). Version 5 can do some neat things that aren't possible with prior versions. Chapter 1 talks a bit about the various versions of Quattro Pro.

A Blatant Plug

Do you like the concept behind *Quattro Pro for DOS For Dummies*? If so, you'll be glad to know that IDG Books has a whole slew of books in this vein. Their Dummies series includes titles such as *DOS For Dummies*, *PCs For Dummies*, *WordPerfect For Dummies*, *Windows For Dummies*, and lots more. If you're in a bookstore and start seeing yellow, chances are you've found the IDG Books floor display. The books are great for people who want to learn the basics (and you don't have to prove you're a dummy to buy them).

How This Book Is Organized

Personally, I think that my editors and I are the only ones who really care how this book is organized. But if you're among the dozen or so human beings who actually read sections like this and you're too lazy to turn back to the Contents at a Glance section (which is right before the overly detailed Table of Contents), here's a brief synopsis of what you're in for.

Part I: You Gotta Start Somewhere

The three chapters in this section are for people who don't have a clue as to what a spreadsheet — much less Quattro Pro — is all about. You'll learn lots of interesting things that will let you hold your own should you ever find yourself at a cocktail party populated with spreadsheet junkies. You'll also learn how to start the program and (importantly) how to quit it when you've had enough. If you would like to get some quick and dirty spreadsheet experience, check out Chapter 3. I'll walk you through a real-life Quattro Pro session, and you can pretend I'm standing over your shoulder telling you what to do.

Part II: Basic Stuff That You Must Know

Like it or not, you can't just jump into Quattro Pro and expect to start doing meaningful things immediately. There is some basic background information that you need to have. Part II imparts this knowledge to you in the form of eight (usually) short chapters. You'll learn about entering data, using menus, saving files, creating formulas, using built-in functions, printing, and lots of other things that you may or may not be interested in (but you should know about). You'll also get the scoop on Quattro Pro's cool 3-D notebook feature. You don't have to read everything in these chapters, and you can always refer to them when the need arises.

Part III: Things to Impress the Easily Impressed

The four chapters in this section can be described as "gee whiz" stuff (with a bit of "jeepers" stuff thrown in for good measure). You can probably get by for quite a while by pretending these topics don't even exist. But sooner or later, you might need to expand your horizons. If so, you'll learn how to make your worksheets look great (or at least reasonably good), how to create and customize graphs, and even how to work with files that come from other software (a great skill that will make you very popular in the office). Also included in this section are all kinds of shortcuts that can save you valuable minutes each day.

Part IV: Faking It

Aptly named, this is the part where I tell you just enough about some of the more advanced topics that let you get by (and make you somewhat dangerous). If you're so moved, you can learn about databases, steal some nifty formulas that I developed, and even learn how to use and create (horrors!) macros. This section wraps up with a chapter that answers the musical question, "How do I?"

Part V: Mini-Chapters with Maxi-Info

For reasons that are mainly historical, most of the books in the ... *For Dummies* series include short chapters with lists of 10 or so things in each. Since I'm a sucker for tradition, you'll find a few such chapters all collected together in Part V.

Appendixes

And what's a computer book without appendixes? Here you'll find three of them: one on installing Quattro Pro, one that covers all of the built-in @functions (not the most exciting reading experience you'll ever have), and a special bonus appendix that can help you convince people that you know what you're talking about when you really don't.

Are You Like Pat? (Or, What I Assume About You)

People who write books usually have a target reader in mind. In the case of this book, my target reader is a person named Pat. If you're anything like Pat, you and this book will get along just fine. Here's a description of Pat:

- Pat has access to a PC at work but doesn't show a whole lot of interest in it.
- Pat's computer has a hard drive, a printer, and some version of the DOS operating system.

✔ Pat has only a little experience with computers (word processing mostly) and has even copied a few files from the hard drive to a floppy.

✔ Someone just installed Quattro Pro Version 5 on Pat's computer — and Pat has never used a spreadsheet before.

✔ Pat needs to get some work done, yet doesn't want to waste time plodding through thick manuals or overly technical books.

Conventional Wisdom

As you work your way through the book, you may notice that different type-faces are used. This book uses different typefaces for two purposes: to show off the typographic skills of the production house and to make it easy for you, the reader, to identify various parts of the book.

Often I instruct you to enter text into a cell. Text that you must type into a cell sometimes appears on a line by itself. This text uses a distinctive typeface and is screened like this:

```
@SUM(income)-@SUM(expenses)
```

You type exactly what you see. Most of the time, you also need to press Enter to signal when you're done.

If I want you to enter text that's short, I simply include the text to be typed within the paragraph. This text appears in bold type — "Enter **256** into cell A1," for example. In this case, you just type the three numbers and press Enter.

Occasionally, Quattro Pro displays messages. When I talk about such messages, I'll use a distinctive typeface, like this: READY.

Sometimes, you'll be asked to press a key combination — which means to hold down one key while you press another. For example, Alt-Z means that you should hold down the Alt key and then press Z.

Of Mice and Keyboards

You can use Quattro Pro with or without a mouse. To select the command to save a file, for example, you can press **/FS** (which stands for the **F**ile⇨**S**ave command), or you can use the mouse to click on the **F**ile menu and then click on the **S**ave command.

When I ask you to perform specific tasks, I won't waste time by giving **directions** for both keyboarders and mouseketeers. Rather than say "If you're using the keyboard, press **/FS** to save your file. If you're using the mouse, click on **File** and then click on **Save**," I say, "Save your file by issuing the **File⇨Save** command." A lot simpler, no?

I Think Icon, I Think Icon

The left margins of this book are packed with *icons* — small pictures that draw your attention to various features or help you decide whether the topic is worth reading. Following are the icons you encounter in this book:

This icon signals material that no one in his right mind should care about. One or two of you, however, might get real excited about this information.

Don't skip these. These icons tell you about a shortcut that can save you lots of time and make you a hit at the next party.

This icon tells you when you need to store something away in the deep recesses of your brain for later use.

When you see a Warning icon, read the text. Otherwise, **you may** lose your data, short circuit your computer, cause a nuclear holocaust, or worse.

This icon alerts you to features that are found only in Quattro Pro 5. (If you're using Version 4, this information doesn't apply to you.)

Now What?

You're now ready to move on to something a bit more meaty. (I don't know about you, but I'm ready for a cold one.)

If you've never used a spreadsheet before, consider reading Chapters 1 through 3 before you do anything else. Chapter 1 tells you what a spreadsheet is and exactly what Quattro Pro can do. Chapter 2 tells you how to start and stop Quattro Pro, and Chapter 3 gives you some on-the-job experience by walking you through a typical spreadsheet session.

But it's a free country, so we won't send the Book Police after you if you choose to thumb through the book randomly and read whatever strikes your fancy. By the way, the cartoons and limericks are the best parts.

If you have a particular task in mind — such as, "How do I sort all of these numbers?" — go to the index. Go directly to the index. Do not pass Go. Do not collect $200.

Good luck, and have fun.

Part I:

You Gotta Start Somewhere

The 5th Wave — By Rich Tennant

THE SYSTEM CAME BUNDLED WITH A GRAPHICS BOARD, A SPREADSHEET, AND THE DEVELOPER'S OUT OF WORK NEPHEW.

In This Part...

This part has only three chapters. If you've never used a spreadsheet before or need a refresher course, you don't want to miss these chapters. Chapter 1 gives you some essential — and some not so essential, but very interesting — background information. Chapter 2 tells you how to start and stop Quattro Pro. In Chapter 3, you can get some hands-on experience with Quattro Pro. Work your way through this chapter, and you can honestly say, "Yeah, I've used Quattro Pro."

Chapter 1
Quattro Pro: The Good, the Bad, and the Ugly

A musician from France, I did learn,
Took an unusual, incredible turn.
He did a corporate gig
And hit it quite big,
And now he's got money to burn.

In This Chapter

▶ A description of what Quattro Pro is, where it came from, and what you've gotten yourself into

▶ Things that you can and cannot do with this program

▶ How to tell what version of Quattro Pro you have and whether it matters

Since it doesn't have any hands-on computer stuff, this is the one chapter of the book that you might want to curl up in bed with on a cold winter's night with a fire blazing in the fireplace — unless, of course, you have better things to do in bed (like sleep).

Here's the incentive for making it through these pages: You'll have more background information about Quattro Pro and Borland International than 99.9 percent of the people on this planet (true fact). That, and about two bucks, will get you a cup of cappuccino at Starbucks. Actually, there's a slight chance that you may find this stuff interesting. But you'll definitely have a semi-solid foundation for what comes later in the book. So read it.

Okay, I'll Bite: What Is Quattro Pro?

Glad you asked. Quattro Pro is an electronic spreadsheet. Think of a large sheet of accountant's paper that has grid lines drawn on it. Then try to envision an electronic version of this page that you can see on your computer monitor. The electronic version is huge — so big, in fact, that you can see only a tiny portion at one time on your screen. You can use the keyboard or mouse to move around this worksheet so you can see the other parts of the spreadsheet.

In place of the grid lines, the electronic spreadsheet — that is, Quattro Pro — has rows and columns. The place where each row and column intersects is called a *cell*. You enter numbers and words into the cells. You can print the information in the cells if you want others to see it. It's also very easy to copy and move cells around. You can save the results of your efforts in a file on your hard disk and work on it later. So far so good, but any decent word processing software can do this sort of thing.

The real fun starts when you learn how to enter formulas into cells. Formulas bring a spreadsheet to life since they perform calculations on other cells. Suppose that you want to display the average of the numbers in a column, for example. You might enter into a cell a formula that says, in effect, "Add up all the numbers in the first column, and then divide by the number of values in the column." This formula displays in its cell the average of the numbers.

Best of all is that formulas recalculate the results if you change the numbers in any of the cells that the formulas use. You may not appreciate this now, but you will later on (trust me).

But wait, there's more (he says in a Ginsu knife pitch man's voice). Quattro Pro also lets you apply slick formatting to the cells, and you can make graphs that look like they came from a professional artist.

Why the weird name?

Many software products have names that describe what they do. WordPerfect makes perfect words, and Harvard Graphics creates graphics for Ivy League professors. Other products have names that were assigned for no apparent reason — for example, Quark Express. And some products have misleading names. XTree, for example, is not a program that lumberjacks use to determine which trees need to be chopped down (it's actually a program that helps you manage the files on your disks).

To understand where the name Quattro came from, you have to know that Quattro was originally developed to compete with Lotus 1-2-3 — which has always been the biggest selling spreadsheet program (the sheet to beat). My guess is that someone at Borland was trying to come up with a name for this new product and thought, "Let's see now, what comes after 1-2-3?" As fate would have it, this person happened to be listening to "Woolly Bully," the classic tune by Sam the Sham and the Pharaohs. If you're as old as I am, you know the rest of the story.

How big is a worksheet?

Imagine, for a minute, that you entered a number into every cell in a Quattro Pro worksheet. With Version 5, you're talking 256 pages, each with 256 columns and 8,192 rows — which works out to be 536,870,912 cells. (Filling every cell is actually impossible because your computer doesn't have nearly enough memory to hold all of this information. But bear with me on this, okay?)

If you enter the numbers manually into each cell, the task takes about 34 years (figuring a relatively rapid two seconds per cell, with no coffee breaks or time out for sleep). Hopefully, you save your work often while entering this amount of data since it would be a shame to have to repeat five or six years of data entry due to a power failure.

You would hate to lose all this work, so you make a backup of this 5.9 gigabyte file. Before you start the backup procedure, however, you make sure that you have about 4,765 blank floppy disks on hand. (I suggest you use high-density floppies.)

You want a hard copy of the data to give to your boss. Using the default column width and row height, Quattro Pro can print 55 rows and 8 columns (or 440 cells) on a sheet of 8½ by 11-inch paper. Printing the entire notebook requires 1.22 million pages of paper. If you use cheap photocopier paper, your printout is a stack of pages about 407 feet tall—roughly the height of a four story building. If you splurge for better quality paper, your printout is about as tall as the St. Louis Gateway Arch.

Using a standard four-page-per-minute laser printer, printing the entire spreadsheet takes about 530 days (not counting time you spend changing paper and replacing toner cartridges). If you have a faster laser printer, you can easily print the entire job in less than a year.

If this worksheet has formulas in it, you have to take recalculation time into account. I have no way of estimating how long it would take to recalculate the formulas in such a worksheet, but it would probably be a good time to take that round-the-world cruise after pressing F9.

Actually, *quatro* is the Spanish word for *four*. Since 4 comes after 1, 2, and 3, it's a somewhat apropos name for a product that they hoped to be the successor to 1-2-3. But I have no idea why they spelled it wrong. By the way, wouldn't it be cool if *Pro* were the Spanish word for five?

Yes, but does it taste good?

There are several spreadsheet programs on the market, so you may be curious as to how Quattro Pro stacks up against the competition. Quattro Pro is most often compared to Lotus 1-2-3. Most people who know about such things think Quattro Pro is as good (or even better) than 1-2-3 in just about every area. For example, Quattro Pro makes it much easier to make your worksheet look good, its menus are more logical, and you can work with more than one worksheet at time. So you can rest assured that someone made a good purchase decision, and you're using an excellent product.

A Rags to Riches Story

If you're wondering about the relevance of the limerick that opens this chapter, it's referring to Borland's CEO, Philippe Kahn. Mr. Kahn, formerly a teacher in France, is one of the computer industry's most interesting success stories. Besides having a great sense for business, he's an accomplished jazz musician, with several CDs to his credit (I own them all). He started Borland International about a decade ago with a single product: an amazingly fast and inexpensive programming language called Turbo Pascal (I bought it and will admit that it was the best 30 bucks I ever spent). The success of Turbo Pascal paved the way for dozens more software products in all of the major categories. The company grew rapidly and now ranks among the top software companies in the world. Let that be an inspirational lesson to us all.

What Can This Puppy Do?

People use Quattro Pro for lots of things — for business, educational, scientific, personal, illegal purposes, and who knows what else. The following is a quick rundown of its primary uses

Crunch numbers (Beg)

Spreadsheet programs are made primarily for calculating numbers. If you use Quattro Pro to create a budget (probably the most common task people use spreadsheets for), you enter into cells your budget category names and values for each month. Then you include some formulas to add up each month's total and the annual total for each category. (And, if necessary, you fiddle around with the numbers until the formulas come up with the results your boss wants to see.) Figure 1-1 shows an example of an operating budget. It's all pretty easy after you get the hang of it.

Here are a just a few examples of the types of worksheets you can develop in Quattro Pro:

- **Budgets.** These include simple household budgets, corporate department budgets, budgets for a complete company, or even a budget for an entire country.

- **Financial projections.** Figure out how much money you're going to make or lose this year, using formulas that rely on various assumptions.

✔ **Sales tracking.** Keep track of who's selling the most (and how much commission they get) and who's falling down on the job (and when they should get their pink slips).

✔ **Loan amortizations.** How much of that mortgage payment goes to interest (a lot), and how much to principal (not much)? A spreadsheet can tell you for every month of the loan's term.

✔ **Scientific things.** Quattro Pro has several very specialized built-in functions that only white-coated laboratory inhabitants understand.

✔ **Statistical stuff.** Again, there are lots of built-in functions for people who think in terms of standard deviations.

These examples just scratch the surface. If you have a problem that involves numbers, chances are Quattro Pro is a good tool to use — especially if you can't find a Phillips head screwdriver.

Make impressive graphs (Attack)

Quattro Pro can take the numbers you put in a worksheet and transform them into a magnificent graph in just about any style you can imagine. And here's the best part: You can waste hours of your company's time playing around with the

| File | Edit | Style | Graph | Print | Database | Tools | Options | Window | | ? ↑↓ |

| ▲ ◄ ► ▼ | Erase | Copy | Move | Style | Align | Font | Ins | Del | Fit | Sum | Format | PgNm | Grp | Text |

A:E13: (,0) U [W9] +E7-@SUM(E10..E12)

	A	B	C	D	E	F	G	H
1					1994 Operating Budget			
2								
3			Jan	Feb	Mar	Apr	May	Jun	Jul
4	INCOME							
5	Sales	352,348	361,157	343,099	291,634	262,471	196,853	295,279
6	Returns	(1,787)	(1,832)	(1,740)	(1,784)	(1,828)	(1,874)	(1,921)
7	NET SALES	350,561	359,325	341,359	289,850	260,642	194,979	293,359
8								
9	COST OF GOODS SOLD							
10	Materials	85,577	87,716	83,331	70,831	63,748	47,811	49,006
11	Merchandise	11,915	12,213	11,602	9,862	8,876	9,098	9,325
12	Commissions	34,481	35,343	36,227	30,793	27,713	28,406	29,116
13	GROSS PROFIT	218,588	224,053	210,199	178,365	160,305	109,664	205,911
14								
15	EXPENSES							
16	Wages	56,964	58,388	55,469	47,148	42,434	31,825	47,738
17	Office	2,142	2,196	2,250	2,307	2,364	2,423	2,484
18	Telephone	1,456	1,492	1,530	1,568	1,607	1,647	1,689
19	Travel	2,934	3,007	3,083	3,160	3,239	3,320	3,403
20	Maintenance	3,425	3,511	3,598	3,688	3,781	3,875	3,972
21	Gas	345	354	362	372	381	390	400
	Automobile	5,142	5,271	5,402	5,537	5,676	5,818	5,963

A / B / C / D / E / F / G / H / I / G

BUDGET94.WQ2 [3] READY

Figure 1-1: Quattro Pro hard at work crunching numbers.

graphs to make them look just right. Even if your numbers aren't worth a darn, you can still impress your boss with the quality of the graph. And that's what life is all about, right?

Figure 1-2 shows a modest example of a Quattro Pro graph. (I made a vow to avoid using trite phrases such as "a picture is worth a thousand words," so it's up to *you* to figure out how many words a picture is worth.)

Manage your lists (Heel)

Quattro Pro has ready-made rows and columns. Because you can make the columns as wide as you want, Quattro Pro is a natural choice for keeping track of items in lists (even better than a mere word processor). Following are a few lists that you may want to store in a Quattro Pro worksheet:

✓ Things to do today

✓ Things to avoid doing today

✓ Questions to ask the office computer geek

✓ Any of David Letterman's top-ten lists

✓ A list of the logical flaws in the *Gilligan's Island* plots (**Tip:** Use a separate worksheet for each episode — otherwise, you'll quickly run out of room.)

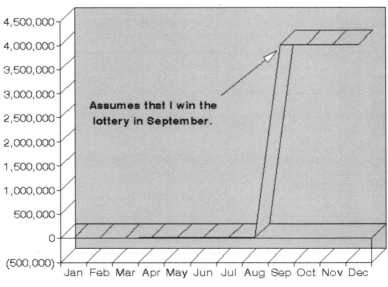

Figure 1-2: Quattro Pro lets you transform dull numbers into more interesting graphs.

Lists (such as the preceding) can include only words, or they can include a combination of words and numbers. If you use numbers in your lists, you can create formulas that perform calculations on the numbers. Here are some list ideas that use numbers:

- Bills you need to pay this month
- Bills you can get by without paying
- Itemized costs for fixing your wrecked car
- The amount of time the person in the next cubicle spends goofing off each day

Figure 1-3 shows a simple list that uses three columns (the third column has formulas that compute a running total of the values in the second column). You'll learn all about formulas in later chapters.

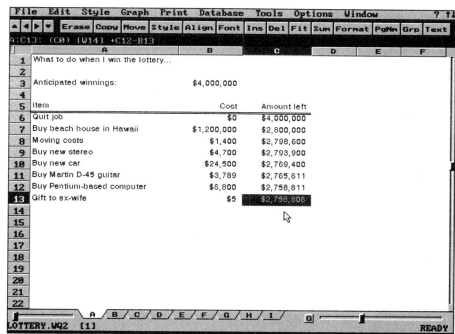

Figure 1-3: Quattro Pro is great for keeping track of things in lists.

Manage databases (Play dead)

If the term *database* conjures up images of dull, obsessively tidy, compulsive people whose socks always match the color of their pocket protector, you're right on track. Actually, a database is nothing more than an *organized* list. If you have a lot of friends, you might use a database to keep track of them, storing their names, addresses, phone numbers, and amount of money they owe you.

Truth is, Quattro Pro is pretty good at helping you work with this type of database. You can sort the data, search for something in particular, display items that meet certain criteria, and so on.

Access other data (Fetch)

If you have to deal with a humongous database — such as your corporate accounting system that lives on a different computer—you probably won't have enough memory in your computer to be able to load it all into Quattro Pro. Fortunately (or perhaps unfortunately), you can still access such "external" databases from Quattro Pro. If you learn how to work with external databases in Quattro Pro, you may not even have to buy a real database program.

Automate with macros (Sit)

For hard-core spreadsheet junkies, Quattro Pro provides a feature known as macros. A *macro* consists of instructions that tell Quattro Pro what to do — kind of like a computer program. If you want to take the time to learn, you can write macros for Quattro Pro, although the average user has no need for this sort of thing. You might, however, need to *execute* a macro that someone else wrote. Those with inquiring minds will learn how to execute macros (and even create simple ones) by going no further than this book.

Manage your files (Stay)

Quattro Pro includes a fairly proficient file manager that lets you do things with the files on your hard drive and floppy disks. You can copy files, erase files, rename files, and do many other file-related chores in the comfort and privacy of Quattro Pro.

Who knows what else? (Roll over)

The neat thing about spreadsheets (including Quattro Pro) is that they are so versatile. Even after using these things for more than a decade, people are still showing me new uses for spreadsheets that I had never dreamed of. Once you learn the basics, don't be surprised if you come up with a brand new use for Quattro Pro. (Let me know if you do, so I can put it in my next book.)

Note: Try not to be overwhelmed by the potential of Quattro Pro. Sure, it's a complex product, and people do some amazing things with it. But the vast majority of users (including yourself, I would bet) can get by just fine by using only a small fraction of its features. As you'll see, you can do quite a bit with this small fraction of features.

What Quattro Pro Can't Do

Quattro Pro is a great program, but it can't do everything. While it can deal with small amounts of text, it's no substitute for a real word processor. And if your database needs are more than moderate, you'll be better off with a dedicated database program. And, of course, Quattro Pro doesn't offer much in the way of entertainment. In other words, learning Quattro Pro is no reason to close your mind to other types of software (especially all of the cool games available).

Excursions into Versions

Software companies continually come up with new versions of their products because computer users are a demanding bunch who always gripe that their favorite software doesn't do enough. Software companies also release new versions so that they can correct bugs in the previous version and charge their loyal customers for upgrades at the same time.

The latest version of Quattro Pro is Quattro Pro 5. To find out which version you have, try to find the box the program came in and read the version number off the box. If you trashed the box, try to find the original disks and read the version number off one of the disks. If you lost the original diskettes or acquired the product through illegal means (which I do not condone), you can tell what version you have by typing **@VERSION** into any cell in any Quattro Pro worksheet. The version number then appears in that cell.

So you can get an idea of where this product came from, I've pulled together a quick rundown of the differences between versions of Quattro and Quattro Pro.

✔ **Quattro Version 1.0:** This was the original Borland spreadsheet. First released in 1987, Borland spreadsheets have come a long way since this one.

✔ **Quattro Pro Version 1.0:** This version directly followed the original Quattro and was released in 1989. But because it was so much better, they decided this version was worthy of a new name that included the word *Pro*.

- ✓ **Quattro Pro Version 2.0:** This version appeared in 1990 and had lots more features.

- ✓ **Quattro Pro Version 3.0:** Appearing a mere six months after Version 2.0, this edition featured a slick what-you-see-is-what-you-get (WYSIWYG) graphical user interface (GUI).

- ✓ **Quattro Pro Version 4.0:** This 1992 version offered still more features: SpeedBars, better graphs, auditing, and other nifty things.

- ✓ **Quattro Pro Version 5.0:** Borland released this version — the latest and greatest — in 1993. This version literally adds a new dimension by letting you work with a 3-D stack of 256 worksheets in a single file. That's about all that's new, but it's well worth upgrading.

- ✓ **Quattro Pro for Windows Version 1.0:** This version requires Microsoft Windows (and a pretty high-powered computer). It also has a 3-D notebook orientation.

- ✓ **Quattro Pro for Windows Version 2.0:** This upgrade to the original Windows version adds lots more analytical power and dozens of ease-of-use features.

Chapter 2
Starting, Stopping, and Throwing in the Towel

There once was a kid named Bart
Who bought his machine at K-Mart.
He poured through the docs
And asked PC jocks
"Just how in the heck do I start?"

In This Chapter

▶ How to start Quattro Pro

▶ How to quit Quattro Pro (the right way and the wrong way)

▶ What to do if you get completely confused

Before you can use Quattro Pro — or any software for that matter — you must install it on your computer. If you're lucky, Quattro Pro is already installed on the computer you are using, and you can proceed with this chapter. If Quattro Pro isn't installed on your computer, see Appendix A for installation instructions before you proceed.

Quattro Pro must be installed before you can use it. You can't just run it from the floppy disks it comes on.

On Your Mark, Get Set, GO!

Once you have Quattro Pro installed, you need to *run it* (or start it) in order to do anything with it; otherwise, the program just eats up space on your hard disk and you (or your company) wasted several hundred dollars. You can start Quattro Pro in a number of ways, which I explain in the following sections.

Starting from a menu

This is the best way to start Quattro Pro. If someone else installed Quattro Pro on your computer, he or she may have placed it on some type of menu system that appears whenever you turn on your system.

There are lots of these menu systems available, so I won't even begin to describe what yours might look like. In most cases, however, the menu displays a list of programs installed on your computer. Simply choose Quattro Pro from the list, and you're off to the races. If you installed Quattro Pro yourself, *you* have to add it to the menu system. Consult the manual that came with your menu software for instructions.

Starting from DOS

If your computer starts up with a fairly blank screen, with only the DOS prompt showing, you can start Quattro Pro directly. Just type **Q** (upper- or lowercase) and press Enter. Figure 2-1 shows what this might look like.

If it doesn't work

If you type **Q** at the DOS prompt and you get the message `Bad command or file name`, this means that DOS can't find the program — assuming, of course, that you successfully installed the program.

Here's how to solve the problem. First, try restarting your computer. Remove the floppy disk from the A drive if you haven't done so already, and then press Ctrl-Alt-Del. When you see the C:> prompt, type **Q**.

If you still get the `Bad command or file name` message, try this: At the DOS prompt, type CD C:\QUATTRO and press Enter. If you don't get a message that says `Invalid directory`, you're in good shape. Now, type Q, and Quattro Pro should start up.

What you did was move to the directory that holds the Quattro Pro program files. You need to do this if the QUATTRO directory is not in your DOS path.

If you got the `Invalid directory` message, there are a number of things to check:

- ✔ Quattro Pro may be installed in a directory named something other than QUATTRO. If Quattro Pro is installed in a directory with a different name, substitute that name for QUATTRO in your CD command. For example, if the program's installed in a directory named QPRO, you would type **CD C:\QPRO** instead.

- ✔ Quattro Pro may be installed on a different hard disk. Some systems have more than one hard drive, labeled D:, E:, and so on. Type **D:** (to change to drive D:), and then type **CD D:\QUATTRO**. Hopefully, you can now start up Quattro Pro by typing the **Q** command.

- ✔ Are you sure Quattro Pro is actually installed? Refer to Appendix A for more information on installing this software.

Figure 2-1:
Entering
the single
character Q
is all it takes
to start
Quattro Pro.

```
c:\>q
```

Starting automatically

If Quattro Pro is the only program that you ever use (what a boring life you must have), you can set things up so that Quattro Pro is started whenever you turn on your computer. You need to use a file editor and modify the AUTOEXEC.BAT file. At the end of the AUTOEXEC.BAT file, simply insert an additional line that contains the single letter **Q**. If this is totally foreign to you, bribe your office computer guru with a six-pack or a pizza.

If you don't know what you're doing, do not mess with your AUTOEXEC.BAT file. This file contains lots of cryptic lines, and if you change even one, your system may no longer work correctly.

Whenever you turn on your computer, two files that are stored in your C:\ root directory are very important: AUTOEXEC.BAT and CONFIG.SYS. These files both hold commands that are executed by the operating system to get things set up so everything operates correctly. Novices shouldn't attempt to modify these files, but they should know what they do.

CONFIG.SYS holds special commands that load files into memory that control various parts of your computer. For example, commands in this file may load the software that your sound card uses, set up memory, and lots of other things. AUTOEXEC.BAT holds lines of text which are actually commands that are run at the DOS prompt immediately after your computer starts. Therefore, if you place a DOS command in your AUTOEXEC.BAT file, that command will be executed every time you start your computer.

Starting from Windows

If your company has jumped on the Microsoft Windows bandwagon, your system might be set up so that you run your programs from the Windows Program Manager. If so, there will be an icon that says *Quattro Pro*, which probably looks like the icon in Figure 2-2. Just use your mouse to double-click on this icon, and Quattro Pro starts. Windows will still be running, and you can return to it by pressing Ctrl-Esc and then selecting Program Manager from the menu that appears.

Figure 2-2:
If you use Microsoft Windows, start Quattro Pro by double clicking on this icon in the Windows Program Manager screen.

Whoa! Quitting Quattro Pro

After you get Quattro Pro started, you'll be staring at a blank worksheet. Later on, you'll find out what you can do with a blank worksheet (the possibilities are virtually unlimited). But there's one more very important thing you need to know: how to quit Quattro Pro.

The right way

One way to get out of Quattro Pro is to issue a command using the menu (which is explained in Chapter 4). But a much quicker way is to simply press Ctrl-X to tell Quattro Pro that you've had enough. Ctrl-X, by the way, is a shortcut for issuing the **File⇨Exit** command.

As you'll see, Quattro Pro has lots of shortcut keys that you can use instead of the normal menu commands. As the name implies, the shortcut keys let you do things faster and more efficiently. You'll learn about these later, but for now, just remember Ctrl-X, okay?

If you haven't done anything in Quattro Pro, or if all of the work that you've done has already been saved to disk, Quattro Pro comes to a screeching halt and bring you back to the place you were when you started the program (a menu, the DOS prompt, or the Windows Program Manager).

But if you've been working on something and you haven't yet saved it to disk, pressing Ctrl-X causes Quattro Pro to display a message like the one shown in Figure 2-3.

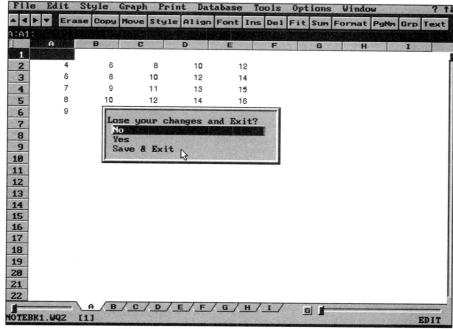

Figure 2-3:
You'll get
this
message if
you try to
quit before
you've
saved your
work to disk.

If you see this message box, you have three options:

 ✔ Press Y for **Yes** if you want to abandon your work. You'll never see it again.

 ✔ Press N for **No** if you change your mind and decide not to exit. You can then save your file and exit.

 ✔ Press S for **Save** & Exit. Quattro Pro asks you for a filename if you haven't already given your work a name. Just enter a filename (up to eight characters) and press Enter.

This warning message is a nice safeguard that reminds you to save your work before you exit. In other words, Quattro Pro lets you exit before saving your work, but it always warns you if there's a chance you may lose some work. How you respond to this warning message is up to you. Unless the stuff you've been working on is totally bogus or simply for practice, you'll probably want to save it to disk so you can work on it again later.

The work you do in Quattro Pro is stored in your computer's memory, and Quattro Pro doesn't save your work to disk automatically — you have to give the command to do so. The procedure for saving your work to a file is covered in detail in a later chapter (and it's very easy to do).

Baffled by files and directories?

You can't use computers for long without having to deal with files. In fact, just about everything that you do on a computer involves files. Programs, such as Quattro Pro, are stored in files, and the work that you do in programs is also stored in files. A filename can have up to eight characters, plus an extension (up to three characters) separated from the file name by a period. (I know it's weird — but that's life). Here are some valid file names: Q.EXE, RESUME.DOC, JUNK.WQ2, READ.ME, BUDGET1.WQ2.

Files are stored on disks (hard disks or floppy disks). Disks, especially hard disks, are usually broken down into directories. Directories help you organize your files and make locating a file you need easier.

Normally, a directory holds all the files needed for a specific software program. For example, when you install Quattro Pro, the program creates a directory called \QPRO on your hard disk and dumps all of its file there. Directories can also have other directories, which can have other

directories, and so on. In other words, a file may be stored in a directory that's *nested* deeply within other directories. Think of a tree with branches coming out of it, and then turn the tree upside down to envision how a disk's directories are arranged.

You refer to directories using a backslash to separate nested directories (this is known as a *path*). You can also precede the directory path with the disk drive letter and a colon. Furthermore, you can specify a file using all of this information. The following example specifies a file named EXPENSE.WQ2, in a directory named \FILES, which is a directory nested under the QUATTRO directory on drive C:

```
C:\QUATTRO\FILES\EXPENSE.WQ2
```

If you're still baffled by files and directories, be patient. Hang around with computers long enough, buy lots of my books, and it will all make sense — maybe.

The wrong way

One of the worst things you can do when using a computer is to simply turn it off when you're finished with what you're doing. Even if you saved your file first, you should never use the "power switch" method to exit Quattro Pro. Exit gracefully, as they say, by using the File⇨Exit command (or its Ctrl-X shortcut). Then you can turn off your computer and do what you normally do when you turn off your computer — head for the local pub, grab your surfboard and hit the beach, sneak out of the office via the back stairway, or whatever else strikes your fancy.

Only fools turn off their computer before properly exiting from the program they're using.

Totally Confused?

If you've followed along in this chapter and don't have a clue as to what I'm talking about, you might want to find someone who's knowledgeable about computers who can give you some personal attention. The fact is, installing Quattro Pro and getting it set up can be more difficult than actually using the program. (Appendix A might help.) But the good news is that once it's set up and running properly, you don't have to do it again — until you upgrade to the next version.

Chapter 3
Jumping Right In

There was a PC novice named Pruitt
Who was inclined to just say, "Screw it"
Though it was hard to begin,
He finally jumped in
And found it was best to just do it.

In This Chapter

▶ A once-in-a-lifetime opportunity to get some actual experience with Quattro Pro
▶ Step-by-step instructions for creating a useful worksheet

If you can't tell the difference between a spreadsheet and a bed sheet, this chapter will set you straight. Take the time to wade through these words and follow along on your own computer, and you might learn a few things. At the very least, you will have gotten your feet wet with Quattro Pro, and you can decide if it's really something you want to learn.

Note: If you've never used Quattro Pro before, you'll find lots of things in this chapter that you're not familiar with—things that will be discussed in more detail in later chapters. While going through this chapter, it's not important that you understand every aspect of what you're doing. The point of this exercise it to give you a feel for what it's like to do things in Quattro Pro. Also, your screen may look different from the figures shown in this chapter. That's because you can run Quattro Pro in two different modes (you'll learn about these in a later chapter, too). The screens shown here are in WYSIWYG mode. But regardless of what your screen looks like, the instructions are the same.

Get Your Feet Wet

By the time you reach the end of this chapter, you will have created a Quattro Pro worksheet that can help you catalog your music collection. (If you don't have a music collection, just pretend that you do.) If this were a normal computer book, the example in this chapter would be something like a worksheet to calculate monthly payments on a mortgage or to keep track of your business expenses. My example, though certainly not the most exciting spreadsheet you will ever encounter, is slightly more interesting than the run-of-the-mill financial examples.

More specifically, the worksheet you create in this chapter will

- ✔ Let you keep track of CDs, cassettes, and LPs (remember them?) by storing the title, artist, and total time of the recording. (You'll store each recording in a separate row, and each row will occupy four columns.)
- ✔ Calculate the total number of recordings in the worksheet
- ✔ Calculate the total time of the recordings

And a One, and a Two...

I'm assuming that your system is set up to run Quattro Pro and that you know how to start the program. (If you haven't installed Quattro Pro yet, see Appendix A before proceeding.) You start out with a completely blank worksheet — which is the way Quattro Pro normally starts up.

Putting in column headings

This spreadsheet is going to have four columns of information: the artist's name, the name of the recording, the format (CD, cassette, or LP), and the total time (in minutes) of the recording. Therefore, you need four headings. The headings aren't absolutely necessary; they just make clear exactly what's stored in each column.

1. Make sure the cell pointer is in cell A1.

    You can tell where the cell pointer is because that cell appears in a different color. The top part of the display also tells you which cell the cell pointer is in. If this line doesn't say A1 or A:A1, use the arrow keys or press Home to move the cell pointer to A1.

2. Type **Artist**, and then press the right-arrow key to move the cell pointer to cell B1.

    You'll notice that as you type, the letters appear at the top of the screen, not in the cell. But when you move the cell pointer to another cell (or press Enter), the information shows up in the cell. Though you might find this kind of strange, it's perfectly normal, and you'll soon get used to it.

3. With the cell pointer in cell B1, type **Title** and press the right-arrow key again to move to cell C1.

4. In cell C1, type **Format** and press the right-arrow key to move to cell D1.

5. Type **Time** in cell D1 and press Enter.

Underlining the headings

Next, you're going to underline the labels you just entered, using a command. Underlining the headings isn't essential, but it does make the worksheet look more attractive.

1. Move the cell pointer to cell A1 (the cell with the first column heading). Use the arrow keys or press Home.

2. The command to draw lines is Style⇨Line Drawing. Issue this command by pressing /SL. Quattro Pro responds with the message `Enter block to draw lines.`

3. You need to highlight the cells that you want to underline. Press the right-arrow key three times to highlight all four of the label cells, and then press Enter.

4. Quattro Pro displays a pop-up menu in which you specify where you want the lines drawn (see Figure 3-1). Choose **B**ottom by pressing B.

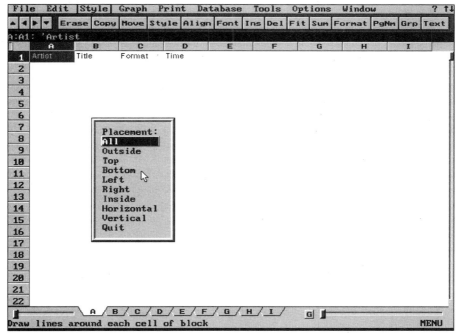

Figure 3-1:
This menu appears when you select Style⇨Line Drawing.

5. Another menu appears, asking what type of line you want. Choose **D**ouble by pressing D. This menu closes, but the preceding menu remains open.

6. Choose **Q**uit to close the menu (press Q).

Your worksheet should now look like Figure 3-2.

Figure 3-2:
Your
worksheet
after
entering and
underlining
titles.

Adjusting the column widths

Unless your music collection consists exclusively of one-word titles by artists with a single name, the column widths aren't going to be wide enough to display the information properly. So you must make them wider.

1. Move the cell pointer anywhere in column A.

2. Press Ctrl-W (this is a shortcut key for the **Style**⇨**Column Width** command).

   Quattro Pro responds with the message `Alter the width of the current column [1..254]: 9`. This message tells you that you can make a column from 1 to 254 characters wide, and it's proposing a width of 9 (which is the default column width).

3. Now you have a choice. You can either enter a number representing how many characters wide you want the column, or you can use the right- and left-arrow keys to adjust the column. Using either method, make the column 26 characters wide.

4. Repeat steps 2 and 3 for column B. Start by moving the cell pointer anywhere in column B, and then press Ctrl-W. Make this column 26 characters wide also.

5. The Format column (column C) is fine as it is, but you can make the Time column (column D) narrower if you want. (Five characters is a good choice.)

Putting Stuff in the Cells

Now you're ready to add some entries into the worksheet. You'll do so by moving the cell pointer to the appropriate cell and then typing in the information. This is exactly what you did earlier when you entered the labels for the column headings, so the procedure should be familiar.

By the way, if your cell entries are too wide to fit into the cell (even after making the columns wider), don't worry. The information is all there, but it may appear to be truncated if the cell to the right is occupied. You can always make the columns wider, using the method you used previously.

But again, don't be too concerned at this point about all these minute details. There's plenty of time for that later.

1. Move the cell pointer to cell A2 and enter the name of a recording artist. If you're just pretending you have a music collection and don't have an artist of your own to enter, type **Eric Clapton**.

2. Move one cell to the right (using the right-arrow key) and enter the title of the recording. *Unplugged* is a good title.

3. Use the right-arrow key to move next door one cell and enter the format. You can type **CD**.

4. Move the cell pointer to cell D2 and enter the total time in minutes (try typing **62**).

When you're finished, go down to the next row (use the arrow keys to do this) and put in another recording. The second recording will start in cell A3. Repeat these steps until you have entered your entire CD, cassette, and record collection. (Not really, you can stop after four or five, or whenever it gets boring.)

After you type in several entries, your worksheet should look something like Figure 3-3. If it looks *exactly* like this figure, congratulations — you have excellent taste in music.

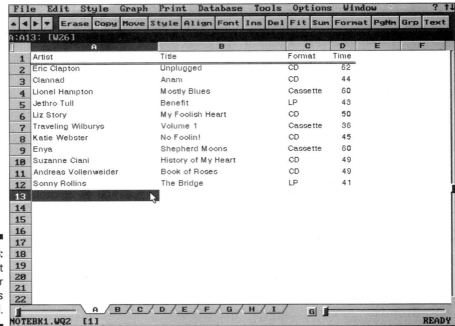

Figure 3-3:
A worksheet
after
recordings
are entered.

And Now, Some Formulas

If you only have a few sample lines of data in this worksheet, you can tell at a glance how many recordings are in it. But what if you have several hundred? Or several thousand? You would have to page down to the end and see what row number the last entry is in and then mentally subtract one from this to account for the column headings. Why do all of this when you can use a formula to do the counting?

The next step in this exercise is to create a formula to count the number of recordings in the spreadsheet. You'll put this formula into a cell (which is the only place a formula can go). A good place for this formula is at the very top of the worksheet. But since the top rows are already used, you'll have to insert some new rows.

Inserting new rows

When you insert one or more new rows, everything below is shifted downward. If you insert two new rows, for example, everything below the place where you insert them gets moved down two rows. Whatever was in cell A1 moves to A3, A2 is moved to A4, and so on. You want the total count to appear at the top of the worksheet, so insert three new rows.

1. Move the cell pointer to cell A1. (Pressing the Home key is a fast way to do this.)

2. Choose Edit⇨Insert from the menu. (You can press /EI or use the shortcut Ctrl-I.)

   Quattro Pro responds by displaying a menu, shown in Figure 3-4.

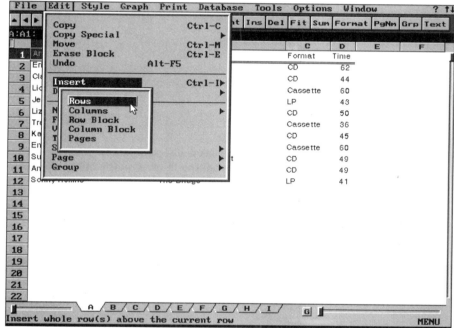

3. Press R to choose **R**ows, or you can just press Enter since **R**ows is already highlighted.

   Quattro Pro displays the message Enter row insert block: A:A1..A1. The program wants you to highlight the number of rows that you want to insert.

4. To add three rows, move the highlight down two additional rows by pressing the down-arrow key twice.

5. Press Enter.

   Quattro Pro moves everything down three rows to accommodate the new arrivals.

Sticking in the formula

Now you have to put the formula to count the number of recordings in cell A1.

1. Move the cell pointer to cell A1.

2. Enter the following text, and then press Enter:

```
@COUNT(A5..A1000)
```

This formula uses a special function that returns the number of non-blank entries in a block of cells. (You'll learn about these special functions later.) You specified a block of A5..A1000, which consists of 996 cells. (Keep in mind that the formula doesn't appear in the cell; rather, the *result* of the formula appears in the cell.)

If you happen to have more than 996 recordings, the formula will not return the correct number.

3. Move to cell B1 and type **Recordings,** and then press Enter. This is just a label that reminds you what the number in the cell to the left is.

Add another record or two to the list and watch as Quattro Pro updates the count automatically. Isn't technology amazing?

Ready for another formula?

Now you'll add a slightly more complex formula that calculates the total time of the recordings, in hours.

1. Move the cell pointer to cell A2.

2. Enter the following formula:

```
@SUM(D5..D1000)/60
```

This formula uses another one of the special functions, @SUM. Quattro Pro evaluates this formula as follows: First, it calculates the sum of all the values in the block D5..D1000. Then it divides this number by 60 (since the times entered are in minutes, and an hour has 60 minutes).

3. Move to cell B2 and enter the label **Total time in hours**.

4. To see whether the formula works, add another record or two and watch as Quattro Pro updates the formula's result to include the new times.

Now the worksheet should look something like Figure 3-5. The actual numbers that appear in cells A1 and A2 depend, of course, on how many recordings you entered and how long the recordings are.

| File | Edit | Style | Graph | Print | Database | Tools | Options | Window | ? ↑↓ |

| ▲ | ◄ | ► | ▼ | Erase | Copy | Move | Style | Align | Font | Ins | Del | Fit | Sum | Format | PgNm | Grp | Text |

A:A2: [W26] @SUM(D5..D1000)/60

	A	B	C	D	E	F
1	13	Recordings				
2	10.9	Total time in hours				
3						
4	Artist	Title	Format	Time		
5	Eric Clapton	Unplugged	CD	62		
6	Clannad	Anam	CD	44		
7	Lionel Hampton	Mostly Blues	Cassette	60		
8	Jethro Tull	Benefit	LP	43		
9	Liz Story	My Foolish Heart	CD	50		
10	Traveling Wilburys	Volume 1	Cassette	36		
11	Katie Webster	No Foolin!	CD	45		
12	Enya	Shepherd Moons	Cassette	60		
13	Suzanne Ciani	History of My Heart	CD	49		
14	Andreas Vollenweider	Book of Roses	CD	49		
15	Sonny Rollins	The Bridge	LP	41		
16	Chick Corea	Three Quartets	CD	61		
17	Wendy Carlos	Switched-On Bach 2000	CD	54		
18						
19						
20						
21						
22						

A / B / C / D / E / F / G / H / I /   G

NOTEBK1.WQ2 [1]   READY

Figure 3-5: A worksheet after entering formulas to count the recordings and compute the total time.

Saving This Masterpiece

Everything you've done so far was done in your computer's memory. Your hard disk has been completely idle. If some clod accidentally kicks your PC's plug out of the wall socket, all of this fine work would go down the tube. To prevent such a disaster, save your work to your hard disk.

1. Make sure you're in READY mode. The word READY should appear at the lower right corner of your screen. If it doesn't say READY, press Escape a few times until it does.

2. Choose the File⇨Save command by pressing /FS.

   Since this worksheet hasn't been given a name yet, Quattro Pro displays a box (see Figure 3-6) that lets you enter a name for the file. This box also shows you a list of other worksheet files that may be in this directory.

3. Enter a filename, such as **MUSIC**, and press Enter.

   Quattro Pro saves your work as MUSIC.WQ2 (or MUSIC.WQ1 if you're using Version 4). This filename now shows up at the bottom left of your screen to remind you what you're working on.

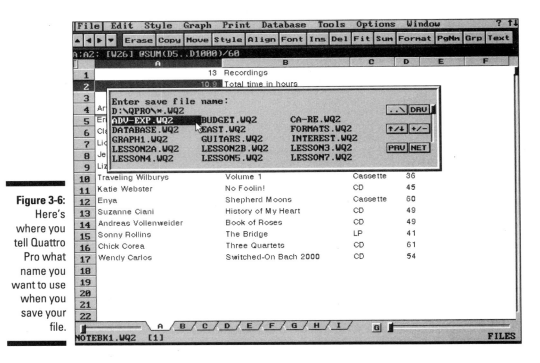

Figure 3-6:
Here's
where you
tell Quattro
Pro what
name you
want to use
when you
save your
file.

Sorting the Stuff

Most of the time, lists (or databases), such as the one you created, are more useful when the items in the list are put into some type of order — or *sorted*, to use the technical term. The next step in this endeavor is to sort the recordings by format. When you sort the list alphabetically by format, all the CDs will be together, all the cassettes will be together, and all the LPs will be together.

1. Move the cell pointer to the first cell of the actual data (not the headings). This is cell A5.

2. Choose the **Data**⇨**S**ort command by pressing /DS.

   Quattro Pro displays another menu, shown in Figure 3-7.

3. Select **B**lock from this menu (you can press B, or you can just press Enter since the option is already highlighted).

   Quattro Pro responds with the message Block of data to be sorted: A:A5. Here's where you point out, by highlighting, the block of cells you want to sort.

4. Press period (.) to anchor the cell pointer at cell A5, and then use the arrow keys to select the entire data block. The actual block you select

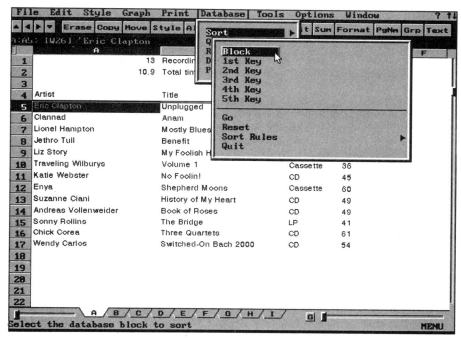

Figure 3-7:
The menu
you use to
sort data.

depends on how many records you entered, but the last column is column D. After you highlight (or select) the block, press Enter.

You return to the sorting menu, which now tells you the block that you selected.

5. Tell Quattro Pro what column to sort on (this is called the *sort key*). You can have up to five sort keys, but you'll only use one for this sort. Choose **1st Key** (by pressing 1), and then press Enter.

Quattro Pro then prompts you with `Column/Row to be used as first sort key: A:A5`. Move the cell pointer to any cell in column C (since this is the column you want to sort on) and press Enter.

Quattro Pro displays a small box in which you specify the order of the sort — ascending (from A to Z) or descending (from Z to A).

6. Press A for **A**scending, and then press Enter.

You return to the previous menu.

7. You've told Quattro Pro everything it needs to know to perform the sort, so choose **G**o by pressing G.

Quattro Pro sorts the data to the specs you gave and rearranges the rows in alphabetical order by column C (the sort key). My sorted data appears in Figure 3-8.

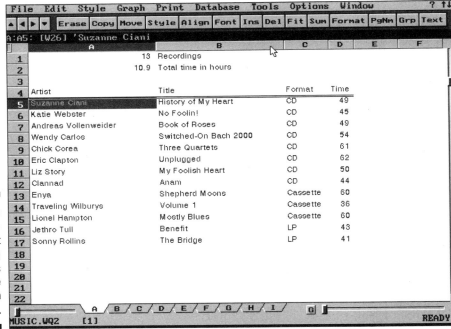

File   Edit   Style   Graph   Print   Database   Tools   Options   Window   ? ↑↓

▲ ◀ ▶ ▼ Erase Copy Move Style Align Font Ins Del Fit Sum Format PgNm Grp Text

A:A5: [W26] 'Suzanne Ciani

	A	B	C	D	E	F
1	13 Recordings					
2	10.9 Total time in hours					
3						
4	Artist	Title	Format	Time		
5	Suzanne Ciani	History of My Heart	CD	49		
6	Katie Webster	No Foolin!	CD	45		
7	Andreas Vollenweider	Book of Roses	CD	49		
8	Wendy Carlos	Switched-On Bach 2000	CD	54		
9	Chick Corea	Three Quartets	CD	61		
10	Eric Clapton	Unplugged	CD	62		
11	Liz Story	My Foolish Heart	CD	50		
12	Clannad	Anam	CD	44		
13	Enya	Shepherd Moons	Cassette	60		
14	Traveling Wilburys	Volume 1	Cassette	36		
15	Lionel Hampton	Mostly Blues	Cassette	60		
16	Jethro Tull	Benefit	LP	43		
17	Sonny Rollins	The Bridge	LP	41		
18						
19						
20						
21						
22						

A / B / C / D / E / F / G / H / I /   G

MUSIC.WQ2   [1]   READY

Figure 3-8:
The worksheet after sorting the records by the information in column C.

All of the recordings of each format appear together, but the order within each grouping doesn't change. If, for example, you want all of the recordings sorted by format and also sorted by artist within each format grouping, you need to specify a second sort key.

Quitting Quattro

Now that you have set up and saved this worksheet, you can call it quits.

To exit Quattro Pro, press Ctrl-X (a shortcut for the File⇨Exit command). At this point, if you have any work that hasn't been saved, Quattro Pro lets you know by displaying the message shown in Figure 3-9 and gives you a chance to save your work before exiting. Choose the Save & Exit option by pressing S. If the file has already been saved, Quattro Pro displays yet another message asking if you want to replace the file on disk with your changed file. Usually, you want to answer in the affirmative.

If your work has already been saved, the program ends immediately when you press Ctrl-X, and you'll be back at the DOS prompt (or a menu system if your system is set up with one).

A personal anecdote

At one point in my college days, I had four roommates who also happened to be music lovers and computer buffs. Between the five of us, we had approximately 3,000 LPs (this was long before CDs were available). One of these guys was taking a computer class and needed a project. Believe it or not, we actually keypunched all of the titles, artists, and other information onto IBM cards and created a data file on the campus mainframe. Using FORTRAN (an ancient computer language), we wrote a program to summarize and print the data. Then when we were all sitting around in various states of consciousness and couldn't decide what to listen to, someone would call out a random number. We had a mutual agreement that we would play the record that corresponded to the number on the printout.

Since our musical tastes were all pretty good, this usually resulted in an agreeable outcome, and we often heard an album that we would never think of playing otherwise. Occasionally, however, the scheme backfired, and we had to endure 45 minutes of the Carpenters or something equally obnoxious.

The point of this story is that we all learned a great deal about programming from this project because it involved something that we were *interested* in. The same goes for learning Quattro Pro or any other software for that matter. If you try to learn software by using stupid examples, you probably won't get too far. The best way is to work on projects that are important to you.

Figure 3-9:
If you try to quit Quattro Pro before you save your work to disk, you'll know about it.

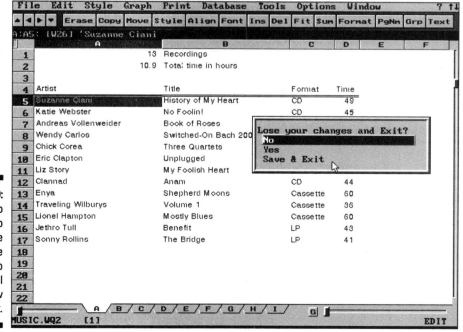

Come Back, Elvis

The next time you start Quattro Pro, you can work on this worksheet again by issuing the File⇨Open command. Simply type in the filename you saved the spreadsheet under (or use the arrow keys to highlight the name in the list shown) and press Enter.

Other Stuff for the Really Ambitious

The worksheet you developed in this chapter is only a start. Here's a list of some potential additions you can make to it:

- Add a formula to calculate the average recording length (**_Hint:_** use the @AVG function).

- Add another column to hold the year that recording was recorded. By doing this, you can sort your collection from newest to oldest (or vice versa).

- Add another column to hold your evaluation of the recording: Excellent, Good, Poor, Pure Garbage, and so on. If you use numerical ratings, you can sort by this column and instantly see your recordings from best to worst.

- Add another column labeled SortField. A SortField column is handy if you want to sort the records by artist. As it stands, if you sort by artist, Eric Clapton comes before The Beatles. Normally, you want The Beatles (B) to come before Eric Clapton (C). If you add the additional column, you can insert the word that you want to sort (_Clapton_ and _Beatles_, for example) and then sort by this column.

Even More Stuff for Overachievers

The formulas you put into the worksheet aren't really foolproof. As I pointed out, if you put data beyond row 1,000, it is not accounted for in the formulas. By the way, you'll learn all the ins and outs of formulas later — this is for overachievers, remember?

But there's another problem. What if you're strapped for cash and have to sell off some of your old records? You'll need to go to the worksheet and delete the rows by using the Delete⇨Row command. For every row you delete, the formulas adjust themselves automatically. Delete one row and the formula that originally read @COUNT(A5..A1000) turns into @COUNT(A5..A999). In other words, for every row you delete, the formula makes its block one row shorter.

But a semi-serious problem occurs if you delete the first row (row 5 of the sample worksheet) or the last row (row 1000) in the block used in the formulas. If you do either of these, both of the formulas return ERR (which means the formula can't calculate) because the rows that they use no longer exist. You then have to correct the formulas manually.

In this example, it's no big deal. The world won't come to a screeching halt if your worksheet doesn't compute the correct number of recordings you own. But if this worksheet were doing something less trivial — like adding up the investments made by your company — returning a wrong value can have serious consequences. The good news is that the formulas don't return wrong values; they don't return _any_ values. This is a sign that something is wrong.

Now What?

If you made it through this first exercise, congratulations. The rest of the book will help you understand exactly what you did here. If you got lost somewhere along the way, it's probably easier to start again from scratch, making sure you follow the instructions exactly. You've now done some actual work in Quattro Pro, and you're ready to move on to bigger and better things.

Part II:

Basic Stuff That You Must Know

The 5th Wave By Rich Tennant

"EXCUSE ME — IS ANYONE HERE **NOT** TALKING ABOUT THEIR PERSONAL COMPUTER?"

In This Part...

The information in these chapters can best be described as fundamental. In other words, you won't get too far with Quattro Pro unless you know how to do the basic operations. Here's another way of saying it: If you're just starting out with Quattro Pro, this is not the section to skip.

Chapter 4
Ordering from the Menu

There once was a fellow called Nash
Who thought all computers were trash.
He was always complaining
Till he learned through some training
Just what you can do with a slash.

In This Chapter

▶ How to use Quattro Pro's menu system (and why you would want to)

▶ Discovering what *all* those commands — well, at least the important ones — do

▶ New insights into the age-old question: Mouse or keyboard?

Using Quattro Pro is kind of like training a dog. You can give commands all day long, but unless you give the right commands, nothing happens. Quattro Pro understands hundreds of commands — but you have to know how to give these commands. That's why you need to know about menus.

Since Quattro Pro can't understand English, you have to communicate with it by using commands it understands. These commands are located on the menu.

Some day, computers will be able to recognize speech and respond to your verbal commands. You'll be able to say something like "Hey PC, load up that spreadsheet I was working on yesterday afternoon and change the colors on the graph to the ones I like." Until that time, you have to settle for communicating with your PC using more mundane methods: a keyboard or a mouse.

Using the Menu

Figure 4-1 shows the Quattro Pro menu bar. This menu bar always appears at the top of your screen and consists of nine words, also known as *menu items*. When you select a menu item, it displays more words in a list that drops down. More technically, these are known as *commands*. Quattro Pro has many commands — and you can probably lead a long and fulfilling life without using most of them.

Figure 4-1:
Quattro
Pro's menu
bar.

File   Edit   Style   Graph   Print   Database   Tools   Options   Window   ? ↑↓

Throughout this book, I talk about issuing commands. This simply means choosing a menu item and then selecting one of the commands from the list that drops down.

The main menu has nine menu items, and each of these leads to several more commands.

So what kind of commands are available? Glad you asked.

A good way to get a feel for what commands are available is to take a look at the menu items displayed at the top of the Quattro Pro screen.

Before you get too overwhelmed with the menu choices, keep in mind that you probably have no need for the majority of the commands. And besides, Quattro Pro has lots of shortcuts for commonly used menu commands and even has a SpeedBar for mouse users. If you learn these shortcuts, you can make fewer trips to the menu and save valuable seconds of your company's time.

Selecting one of these menu items usually leads to more choices than you care to know about:

File menu: Use this menu when you need to do something that involves a file (gee, this book is just *filled* with revelations). Commands in this menu let you load a file from disk, save your work, delete a file from disk, and lots of other things.

Edit menu: This menu has loads of commands you use to manipulate a worksheet. For example, you can copy cells, move cells, insert new rows or columns, delete entire rows or columns, and search the worksheet for specific numbers or words.

Style menu: As the name implies, this menu is used for making stylistic modifications. These include changing how numbers appear (number of decimal places, commas, dollar signs, and so on), changing the column width, drawing lines, shading cells, and changing the type font, for example.

Graph menu: This menu is your doorway to all the commands used for creating graphs from numbers in your worksheet.

The 5th Wave
By Rich Tennant

Print menu: Take a guess what this menu does.

Database menu: When you use Quattro Pro to work with database-type information, you can use this menu to work efficiently with the data. This menu also contains the command that you use to sort a block of cells.

Tools menu: This menu might as well be called Miscellaneous because it contains a bunch of commands — most of which fall into the Not-For-Beginners category.

Options menu: This menu is where you go when you need to change how Quattro Pro operates. You can change to and from WYSIWYG mode here, and you can turn Undo on and off. The most entertaining command here, however, is the one that lets you change the colors that Quattro Pro uses. You can waste a lot of time adjusting the colors until they are just right for you (and completely obnoxious to the person in the next cubicle).

Window menu: You use this menu mainly when you have more than one worksheet open. Each open worksheet lives in its own window, and the Window menu lets you adjust these windows.

When the menus don't match

If your menus aren't anything like the ones I'm talking about, someone probably created a new menu system. Quattro Pro has a feature that lets you rearrange the menu commands to a configuration that's more to your liking. You rearrange menus by using the **O**ptions⇨**S**tartup⇨**E**dit Menus command (a command that all but those with a Ph.D. in Quattro Pro should avoid like the plague).

You can reload the normal menus by using the **O**ptions⇨**S**tartup⇨**M**enu System command. Choose the Quattro option (which loads the QUATTRO.MU menu file).

Slashing and Mousing — Accessing the Menu

In order to issue a command by using the menu, you must first activate the menu bar. You can do this in two ways:

✔ Press the slash (/) key in READY mode

✔ Point to any menu item with your mouse, and then click the left mouse button

You can access the menu from the keyboard by pressing slash, or you can use your mouse to click on a menu item.

With the keyboard

When you press slash (/), the first word in the menu bar (**F**ile) is highlighted. You can use the left- and right-arrow keys to move this highlight to different menu items. As you highlight the commands, notice that a brief explanation of the highlighted menu item appears at the bottom of your screen in the status line. For example, the description for the **P**rint menu is Print a spreadsheet or graph. When you get to the last menu (**W**indow), pressing the right arrow causes the highlight bar to wrap around to the beginning of the list (back to **F**ile).

You select the highlighted menu item by pressing Enter (or the down-arrow key). When you do this, the highlighted menu item displays a list of commands. You can use the up- or down-arrow keys to scroll through this list. Press Enter to issue the highlighted command.

Colored letters

If you look at the menu, you see that the first letter of each command appears in a different color. This means that, after you activate the menu by pressing the slash key, you can simply press this highlighted letter to execute the command. For example, you can press / to activate the menu and then press E to access the Edit menu. Therefore, pressing /E drops down the Edit menu (see Figure 4.2).

Notice that each command in the list that drops down also has one letter that is highlighted (notice that it's not always the first letter, however). After the menu drops down, you can press one of these highlighted letters instead of scrolling through the list by using the up- and down-arrow keys. If you press the highlighted letter, you don't have to press Enter to issue the command (hey, every timesaving tip helps).

Every menu command has a highlighted letter, which you can press to issue the command.

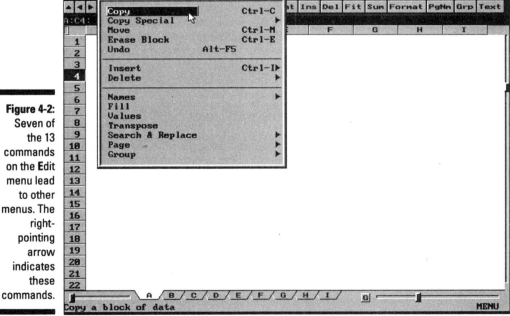

Figure 4-2: Seven of the 13 commands on the Edit menu lead to other menus. The right-pointing arrow indicates these commands.

More menus

Some of the commands have small arrows that point to the right. These **arrows** tell you that issuing this command (by pressing Enter or pressing the high-lighted letter) leads to yet another menu. As you can see in Figure 4-2, seven of the commands in the **E**dit menu have these arrows, which lead to another menu. In some cases, the next menu also leads to another menu. So occasionally, you may find yourself in a menu that's "nested" several levels deep.

When you're dealing with these nested menus, you can *back up* to the previous one by pressing Esc.

To demonstrate, Figure 4-3 shows the additional menu that appears when you select the **S**earch & Replace command from the **E**dit menu. Nested menus usually pop up over the previous menu, but they never completely obscure them.

If you see a small arrow pointing to the right, the menu leads to another menu.

Shortcut keys

In some cases, Quattro Pro displays a key combination at the right of the menu. Did you notice the Ctrl-C at the right of the Edit⇨Copy command? This key combination means that you can simply press Ctrl-C and avoid the whole menu business altogether. Quattro Pro provides theses shortcuts for commonly used commands. For example, pressing Ctrl-C is the same as pressing **/EC**.

Many of the more popular menu commands have shortcut keys that let you execute a command and avoid the menu altogether.

Besides displaying shortcut-key combinations, some commands also display their current settings (in a different color). For example, in Figure 4-3, the **L**ook In command currently has a setting of Formula. Quattro Pro's displaying the current setting is actually quite useful since you can tell at a glance what the current setting is for a particular command.

If you don't like to see the settings displayed in your menus, you can press the minus key (-) when the menu is displayed. Besides removing the settings, pressing the minus key also makes the menus narrower. To display the settings again, press the plus key (+).

With a mouse

You may prefer to use a mouse for your menu work. If so, simply click on the menu command, and the menu drops down to display additional commands. Use the mouse to click on one of these commands.

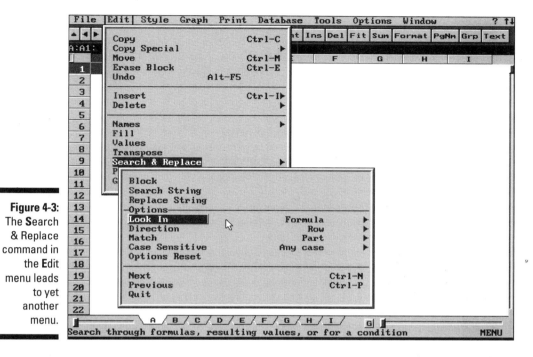

If you start a command with a mouse, you don't have to continue with a mouse.
In other words, Quattro Pro lets you mix and match mouse and keyboard
selection procedures.

Getting Out of the Menu

Okay, you know how to activate the menu. But how do you get out of it? You
can

- ✔ Issue a command by going through all of the menus required. When a
  command is successfully executed, you return to READY mode and can
  continue on your merry way.

- ✔ Press Esc if you change your mind. In some cases, you may have to bang
  away at Esc several times to cancel all the menus that are displayed. When
  you see the READY mode indicator, you're home free.

- ✔ Press Ctrl-Break. This cancels all the menus and immediately returns you
  to READY mode.

Chapter 5
Entering Numbers, Words, and Other Things

There was a young man from Minnerck
Who hated to get down to work.
So he stared at his screen
And made such a scene,
He was finally diagnosed as berserk.

In This Chapter

▶ The obligatory tour of the screen, including the difference between Text display mode and WYSIWYG display mode

▶ Instructions of what to do when a blank worksheet is staring you in the face

▶ An explanation of how to move from cell to cell (a common pastime among restless prisoners *and* Quattro Pro users)

▶ An explanation of how to put numbers and words into cells

▶ An explanation of how to get rid of a cell's contents

▶ Marginally useful terminology that you can forget

Chapter 2 showed you how to start and quit Quattro Pro. And if you took my sage advice and worked your way through Chapter 3, you have had some first-hand experience with Quattro Pro — and you even have a fairly lame worksheet that keeps track of your music collection. Chapter 4 answered all your burning questions about the menu system. This chapter provides enough information to make you feel safe going off on your own to make prize-winning spreadsheets out of the vast wasteland that is innocuously called a blank worksheet.

Modus Operandi: Text or WYSIWYG?

Federal Statute CB324.21.190 states that every computer book published in the U.S. must include a tour of the screen within its first 50 pages. Quattro Pro has two screen modes — WYSIWYG and Text mode. Because I'm a fairly law-abiding citizen, I've included screen shots of both (see Figures 5-1 and 5-2).

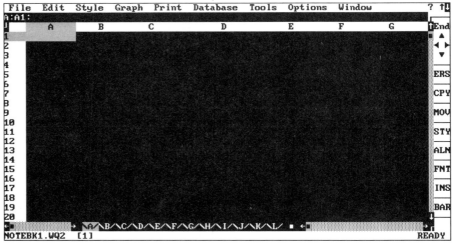

Figure 5-1:
This is your
worksheet
in Text
mode.

When you start Quattro Pro, your screen looks something like Figure 5-1 or Figure 5-2. In either case, the worksheet is blank, an empty slate.

Note: Your screen will look slightly different if you don't have a mouse installed.

Only Quattro Pro 5 screens have the tab display with the letters of the alphabet at the bottom of the screen. If you're using Quattro Pro 4, your screen doesn't contain this element.

Text display mode is the most common display mode and runs the fastest. You can't see fancy things like big type, italics, or colors. In other words, everything is in plain text.

One of the more common acronyms in personal computing is *WYSIWYG* (pronounced "wizzy-wig"), which stands for *What You See Is What You Get.* In WYSIWYG display mode, you can see on-screen how your spreadsheet will look when you print it out. This display mode is somewhat slower, but you can see different sizes of type, bold and italic characters, lots of colors, and so on.

Fire up Quattro Pro and compare your screen to the screen shots in Figures 5-1 and 5-2 to determine which display mode you are running. Most of the time, this book assumes that you are using WYSIWYG display mode, which is the default; almost all the screen shots illustrate in this mode.

If your screen doesn't look anything like either of these figures, make sure that you're actually running Quattro Pro and not a word processor or game.

See you on the flip-flop

Select the **O**ptions⇨**D**isplay Mode command. In the list that appears, choose the A: 80x25 option. Your screen should look something like Figure 5-1.

Back home again

Select the **O**ptions⇨**D**isplay Mode command. Then choose the B: WYSIWYG option. Your screen should look like Figure 5-2. If nothing happens after you choose B:WYSIWYG, your system isn't capable of displaying graphics, and you're doomed to a life in Text mode.

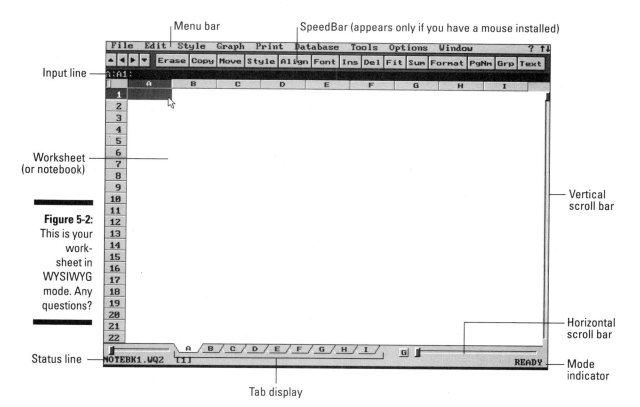

Figure 5-2: This is your worksheet in WYSIWYG mode. Any questions?

WYSIWYG: Why?

I started this chapter by showing you two screens: one in Text display mode and the other in WYSIWYG display mode. Whoever installed Quattro Pro on your system may have set it up so it always starts in WYSIWYG mode, which is the default mode at installation time.

Which mode should you use? Here are some general guidelines:

- If your computer has an old monochrome monitor (usually with a green display), you don't even have a choice. You have to use Text mode because WYSIWYG mode requires a graphics monitor.

- If you're using an AT class computer (one that uses the 80286 microchip), you'll definitely want to use Text mode. Otherwise, things seem to occur in slow motion. If you don't know what kind of computer you have, ask someone who would know (every office has at least one person like this).

- Even some 80386 computers (especially 80386SX-based PCs) are too slow for WYSIWYG mode. If you like things to happen immediately, use Text mode.

- If you really care about seeing things like different fonts and colors (and have a fast enough PC), you'll like WYSIWYG mode.

- For the most part, the examples in this book use WYSIWYG mode. So if you want your screen to look like the screen shots in the book and they don't, go for WYSIWYG mode.

- Remember that you can always change back and forth between these two modes, so it's not really a big deal which mode you have set up.

The Screen Tour (It's the Law)

Like the human body, a spreadsheet is made up of various parts, which more or less work together. Continuing with this analogy, some parts are definitely more interesting than others. Table 5-1 lists the parts that you'll eventually need to be familiar with. Don't be too concerned if you don't understand the terminology. It'll become crystal clear as you go through this chapter.

You can call me...

What do you call the thing that you're working on in Quattro Pro? The official name is a *worksheet*, but lazy types often call it just a *sheet*. Some people call it a *spreadsheet*, and others simply call it a *file*. A few even call it a *document*. Call it what you want. Nobody cares.

Table 5-1	Parts of Quattro Pro
Part	*What It Does*
The worksheet	This is the big fellow, the thing that holds your work. The worksheet (or *notebook*) contains 256 columns and 8,192 rows, which make up lots and lots of cells (536,870,912 cells, in fact).
Input line	This area shows the current cell and is the place where you enter information into the cell (and edit information that's already in a cell). The input line also displays messages and prompts when Quattro Pro needs information from you.
Status line	This area tells you all sorts of information (some useful, some not): the name of the active worksheet, the status of settings (such as NumLock and CapsLock), and the mode, such as READY, that Quattro Pro is in. (Do not confuse this mode with the display mode — Text or WYSIWYG — which is different.)
Menu bar	This area contains menu items, which contain commands that you give to Quattro Pro when you want to do something in your worksheet.
SpeedBar	This element contains words or symbols that you will probably find very useful. Eventually, you'll learn how to save time by using a SpeedBar (hence, the name). In Text mode, the SpeedBar appears as text down the right side of the screen.
Vertical scroll bar	Mouse users can click here to move up and down in a worksheet.
Horizontal scroll bar	Mouse users can click here to move left or right in a worksheet.
Tab display	This provides quick access to the additional pages in your worksheet. Because Version 4 has only a single page per file, it doesn't have these tabs.

Rows, columns, and cells

A worksheet is made up of a bunch of cells. Each cell is at the intersection of a row and a column. Rows are numbered 1, 2, 3, and so on up to 8,196. Columns are numbered A, B, C, and so on.

There are actually 256 columns in a worksheet, but since the English alphabet stops at Z, an international committee was formed to determine how to label spreadsheet columns when the letters run out. This committee arrived at an ingenious solution: use two letters. After column Z comes column AA, which is followed by AB, AC, and so on. After AZ comes BA, BB, BC, and so on. If you follow this to its logical conclusion, you'll discover that the 256th column is column IV.

Every Quattro Pro 5 worksheet has more pages stacked behind the first one. In fact, there are 255 more pages lurking behind the first page. If you're using Version 4, your worksheets only have one page. But you can have more than one worksheet open at a time, if you like.

So how may cells are in a worksheet? If your math is rusty, I'll do the calculation for you: 8,196 rows × 256 columns × 256 pages = 537,133,056 cells (or a tad more than half a billion). If you need more than this, you're reading the wrong book.

Only Version 5 has 537,133,056 cells. If you are a Version 4 user, you'll have to learn to live with a mere 2,098,176 cells.

Gimme your address

With around half a billion cells in a worksheet, the normal person might have trouble keeping track of them. Actually, keeping track isn't all that hard, thanks to the fact that each cell has its own address (but not its own ZIP code).

The *address* of a cell is made up of three things: the page letter, the column letter, and the row number. A colon follows the page letter, but the column letter and row number are stuck together with no space in between. Therefore, the upper left cell of the first page is cell A:A1. The last cell, down at the bottom of the last sheet and in the last column, has an address of IV:IV256.

You can usually omit the page letter part of a cell address. If you don't include it, Quattro Pro simply uses the current page.

You only have to worry about page numbers if you use Version 5. If you use Version 4, your life will be a bit simpler since you can't have more than one page in a worksheet. Therefore, in Version 4, you don't have to worry about page letters in cell addresses. For example, you can refer to the upper left cell as A1. (If you've ever attended a Bingo game, you've already been exposed to some valid cell addresses.)

The active cell

Take a look at the worksheet in Figure 5-3. Notice that one of the cells is a different color than the others? This is the *active cell*. The active cell is the cell that you can do things to. For example, you can enter information into the active cell, or you can edit what's already in the active cell.

In this case, the active cell happens to be cell C4 (I'm leaving off the page letter part of the cell address since I'm talking about only one page). The active cell is the cell where the pointer is. The input line also tells you what cell is active. When you move the cell pointer around, the active cell changes.

Move it along

So how do you move the cell pointer? Easy, with a mouse or the keyboard.

Moving around with a mouse

If you have a mouse connected to your PC, move the mouse around and notice the cell pointer move. (In WYSIWYG mode, the cell pointer is an arrow; in Text mode, it's a dot.) When the pointer is over one of the cells, click the left mouse button. The cell, which is magically transformed into the active cell, turns a different color.

Mouse fanatics can also use the scroll bars to move to other cells. There are two scroll bars: a vertical scroll bar and a horizontal scroll bar. To move down 20 rows in a worksheet, click towards the bottom of the vertical scroll bar. To move up 20 rows, click towards the top of the scroll bar. To move one screen to

Figure 5-3:
The active cell address is shown in the input line. In the worksheet, the active cell appears in a different color than the other cells.

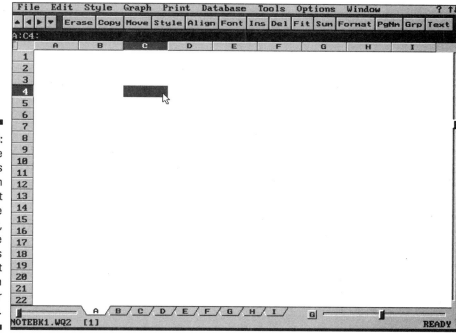

the right, click on the right side of the horizontal scroll bar. To move one screen to the left, click on the left side of the horizontal scroll bar. Using the scroll bars is actually easier to do than it is to describe, so play around with clicking the scroll bars until you get the hang of it.

You can activate and move to another worksheet page by clicking on the appropriate tab at the bottom of the screen. Most of the time, one page in your spreadsheet will probably be enough for you. But don't overlook Chapter 11, which discusses some ways to use these extra pages.

Moving around with the keyboard

Even if you have a mouse, you might find it easier to use the keyboard to move around a worksheet (I do, and I'm an expert). Use the cursor-movement keys. These are the PgUp and PgDn keys and the arrow keys.

> ***Note***: There are lots of different styles of keyboards. One common keyboard has two sets of cursor-movement keys. Most keyboards have a separate numeric keypad at the right.

The keys with the arrows move the cell pointer one cell at a time in the direction of the arrow. (Making the cell pointer movement correspond to the arrow direction was an ingenious idea, eh?) Hold down one of the arrow keys, and the cell pointer zips along until you let go.

A better way to move the cell pointer long distances is to use the PgUp and PgDn keys. These keys move the cell pointer 20 rows at a time.

To move one screen to the right, use the Tab key (or press Ctrl-right arrow). And to move quickly to the left, use Shift-Tab (or press Ctrl-left arrow).

When the arrow keys don't work

If your arrow keys spit out numbers when you press them, you need to press the Num Lock key. Most keyboards have a little light that tells you the status of the Num Lock key (it's either on or off). If your Num Lock light is on, the numeric keypad produces numbers. If the Num Lock light is off, the numeric keypad produces cursor movements. It's as easy as that.

Express routes to distant cell addresses

If you need to move the cell pointer to some off-the-wall cell address such as R:FE459, you could bang away on the cursor-movement keys all day and still not find your way there. You can use this shortcut: Press the F5 key on your keyboard. You can find this key either in a row along the top of your keyboard or in a separate section along the left side. Quattro Pro displays a message in the Input Line that says Enter address to go to. Now simply type **R:FE459** (or whatever cell address you want to get to) and press Enter. *Voila!* You're there. This is magic, and nobody else knows about it, so let's keep it our little secret, okay?

At some point in your life, you may find yourself lost deep in the bowels of a worksheet and want to get back home (that is, get back to cell A:A1). Here's how to take the express route: press Ctrl-Home. You return safe and sound to cell A1 of the first page. To quickly jump to cell A1 of the *current* page, just press Home.

Filling the Void: What to Do with a Blank Worksheet

Okay, I've covered a lot of ground so far. You're familiar with the parts of a worksheet, and you even know how to move the cell pointer to any cell in the worksheet. Lot of good that does, right? After all, you didn't buy Quattro Pro or this book so that you can wander aimlessly from cell to cell. Nine times out of ten, you'll want to put stuff in the worksheet cells (or at least your *boss* will want you to).

Worksheet modes

If you're really observant, you may have noticed the little word (READY) in the bottom right corner of your screen. This is the *mode indicator*. Up until now, Quattro Pro has been in READY mode, which means that Quattro Pro's ready for you to do something like move to another cell (which you already know how to do) or put something into a cell (which you're about to learn).

Quattro Pro is always in one mode or another, and you can tell by looking at the mode indicator (what else?). Table 5-2 is an exhaustive summary of every possible mode indicator (well, at least the important ones) that you will run across in your lifetime. By the way, these modes have absolutely nothing to do with the two display modes (Text and WYSIWYG) discussed earlier.

Table 5-2	Quattro Pro Mode Indicators
Mode	*What It Means*
READY	Quattro Pro is waiting for you to do something with the worksheet.
VALUE	You're entering a number into a cell.
LABEL	You're entering a label (or words) into a cell.
EDIT	You're in the process of changing something that's already in a cell.
WAIT	Quattro Pro is thinking. Normally, you can't do anything in this mode.
MENU	You pressed the slash (/) key and Quattro Pro is waiting for a command from the menu. Press Esc to get back to READY mode.
POINT	You're pointing out a cell reference to Quattro Pro.
MACRO	A macro is running. Unless you're working on somebody else's worksheet, you probably won't see this one.

Besides Bubba, what goes in a cell?

A spreadsheet cell can hold four types of items:

- A number (also known as a *value*). You won't have to stray any further than this chapter to learn how to enter numbers.

- A label (which you may recognize as normal words). Labels are also discussed in this chapter.

- A formula (which does miraculous things, using the contents of other cells). You'll have to wait until Chapter 6 to learn about formulas.

- Nothing (zip, nada, zilch, nil). Cells can be completely empty, void of all content.

A cell can hold only one of these four things at a time. If a cell has a number in it, it can't have a label. If it has a label, it can't hold a formula. If it's empty, it can't have anything. Well, you get the idea.

So why the distinction between numbers and words? When would you need numbers and when would you need words? And do you really need formulas?

You use numbers when you work with something that represents a quantity or a value. If you're making a worksheet to keep track of your gambling losses, you would enter a number for the amount of each bet that you lost. The nice thing about numbers is that you can refer to them in your formulas. For example, you can enter in a separate cell a formula that adds up a bunch of numbers and displays the answer.

Note: Some numbers aren't really numbers. For example, consider Social Security numbers or phone numbers, which aren't *really* numbers. Think about it — when was the last time you needed to add two phone numbers together? Numbers like these are actually labels that just happen to contain numbers. Keep reading for more information on how to tell Quattro Pro that your numbers aren't really numbers. (***Hint:*** It involves using a label prefix.)

Labels, on the other hand, are most useful for describing what the numbers are and for adding titles to your work. In your gambling loss worksheet, you could put labels like these next to your numbers: *Las Vegas slots*, *Del Mar Racetrack*, and so on. You can also use labels when you just want to make a simple list without numbers (those who made it through Chapter 2 will know a bit about labels).

You leave cells blank when you don't have anything to put in them or when you want to have space between cells that contain information. By default, all cells are blank.

Figure 5-4 shows a worksheet with numbers, words, formulas, and blank cells. Notice that you can't see formulas; you only see the *result* of the formulas.

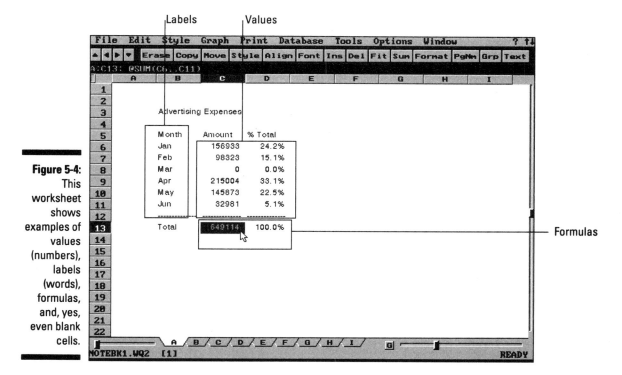

Figure 5-4: This worksheet shows examples of values (numbers), labels (words), formulas, and, yes, even blank cells.

The Quattro Pro manual refers to non-numeric cell entries as *labels*. Some people call it *text*. I've been calling it *words,* but you might also catch me using the term *string.* The bottom line? Call it whatever you want.

Typing in a number

Throughout the course of history, spreadsheets have acquired a reputation of being good with numbers. Therefore, it's only fitting that you start by learning how to enter a number into a cell.

Before you put anything into a cell, make sure you're in READY mode (check the status line at the bottom of the screen to see what mode you're in). You can usually press Esc once or twice to get into this mode.

When you're ready to enter a number, you have two choices:

- ✔ Use the number keys along the top of your keyboard. Be sure not to use the Function keys (the keys with *F*s on them).
- ✔ If your NumLock light is on, you can use the keys on the numeric keypad to input numbers.

Enter a number. Move to a cell — use cell B3 just for fun. Now enter a number such as **236**, but don't press Enter. Notice that you're now in VALUE mode (VALUE appears in the status line). When you entered the first number, Quattro Pro read your mind and realized that you are entering a number (or value) into a cell. Press the Enter key to make the number stick in the cell. Take a peek at the mode indicator, and you'll see that you're back in READY mode.

When you press Enter after typing in a number, the cell pointer stays in the same cell. Use the down-arrow key to move to the cell below (cell B4), and then enter another number — try **314** — and press Enter. Repeat this until you get the hang of it. Remember, you can use any of the techniques you already know to move to any cell in the worksheet before entering a number into it.

You may not realize it, but you've come a long way; you now have enough knowledge to fill the entire worksheet with numbers. (But don't try it; it gets boring pretty fast.)

Making numbers look right

When you start entering numbers into cells, you may not be happy with how the numbers look. If you have a really long number, you might want to put commas in it. And accountants usually like to see dollar signs tacked on to their numbers. And what if you work with percentages? The answer, my friend, is formatting.

But can it calculate the national debt?

The perennially curious readers are probably wondering just how large a number you can put into a cell. The experimentally inclined readers have probably already tried entering some humongous numbers. But most readers have already decided to skip over this section.

Actually, the largest number you can enter into a Quattro Pro cell is 1E308, which is scientific notation for *1 times 10 to the 308th power*. In more common terms, this number looks like this:

100,000,000,000,000,000,000,000,000,000,000,
000,000,000,000,000,000,000,000,000,000,000,
000,000,000,000,000,000,000,000,000,000,000,
000,000,000,000,000,000,000,000,000,000,000,
000,000,000,000,000,000,000,000,000,000,000,
000,000,000,000,000,000,000,000,000,000,000,
000,000,000,000,000,000,000,000,000,000,000,
000,000,000,000,000,000,000,000,000,000,000,
000,000,000,000,000,000,000

I have no idea how you would pronounce this number. Let's just say that it's the mother of all numbers.

Figure 5-5 shows some numbers. The numbers in the first column are plain old numbers, and the numbers in the second column are formatted. Which do *you* like better?

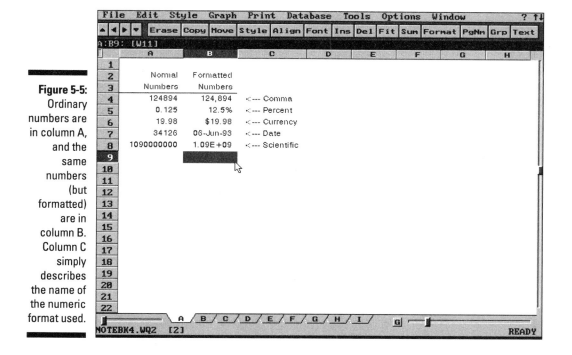

Figure 5-5: Ordinary numbers are in column A, and the same numbers (but formatted) are in column B. Column C simply describes the name of the numeric format used.

Formatting only affects how the numbers look. Formatting does *not* change the actual number in any way. In the figure, the cells in each row both hold exactly the same number. The only difference is the appearance of the numbers (one is formatted and the other isn't).

Formatting numbers

The details of formatting numbers come later in the book. But if you're really interested and can't wait, I'll tell you how to format numbers so you can play around with them on your own.

First, move the cell pointer to the cell that has the number you want to format. Next, select the **Style⇨Numeric Format** command. Quattro Pro displays a little pop-up window that lists a bunch of names for numeric formats (see Figure 5-6).

Figure 5-6:
From this
menu, you
can select
the numeric
format you
want.

You can save a few milliseconds by using Ctrl-F to format cells. This is exactly the same as issuing the **Style⇨Numeric Format** command.

You can press a command's highlighted letter to select a format, or you can move down this list with the arrow keys and press Enter to select the format that is highlighted. Usually (and depending on the format you select), Quattro Pro asks you how many decimal places you want to display. Just enter a number or accept what Quattro Pro proposes (two decimal places) and press Enter.

Quattro Pro displays the message Block to be modified. You can then use the arrow keys to highlight even more cells that you want to apply the formatting to. Press Enter, and you see the results of this command.

> *Note*: You may be interested to know that Quattro Pro's input line displays a code that tells you about the numeric format of the active cell. This code appears in parentheses directly to the right of the display of the active cell's address.

Once you format a number, you're not stuck with it. You can keep applying different numeric formats until you get one you like.

You can even format empty cells so that if you ever decide to put a number in, the number appears in the format that you gave it when the cell was empty.

Entering labels

Spreadsheets are boring enough, but just think how bad it would be if they could only hold numbers. As you already know, Quattro Pro's cells can cope with labels (or words) as well as numbers. To enter a label into a cell, move to the cell you're interested in and start typing letters (Quattro Pro read your mind and changes the mode indicator to LABEL). When you're finished, press Enter. (By the way, a cell can hold more than one word, so you can use the spacebar just as you normally would.)

As you'll learn later on this book, you can do all sorts of things to change the way your labels appear. You can make them bold, italic, a larger size, and so on. The secret here is to use the **Style**⇨**Font** command — but I'm getting ahead of myself.

What if it doesn't fit?

Try this: Move the cell pointer to any cell in a row that's completely empty, and enter the following:

Bills I Need to Pay This Month

You notice that this text seems to spill over into the cells to the right of it. Actually, the text is all contained in the one cell. Since the adjoining cells are empty, Quattro Pro simply borrows their space to display the spill over from the cell.

Now, go to cell B3 and enter a number such as **198** into the cell. Move the cell pointer one column to the left (to cell A3) and enter **Car Payment Amount** into this cell. Since cell B3 is occupied, Quattro Pro can't borrow its space to display the spill over from cell A3. Therefore, it truncates its display for this cell. Don't worry; all of the text is still in there — it just doesn't show up on the screen.

When you start with a new worksheet, all the columns are wide enough to display nine characters. The solution to the failure-to-spill-over problem is to make the entire column A wider. But I need to save some topics for later.

If you really must know

Okay, if you can't wait, here's how to make a column wider. Make sure you're in READY mode and move the cell pointer to any cell in the column that you want to widen. Select the Style⇨Column Width command. Then type in a number (try **15**) that represents the number of characters wide you want the column to be. Then press Enter and marvel at your new, wider column. (By the way, the shortcut key combination to change the column width is Ctrl-W.)

It's a label, you #%!*&% computer!

Sometimes when you enter a label into a cell, Quattro Pro merely beeps and displays an error message like the one shown in Figure 5-7.

Figure 5-7:
This
message
appears
when
Quattro Pro
doesn't like
your label.

If you still operate under the belief that computers are smart, try it yourself: Move to any blank cell and enter the following label:

1st Quarter Sales Report

Press Enter. You'll hear the beep and witness the verbal complaint. Try as you might, you're stuck. The only thing that can save you is to abort your efforts by pressing Esc — or, I suppose, you could fix the problem.

But what *is* the problem? Well, since this particular label starts out with a number, Quattro Pro assumes that you want to enter a value and that *you're* the dumb one. So beeping is the program's way of telling you that it won't let you continue until you correct *your* "mistake."

Does this mean you're doomed to a life with labels that never start with a number? Hardly. All you need to do is begin such a label with a *label prefix*. Table 5-3 is an exhaustive list of all of the label prefixes that you can use. By the way, *label prefix* is definitely a term that you can forget as soon as you finish with this chapter.

Table 5-3	Label Prefixes and What They Do	
Label Prefix	**English Translation**	**How the Label Is Displayed**
'	Single quote	Left aligned in the cell
"	Double quote	Right aligned in the cell
^	Caret	Centered in the cell

Labels can consist not only of letters and numbers, but other characters as well. These characters are listed in Table 5-4. But there's one hitch. Like beginning a label with a number, you can begin a label with any of these characters only if you put in a label prefix first.

Table 5-4	Other Characters That Need Label Prefixes
Character	**English Translation**
/	Forward slash
+	Plus symbol
-	Minus symbol, or hyphen
$	Dollar sign
(	Open or left parenthesis
@	At symbol
#	Pound or number symbol
.	Period

So the moral of this story is *When a label begins with a number or any of the characters listed in Table 5-4, always start it with one of the three label prefixes.* And don't worry about these funny characters messing up the looks of your worksheet — they don't display in the cell.

If you haven't figured it out by now, label prefixes are the key to putting in numbers that aren't really numbers — Social Security numbers, phone numbers, and street addresses, for example. If you want to put your Social Security number into a cell, start it with one of the label prefixes (I suggest a single quote). Quattro Pro will interpret it as a label, and everyone will be happy.

Always use a label prefix when you want to begin a cell entry with a number or any of these characters:

> / + - $(@ # and .

It seems to me that a program that's smart enough to compute natural logarithms, perform linear regressions, and invert matrices could also figure out that you want to enter a label rather than a value. But, alas, it can't.

Using label prefixes for personal gain

The astute reader may have realized that he or she can take advantage of label prefixes. If you want a label centered in a cell, simply start the label with a caret (^). To make the label butt up against the right side of the cell, start it with a double quote ("). In other words, you can use label prefixes even for labels that don't start with a number. In fact, every label has a label prefix whether you add one or not. If you don't insert a label prefix, Quattro Pro automatically inserts a single quote (') for you. This left-aligns the label — the default.

For the insatiably curious, check out the labels in the worksheet shown in Figure 5-8, which shows the effects of the label prefixes. Note that the double quote (") only works if the column is wide enough to display the full label. Otherwise, the label still looks like it's left-aligned.

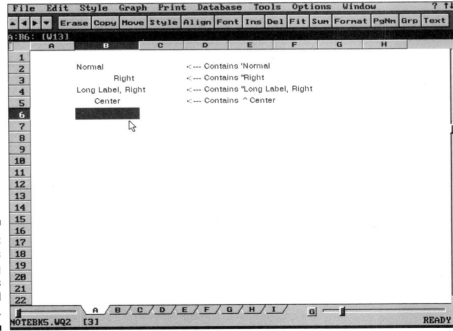

Figure 5-8:
The results
of using
various
label
prefixes.

When Enter isn't good enough

Up until now, you've probably been using Enter to signal the end of your numbers and labels. Actually, you can also use any of the arrow keys instead of Enter. Using the arrow keys has a dual effect: it makes the number stick in the cell, *and* it moves the cell pointer in the direction of the arrow key you selected. Over the past 10 years, this technique has saved me a cumulative total of 3 minutes and 18 seconds.

Making Amends

There may be a time when you realize that you entered something incorrectly into a cell (although this has never happened to me, I *have* heard stories about people making such mistakes).

Imagine that you entered the following label into a cell: *Sales Reprot for January.* Your boss, a former grade school spelling bee champ, tells you that you've misspelled a word. To placate him, you have two choices: you can move the cell pointer back to the offensive cell and re-enter the entire label, or you can edit the cell.

Overwriting a cell

To put something else into a cell that already contains material, just move the cell pointer to the cell and enter the new information. The new stuff replaces the old stuff. You can replace a number with a number, a label with a number, a number with a label, and so on.

Editing a cell

If you only need to make a minor change to what's in a cell, you might be able to save some time by editing the cell. Move the cell pointer to the cell you want to change, and then press the F2 key (which is located along the top of your keyboard or along the left side of the keyboard). If you have a mouse, you can just click on the input line to start editing the contents of the active cell.

Figure 5-9 is a live-action shot of someone editing an actual cell. Notice that the contents of the cell appear on the input line. This is where the editing takes place. Notice also that the mode indicator reads EDIT — a sure sign that you are, in fact, editing a cell. When you press F2 to edit a cell, it's just as if you entered the information all over again and you were just about to press Enter to make it stick. But before you press Enter, you need to fix the mistake.

By the way, that flashing underline thingamajig in the input line is known by the provocative term *insertion point*. When you finish with this chapter, you can safely forget the official name for this item.

The editing keys

While you're in EDIT mode, there are a few keys that come in mighty handy. If you're interested, check out Table 5-5. If not, you'll waste lots of time re-entering data. Have it your way.

Table 5-5	Handy Keys You Can Use While Editing a Cell
Key	*What It Does*
Backspace	Erases the character to the left of the insertion point
Left arrow	Moves the insertion point by one character to the left (and doesn't erase anything)
Right arrow	Moves the insertion point by one character to the right (and doesn't erase anything)
Del	Erases the character to the right of the insertion point
Esc	Leaves the cell just as it was before you started this escapade (Press Esc if you royally mess your editing up and want to start over)

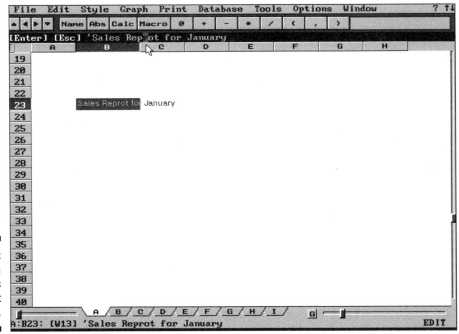

Figure 5-9:
Editing a
cell occurs
in the input
line.

You can use these keys to move around on the input line, erase unwanted characters, and insert new characters. When your entry looks right, just press Enter (or any of the arrow keys).

Ins or Ovr?

As if keeping track of modes such as READY, VALUE, and EDIT isn't confusing enough, here's something else you need to know: Quattro Pro has yet *another* mode, which is entirely unrelated to those that you've already learned. I'm talking about INS (insert) mode and OVR (overwrite) mode. You can tell whether you're in INS or OVR mode by looking at the status line (see Figure 5-10).

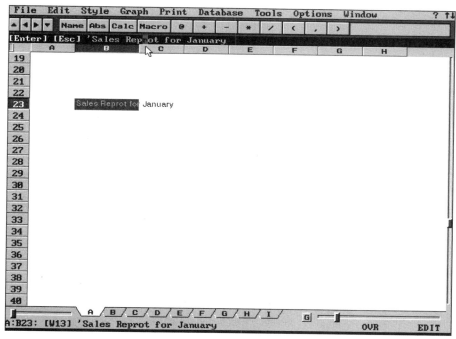

Figure 5-10:
The status line tells you if you're in INS or OVR mode.

What happens when you edit the existing text is partly determined by whether you are in INS or OVR mode:

- In INS mode, when you enter a new character while editing, the new character is inserted into the text, and the characters to the right move over to make room for it.

- In OVR mode, when you enter a new character while editing, the new character replaces the existing character.

Normally, you're in INS mode (which is good because it keeps you from accidentally typing over perfectly good characters). You can get into OVR mode by pressing the Ins (Insert) key.

Why would you ever want to be in OVR mode? It's a minor time-saver because it prevents you from having to erase a character and then type a new one. In OVR mode, you can add a good character and get rid of a bad one with a single keystroke.

> **Note**: A little bit of keyboard trivia: Why do you have to use something as arcane as the F2 key to edit a cell? It all dates back to the dark ages when Lotus 1-2-3 first came out. Back in those days, computer programs relied heavily on these function keys. 1-2-3 used F2 to edit its cells, and Quattro Pro carries on the tradition.

Nuking a cell

You know how to change a cell, but what if you want to wipe the contents of a cell completely off the face of the earth? Easy. Move the cell pointer to the undesired cell, press Del, and kiss it good-bye.

Never erase a cell by hitting the spacebar. Although this appears to get rid of the cell contents, it actually inserts a single character (an invisible space with only a label prefix) into the cell. This can cause you serious problems that are very difficult to diagnose. Take my word for it: substituting the spacebar for the Del key is a no-no.

Ready for More?

If you liked this chapter, even better stuff is only a page-turn away. Keep reading, and you'll learn how to put formulas into your worksheet. Take it from one who knows: Formulas are definitely more fun than getting poked in the eye with an electric drill.

Chapter 6
Formulas: Not Just for Babies Anymore

There once was a girl named Raquel
Who couldn't add or subtract very well,
And then she found out
What a spreadsheet was about
When she put her first formula in a cell.

In This Chapter

▶ Why some people are so fascinated with spreadsheets (or what makes spreadsheets really cool)

▶ What formulas are and why you need them

▶ Two ways to enter a formula (the hard way and the easy way)

▶ A few simple rules about entering formulas

▶ How to use the mathematical operators you thought you were finished with in high school

▶ An exclusive, behind-the-scenes look at what goes on when you enter a formula into a cell

Okay, here's what you've been waiting for. The chapter that makes it all worthwhile. The chapter that will finally make your worksheets come to life. The chapter that gives you the skills necessary to actually do something useful. The chapter that teaches you about formulas.

If you're reading this book from beginning to end, you know just enough about moving around a worksheet to be dangerous. And you also know how to enter numbers and labels into cells with the best of them. Now you're ready for the next logical step.

Formulas: The Definition

When you enter a number or a label into a cell, Quattro Pro simply displays that number or label in the cell. A formula, like a number or a label, is also something that you enter into a cell. But the difference is that a formula doesn't appear in the cell. Instead, it performs some type of calculation and displays the *answer* in the cell (see Figure 6-1). However, you can still see the actual formula in the input line when you move the cell pointer to the cell that holds the formula.

Simple formulas use only numbers and no cell addresses. For example, you can enter the following formula into a cell, and Quattro Pro displays the answer (which is 145):

```
+100+45
```

In this example, the plus sign before the number 100 tells Quattro Pro that what follows is a formula. (Without the initial plus sign, Quattro Pro thinks that you're trying to enter a number and gets confused when it sees too many characters.)

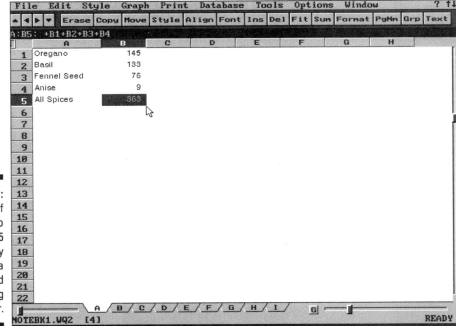

Figure 6-1: A bunch of values? No way. Cell B5 actually holds a formula and is displaying its answer.

But using actual values in formulas isn't all that useful. Formulas are a lot more useful when you use cell addresses instead of actual values. Allow me to demonstrate.

Take a look at Figure 6-1, which shows a worksheet with labels in column A and numbers in column B. But there's something unusual about cell B5: it contains the formula +B1+B2+B3+B4. What you're seeing displayed in cell B5 is the formula's answer (or its result). And because the active cell happens to be cell B5, the content of this cell (that is, the formula) appears in the input line.

What this formula is saying, in plain English, is "Hey Quattro Pro, take the number in cell B1 and add it to the number in B2. Then add the number in B3 to the total. And while you're at it, add the number in B4 to that total. Now, display the final answer in my cell. Thanks, dude."

You may think that entering **+B1+B2+B3+B4** is a rather lengthy way to get the sum of these numbers. But you'll have to admit that it's sure easier than typing out the instructions in English.

Actually, there's a much easier way to get the sum of a bunch of cells, but that's another chapter. (***Hint:*** It involves @functions.)

Hello, Operator?

You've already seen how a formula can use the plus sign to add values together. As you might expect, you can use other mathematical operators to perform even more amazing feats. For example, you can subtract values by using the minus sign and multiply values by using an asterisk (not an *X*, as you might think). And you can't overlook the ever-popular division operation that uses a slash. Finally, those with a penchant for large numbers might be interested in the exponential operator ($^\wedge$) that raises a number to a power. Table 6-1 shows some examples of formulas using these operators.

Table 6-1	Sample Formulas That Use Various Operators
Formula	*What It Does*
+A1*23.5	Multiplies the value in cell A1 by 23.5
+A1-A3	Subtracts the value in A3 from the value in A1
+A4/A3	Divides the value in cell A4 by the value in cell A3
+A3^3	Raises the value of cell A3 to the third power (equivalent to +A3*A3*A3)
+(A1+A2)/A3	Adds the value in cell A1 to the value in cell A2 and then divides the answer by the value in cell A3

Using parentheses

Okay, you caught me. The last entry in the preceding table introduced something new — parentheses. You can use parentheses to tell Quattro Pro what order you want the calculations to occur in. Why is this necessary? Here's how the last example in Table 6-1 would look without any parentheses:

```
+A1+A2/A3
```

In this form, the formula is ambiguous. Do you want to add A1 to A2 and divide the result by A3? Or do you want to divide A2 by A3 and then add A1 to it? Does it matter? Yep. Read on to find out why.

Just for the sake of argument, assume that you have three cells in column A, each with a value. The values are

A1:   4

A2:   10

A3:   2

Take another look at this now-familiar formula: +A1+A2/A3.

If you forget about cell addresses and use the real numbers, the formula would look like this:

4+10/2

Add 4 to 10 and you get 14. Divide 14 by 2 and you get 7. That's the answer, right? Well, yes, except that you *could* look at like this: Divide 10 by 2 to get 5. Then add the 4 to this 5, and you get 9, also a right answer. Hmmmm. The formula can produce either 7 or 9, depending on the order in which the operations are done.

Computers can't handle ambiguity well. Therefore, you need to be very specific. The result of a formula depends on the order in which the arithmetic operations are performed. You can control this by using parentheses around the operation you want to be performed first.

How Quattro Pro deals with ambiguity

So what happens if you leave out the parentheses? Does Quattro Pro go into an endless loop trying to resolve the ambiguity? Not quite. Quattro Pro follows built-in rules that determine how it handles ambiguities such as these. These rules are called *order of precedence* (a term that you can safely forget once you understand the concept).

For example, multiplication has higher precedence than addition; therefore, +2+3*4 produces an answer of 14, not 20. In other words, when Quattro Pro doesn't find any parentheses to guide it, it first does the multiplication (3*4) and then the addition.

Table 6-2 lists some of the world's most popular mathematical operators; the number indicates the precedence level. Operations with higher precedence are done first, and those with equal precedence are performed from left to right. For example, multiplication, which has a precedence level of 2, is performed before subtraction or addition.

Table 6-2	Commonly Used Mathematical Operators and Their Precedence Level	
Operator	*Description*	*Precedence*
-	Subtraction	1
+	Addition	1
*	Multiplication	2
/	Division	2
^	To the power of	3

If a formula doesn't have any overriding parentheses, Quattro Pro always goes for the exponentiation (^) operator first, and then does multiplication and division, and finally subtraction and addition.

Nested parentheses

Frankly, I've been using spreadsheets for a decade, and I can never remember how this precedence business works (and I just don't trust it, for some reason). Therefore, I tend to use more parentheses than are necessary — which isn't bad because it makes it very clear how the formula is calculated. However, it's also easy to get confused when parentheses get nested several levels deep. Examine this formula:

```
(((A1+B1)*2)-((C1+D1)*2))/4
```

Notice that the number of left parentheses is exactly equal to the number of right parentheses. If this isn't true, Quattro Pro lets you know about it and doesn't accept the formula when you press Enter.

When Quattro Pro evaluates a formula like this, it starts in the middle and works its way out. Whatever is enclosed by the most deeply nested parentheses gets first attention, and the result of that is used to evaluate the remaining parts of the formula.

The thing about formulas

Here's the thing about formulas: They always look more complicated than they really are. That's because most people are used to seeing things that have some inherent meaning in them. A cell address such as +F13 is meaningless. Let's face it, things would be much less intimidating if you could write a formula like

+(current-previous)/previous

rather than

+(C12-B12)/B12

If you like the idea of using descriptive words instead of cell addresses, you'll love Chapter 7.

In this example, there are two sets of parentheses at the deepest level: (A1+B1) and (C1+D1). So Quattro Pro finds these two answers and then evaluates the next level. Again, there are two sets of parentheses at the next level. In this case, it uses the answers from the previous level and multiplies them by 2. At the next level up, it takes these two answers and subtracts the second one from the first. At the top level, it takes the previous answer and divides by four. This is the answer that shows up in the cell.

This, of course, all happens in the blink of an eye (actually, faster than that). The point I'm trying to make is that using more parentheses than you really need can actually help you translate gobbledygook formulas like the one above.

Choose Your Poison

Putting a formula into a cell is not difficult, but it can be tricky. One way to enter a formula in a cell is to type it in. Another way, which is often easier, is to *point* to the cells and let Quattro Pro help you build the formula.

The hard way: Typing the formula in

The most straightforward way to enter a formula is to simply type it into a cell. You can enter any of the formulas you've seen so far just by typing them exactly as they appear. This includes all the cell addresses, mathematical operators, parentheses, actual values, and whatever else is required.

What about spaces?

When you enter a formula, you can use spaces to separate cell addresses from operators. For example, if you enter a formula like +A32/B19, Quattro Pro doesn't care if you put a space before or after the slash. But it *does* care if you put a space inside a cell address. In other words, you can't put a space between the row and column (*A 1*, for instance). But there's really no reason to use any spaces since Quattro Pro automatically takes them out anyway. So if you later edit a formula that you entered with spaces, the spaces will have vanished.

The easy way: Pointing and letting Quattro Pro do the work

When you're entering a formula, Quattro Pro offers a slick alternative to typing the actual cell references — which can be very tedious (not to mention error-prone). This method is called *pointing*. The best way to understand this method is to follow along with an example.

You're going to build a formula that adds three cells together and displays the results in another cell. And you'll do it without typing a single cell address. Figure 6-2 shows what my screen looked like when I was trying this out.

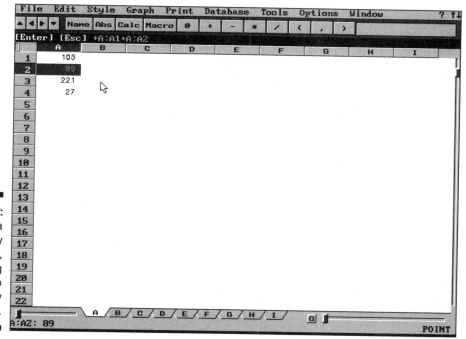

Figure 6-2: Building a formula by pointing (or, letting Quattro Pro do the dirty work).

To build the formula by pointing, follow these steps:

1. Start by entering numbers in cells A1, A2, and A3. Any numbers will do.

2. Move the cell pointer to cell A4.

3. Enter + to tell Quattro Pro that a formula is on its way.

4. Use the up-arrow key to move the cell pointer to cell A1.

   Notice that the mode indicator now reads POINT. Also notice that the formula is being created on the input line before your very eyes.

5. Enter + again (the addition operator).

   The cell pointer jumps back to cell A4, where you're building the formula.

6. Use the up-arrow key to move the cell pointer to cell A2.

7. Press + again.

8. Use the up-arrow key to move the cell pointer to cell A3.The input line should now read, +A1+A2+A3 (which is just what you want).

9. Press Enter to stick the formula into cell A4.

Using this pointing technique means that you never have to be concerned with the actual cell address — just point to the cells you want and Quattro Pro takes care of the ugly details. This method also cuts down on errors. After all, it's pretty easy to make a typing mistake when you enter a formula manually (and you might not even discover the mistake until your boss asks you how 12+12 could possibly equal 197).

How to start a formula

You may have noticed that all the formulas so far have started with a plus sign. A plus sign is one way of telling Quattro Pro that a formula is on its way. In fact, you can start a formula with either a plus sign or a minus sign.

If you use a minus sign to start a formula, you're basically telling Quattro Pro to multiply the first cell address by –1. Check out this formula:

```
-A1+A2
```

This formula says, "Take the value in A1, make it negative, and then add it to A2." Unless that's *really* what you want to do, you'll probably start most of your formulas with a plus sign.

If you want to save what you do

Oddly enough, this book doesn't actually discuss critical things like saving files until Chapter 9. In the course of working your way through this chapter, you might do something that's worth saving. In the unlikely event that this happens, here's a quick rundown on how to save your work and retrieve it later on.

To save a file, make sure you're in READY mode. Then issue the File⇨Save command. Quattro Pro displays a box. Simply type in a filename, up to eight characters in length, and press Enter. You can call the file anything you want, but to be on the safe side, use only letters and numbers for your filename.

Later on, you can bring this file back when you want to work on it some more. Again, make sure you're in READY mode, and then issue the File⇨Retrieve command. Quattro Pro displays a box, and you can use the arrow keys to move around until the filename you want is highlighted. Then press Enter to bring the file in. You can continue working where you left off.

You can also start a formula with an opening (or left) parenthesis, but just make sure that it has a closing (or right) parenthesis to match it.

You can start formulas with a plus sign, a minus sign, or a right parenthesis.

Why Use Formulas?

When you enter a formula, the answer that gets displayed isn't carved in stone (and you shouldn't take it for granite). The answer that's displayed changes when you change a number in any cell that the formula uses. This, gentle reader, is what makes spreadsheets so darned appealing. Once you get your formulas set up, you're free to play around with the numbers and change them without having to re-enter the formulas.

Now that you understand something about formulas, you can appreciate the rest of this section, which tells you why you would want to use formulas in your worksheet.

Because you have to

The most important reason to use formulas is because it's the only way that you can produce the results you need. If you want to add up a column of numbers manually, you could use a hand calculator and a word processor and forget about Quattro Pro altogether.

If you use this low-tech (non-formula) method, you can count on the fact that your boss will want you to change a number or two — and she needs a new

Calculating formulas

One or two of you may be curious about what goes on behind the scenes when you enter a formula into a cell. If you've ever wondered what a computer thinks about, you find out here.

When you enter a formula into a cell, Quattro Pro goes through the following thought process:

1. Okay, this person is entering a formula. Oh, boy! Oh, boy! It's not just a number or a label.

2. Is he using POINT mode? He must be really bright (or reading a *really* phenomenal book) If so, I need to show him the cell addresses as he points to them and stick them in the formula (sheesh, I have to do *all* the work)....

3. He just pressed Enter. That means he's finished with the formula.

4. I'll just check this formula to make sure it follows all of my rules. If it doesn't, I'll beep and make him feel foolish.

5. Looks okay to me. Now I'll calculate the results using the values in the cells he specified.

6. Now I'll finish up by displaying the answer in the cell.

7. Nap time yet?

report in five minutes for the board presentation. Do it with formulas, and you can send your thank-you letters to me care of IDG Books.

To play "what-if"

You can create a worksheet with formulas that use the values you enter. Then change the values to see what happens to the formulas under various scenarios. In a budget, for example, you might ask, "What if all salaries get cut by five percent?" If you have the formulas set up right, you can get the bad news in an instant.

To handle uncertainty

Often, you don't have all the information you need to finish a project. This won't stop you from getting your worksheet all set up. Just plug in dummy values for the missing numbers and create the worksheet, pretending that you have the missing numbers. Then, when they finally show up, you can stick them in, and everything will recalculate like magic.

To make a "fill-in-the-cells" template for someone else

Suppose that you're about to buy a car, so you set up a worksheet to figure out how much your monthly payment will be based on loan amount, interest rate, and the term of the loan. You do it, make your decision, and buy the car. Next week, Lori down the hall says she's interested in buying a car. You can just hand her your worksheet and tell her to punch in her own numbers. She'll think you're pretty smart for developing this model, and even smarter for saving it in a file. And she'll invite you over for dinner next weekend.

Just How Complex Can They Be?

Like relationships, formulas can be simple or complex. All of the formulas you've seen so far in this chapter fall into the simple category. Yes, even the formula that demonstrated nesting parentheses is pretty elementary in the whole scheme of things.

I created a monster

Here's an example of an actual formula that I once developed in a moment of boredom (actually, it was quite a few moments). This entire mess goes into one cell:

@IF(B$25<>$A27,((@COUNT(@@(B$25))*@SUM
PRODUCT(@@(B$25),@@($A27)))(@SUM(@@
(B$25))*@SUM(@@($A27))))(@SQRT((@COUNT
(@@(B$25))*@SUMPRODUCT(@@(B$25),@@
(B$25)))-@SUM(@@(B$25))^2)*@SQRT
((@COUNT(@@(B$25))*@SUMPRODUCT(@@
($A27),@@($A27)))-(@SUM(@@($A27))
^2))),"   --")

This formula is used to calculate correlation coefficients using indirect referencing. Believe it or not, some people actually have a use for this sort of thing. But the most amazing thing is that this monster actually works — although I no longer understand exactly *how* it works.

The point of presenting this formula is not to impress you with my formula-building prowess (although any perceptive, intuitive, and creative person will definitely be awestruck and mesmerized by this Herculean accomplishment), but to demonstrate that you really don't have to worry about creating formulas that Quattro Pro can't handle. Actually, you're limited to 254 characters. When you hit this limit, you can't enter anything more.

Relative vs. Absolute References

There's one additional topic that I can't put off any longer: relative versus absolute references. This can be rather confusing, but it's pretty important stuff.

Up till now, all of the cell references you've used in formulas have been *relative*. If you copy a formula that has relative references, the copies of the formula change to reflect their new position. Here's an example. Assume the following formula is in cell A3:

```
+A1+A2
```

If you copy this formula to the cell next door (B3), the formula in cell B3 reads

```
+B1+B2
```

In other words, copying the formula changed the cells in a relative manner. No matter where you copy the formula, it always computes the sum of the two cells directly above it.

By default, all cell references are relative.

But what if you want the copy of the formula to return the sum of A1 and A2? In this case, you want to use *absolute* references. The same formula with absolute references would be

```
+$A$1+$A$2
```

Using dollar signs tells Quattro Pro that the cell reference is absolute — that it will always refer to those specific cells, even if you copy the formula.

When you get to the point that you want to copy or move formulas, make sure you read Chapter 8, which explains absolute and relative references in more detail.

Further Formula Fare

I'll wrap up this chapter with a few additional random thoughts. This section can be considered lagniappe.

Controlling recalculation

As you know, a formula will display a different result if you change the values in any of the cells that the formula uses. Normally, Quattro Pro automatically does this recalculation. Whenever you change anything in a worksheet, the program quickly scans all the formulas and checks to see whether any of them need to be updated to show a new answer.

Some people, however, create very large worksheets that have hundreds or even thousands of formulas. In such a case, Quattro Pro continues to scan each formula every time you make a change in the worksheet and makes the appropriate recalculations. But since it takes a while — even for a computer — to scan thousands of formulas, you'll notice that you often have to wait for Quattro Pro to do its scanning. The net result is that your computer slows down, and it even takes time for what you type to show up on the screen (a delayed reaction).

The solution to this is to tell Quattro Pro that *you* want to control when it does its recalculation. In other words, you want to turn off automatic recalculation and set it to manual recalculation. In READY mode, issue the **Options**⇨**Recalculation**⇨**Mode**⇨**Manual** command. To switch back to automatic recalculation, use the **Options**⇨**Recalculation**⇨**Mode**⇨**Automatic** command.

But if you do choose to use manual recalculation, it's up to you to remember to recalculate. You do this by pressing the F9 key. Quattro Pro reminds you when a recalculation is needed by displaying CALC in the status line. If the CALC indicator is showing, you know that you can't always trust that what's displayed on the screen is really accurate.

Using built-in functions

Formulas take on even more muscle when you use some of Quattro Pro's built-in @functions (pronounced "at funk shuns"). The reason for the unusual name is that they all begin with an at sign. For example, there are @functions that can calculate the sum of a block of cells, compute the average, do square roots, and lots of other more or less useful things. I cover a few of the more common @functions in the next chapter.

Turning a formula into a value

Assume that you have a formula and you like the answer it's displaying. Also assume that the cells that this formula uses will never change. Therefore, this formula always displays the same answer. You can turn this formula into the value that it displays by using a simple trick.

Edit the cell that holds the formula by pressing F2. Keep your eye on the input line and press F9. You'll see that the formula disappears and is replaced by its answer. Press Enter to make the value stick in the cell. The formula is gone forever.

You can use this technique as sort of a quick and dirty calculator. Assume, for example, that you need to enter the total of three bills into a single cell. You *could* put each bill's amount in a separate cell and then write a formula to add them together. But there's an easier way. Simply enter all three into a formula, like this: **+123.50+75.25+11.92**. But before you press Enter, hit the F9 key to convert this formula to its answer (which happens to be 210.67).

Other types of formulas

This chapter has focused exclusively on arithmetic formulas — formulas that deal with numbers and values. There are actually two other types of formulas.

Text formulas: These formulas work with labels, and you can do some pretty clever things. This topic is covered later in the book.

Logical formulas: These formulas return either *True* or *False*. Most people really don't have much of a need for logical formulas, so this book pretends that they don't exist.

Chapter 7
Making Formulas More Functional

There was a young man from Verblumm
Who most people considered a bum.
But he proved otherwise
And impressed all the guys
When he showed them his skills with @SUM.

In This Chapter

▶ What to do when simple formulas just can't cut the mustard

▶ An overview of @functions — what, why, when, and how

▶ Extending your pointing skills to select complete blocks of cells

▶ Some @functions that just might come in handy

▶ An introduction to the delightful concept of named cells and blocks

Formulas are great — as I tried to convince you in the preceding chapter. But, as the saying goes, you ain't seen nothing yet. This chapter tells you how to coax even more power from formulas by using some of the built-in functions that Quattro Pro provides for your analytical pleasure.

Getting Functional

Sooner or later — probably later — you'll discover that your formulas need something else. Sure, a formula's ability to refer to cell addresses and use numbers is pretty awesome, but there's gotta be more, right? You betcha.

The developers of Quattro Pro, realizing that number crunchers such as yourself might want to actually do useful things with their spreadsheets, included more than 100 @functions to help you out.

These @functions are classified into nine categories, so it's not all that difficult to find the one you want. I discuss these categories later in the chapter, but first there's some groundwork that needs to be covered.

What's with the "at" sign?

It's weird, I admit it. But the built-in functions are called @functions (pronounced "at funk shuns"). Quattro Pro uses the "at" sign (@) to distinguish its functions from other things that you may type into a cell. The reason for this is mainly historical (and slightly hysterical). You see, the original version of Quattro Pro (called simply Quattro back then) was pretty much a clone of the best-selling Lotus 1-2-3 spreadsheet. Since 1-2-3 used the @ symbols to distinguish *its* functions, it was only natural that Quattro did the same. The rest is history.

Don't worry, it doesn't take long to get used to this weirdness. And besides, @ symbols make it very easy to spot an @function in a long formula.

So what is an @function?

You can think of an @function as a shortcut for calculating something. For example, there's an @function called @AVG that computes the average of a list of numbers. This function saves you the trouble of adding the numbers up and then dividing them by the number of elements in the list.

Appendix B tells you more than you want to know about the @functions at your disposal. Of these, some are great — and you'll use them almost every day (except weekends). Others are nice to have, but you won't use them too often. Still others are useful for a small group of people who perform specialized tasks that others don't understand. And then there are @functions (also known as @dysfunctions) that hardly anybody uses.

A functional example

Okay, I'll start with an example so that you can see what's going on here. Study the worksheet in Figure 7-1. It contains a block of numbers that you need to add up to get a total.

The information you've read so far would lead you to create the following formula:

B3+B4+B5+B6+B7+B8+B9+B10+B11+B12+B13+B14+B15+B16+B17

Although this formula would certainly get the job done, there is a better way: using — you guessed it — an @function. In this case, you would use the @SUM function. Instead of entering the unwieldy formula shown above, simply enter the following into any empty cell:

```
@SUM(B3..B17)
```

File   Edit   Style   Graph   Print   Database   Tools   Options   Window   ? ↑↓
▲ ◀ ▶ ▼ │Erase│Copy│Move│Style│Align│Font│Ins│Del│Fit│Sum│Format│PgNm│Grp│Text│
A:B18: (,0)

	A	B	C	D	E	F	G	H
1	Kitchen remodeling costs							
2								
3	Resurface cabinets	2,800						
4	New counter	250						
5	New sink	97						
6	New faucet	69						
7	Flooring	675						
8	Track lighting	285						
9	Drywall repair	225						
10	Paint & supplies	55						
11	Curtains	35						
12	Vertical blinds	233						
13	Table & chairs	645						
14	Room divider	650						
15	Wallpaper	32						
16	Light fixture	75						
17	Miscellaneous	145						
18	GRAND TOTAL:							
19								
20								
21								
22								

A ╱ B ╱ C ╱ D ╱ E ╱ F ╱ G ╱ H ╱ I ╱   G
KITCHEN.WQ2   [1]   READY

Figure 7-1:
An
@function
lets you
determine
the sum of
all these
numbers.

This is a formula which consists of a single @function. The information in the parentheses is called the @function's *argument* (more about this later). In this case, the argument is a block of cells.

You may have already discovered the SUM icon on the SpeedBar. Clicking on this icon automatically builds a formula in the current cell, using the @SUM function. When you click on this icon, Quattro Pro examines your worksheet and figures out what you're trying to add and does the work for you.

Cells, blocks, and cell blocks

A cell is a cell, but a group of contiguous cells is a *block*. A *cell block* is a living area in a prison and has absolutely nothing to do with spreadsheets.

You can tell Quattro Pro that you want to use a block of cells by specifying a block, using the following format:

> FirstCell..LastCell

FirstCell and *LastCell* each represent a normal cell address. A *block reference*, therefore, is simply two cell addresses separated by two periods. Here are some examples of block references:

Block Reference	Refers To
A1..A12	Twelve cells beginning in cell A1 and extending down to cell A12
A1..Z1	Twenty-six cells beginning in cell A1 and extending across to cell Z1
A1..B12	Twenty-four cells encompassing cells A1 through A12 and B1 through B12. In other words, this block consists of two columns and 12 rows.
A1..IV256	A huge block that includes every cell in the worksheet page.

Adding pages to cell references

(None of the information in this section is applicable if you're using Version 4.)

If the reference in your @function extends across multiple worksheet pages (or if you're referring to cells on a different page), you have to tack on a page reference so that Quattro Pro knows which pages to use. As you may already know, adding a page reference simply means preceding the block reference with a page letter and a colon. Here are a few examples:

Block Reference	Refers To
A:A1..A:A12	A block of 12 cells, all on page A, starting in cell A1 and going down to cell A12. You have to use the page letters only if the @function's argument refers to cells on a different page.
A:A1..C:A12	A three-dimensional block of 36 cells beginning in cell A1 of page A and extending down to cell A12 on page C.
A:A1..IV:IV256	A tremendously huge monstrosity of a block that includes every cell in all of the worksheet pages. (You may refer to this as the mother of all blocks.)

Formulas @Functions: The Party Goes On

As you may recall from Chapter 6, when you're building a formula, you can either type the formula into a cell directly, or you can point to the cells that you want to include in the formula. The same thing holds for entering @functions. Plus, there's an added bonus: you can get Quattro Pro to show you a list of @functions that you can choose from (saving you some minor typing duty).

The direct approach

It should come as no surprise that entering an @function directly simply involves, well, entering an @function and its argument(s) directly. If you want to add up the numbers in the block A1..C12 and have the answer appear in cell A13, you could type the following into cell A13:

> **@SUM(A1..C12)**

By the way, you can type the @function in either uppercase, lowercase, or mixed case. It doesn't matter at all because Quattro Pro always converts the function to uppercase.

The pointing method

Sometimes, it's faster to point out the cell or block rather than type it in.

1. Move the cell pointer to cell A13.

2. Type **@SUM(**.

3. Use the arrow keys to move to cell A1, the first cell in the block. Notice that the input line displays the cell address.

4. Now here's the important point. You need to *anchor the cell,* that is, make the first cell stick so that you can point to the last cell in the block. Do this by pressing the period key (one time is enough, although two times also works).

5. Use the arrow keys to move to the last cell in the block — cell C12. Notice that @SUM(A1..C12 is now displayed in the input line.

6. Type a closing (right) parenthesis.

7. Press Enter to insert this formula into the cell.

Getting Quattro Pro to insert an @function

How can you possibly remember the names and correct spelling of all the @functions? Well, chances are you'll only be using a small percentage of the @functions, but there is a way to get a complete list when the need arises.

When you press Alt-F3, Quattro Pro displays a list of all of its @functions (see Figure 7-2). You can use the arrow keys to move down this list until you highlight the function you want. Then press Enter; Quattro Pro types the function in the input line for you. And it even types the opening parenthesis so that you're ready to enter (or point to) the argument(s). The discussion of arguments is coming right up.

Figure 7-2:
Pressing
Alt-F3 gives
you this
handy pop-
up list of all
@functions.

Note: Quattro Pro isn't as smart as you might think: it also inserts an opening parenthesis for @functions that don't use arguments. @RAND and @TODAY are examples of @functions that don't use arguments. If you get Quattro Pro to enter functions like these for you, you'll have to delete the erroneous opening parenthesis yourself.

For argumentative types

The information that an @function uses to perform its duty is called an *argument*. Arguments are always enclosed in parentheses, directly following the @function name. Here are some things to remember about @function arguments:

- ✔ Some @functions need more than one argument. In such cases, you separate the arguments with a comma.

- ✔ Some @functions need a single cell for an argument, and others need a block reference.

- ✔ Some formulas need numbers for arguments, and others need text or labels.

- ✔ You can usually use a normal number or label in place of a cell reference.

Here are some valid formulas that use the @SUM function (pay particular attention to the arguments):

@SUM(A1..A12)	Adds the numbers in the block A1..A12.
@SUM(A1)	Displays the number in cell A1 (admittedly, not a very useful formula, but it *is* valid).
@SUM(A1,A2,A3,A4)	Adds the numbers in cells A1, A2, A3, and A4. This could be done more efficiently by using @SUM(A1..A4).
@SUM(1,2,3,4)	Adds the numbers 1, 2, 3, and 4, and displays the result (which is 10).

@SUM(A1..A12)/2   Adds the numbers in the block A1..A12, and then divides the result by 2.

@SUM(A:A1..C:A12)   Adds the numbers in the three-dimensional block starting in cell A1 on page A and extending through cell A12 on page C. (You can't do this with Version 4.)

You can find out exactly what arguments each @function needs by using Quattro Pro's on-line help (or by referring to Appendix B of this book).

1. Press F1 to access on-line help.

2. Highlight the Functions topic and press Enter.

3. On the next screen highlight the @Function Index topic and press Enter. You'll then get a screen with a bunch of @functions listed.

4. Highlight the one you want and press Enter. (If the one you want isn't listed, select the Next command until you find it.)

   Quattro Pro shows you the @function at the top of the screen, along with a description of the arguments it requires.

Editing formulas that use @functions

It should come as no surprise that you can edit formulas that contain @functions. You do this just like you would edit any other cell — by pressing F2 (or clicking on the input line when the cell is selected). You can use the normal editing keys (the arrow keys, Backspace, and Del, for example) to change the formula. When you get the formula right, press Enter.

As you learned in Chapter 6, you can press F9 while you're editing a formula to convert the formula to its value. This technique also works with formulas that use @functions.

@Function Categories

Quattro Pro divides its @functions into nine categories. These categories make it easier to narrow things down when you know you need an @function, but you don't know the function's name. The categories are shown in Table 7-1.

You can use Quattro Pro's on-line help to figure out which @function is best for the job at hand. Press F1 to access the Help screen, highlight Functions, and press Enter. Highlight one of the nine categories that best describes what you want to do, and then navigate through the Help screens until you find what you're looking for. Sometimes, you'll even find a more or less helpful example.

Table 7-1	@Function Categories
Category	*What It Includes*
Cell and table	Functions that give you information about a particular cell and functions that look up information in tables
Database	Functions that summarize information in databases
Date and time	Functions that deal with dates and times (numbers in Quattro Pro's special serial numbers)
Financial	Functions that deal with money and financial things
Logical	Functions that return either 1 (true) or 0 (false) depending on certain conditions in your worksheet
Mathematical	Functions that deal with numbers (including the trigonometric functions that you forgot all about from high school)
Statistical	Functions that statisticians use, including several functions that normal people find handy
String	Functions that let you work with and manipulate text or labels
System	Functions that tell you things about your computer system

A Few Fun @Functions

So far, you know about @SUM and @AVG. Since you're probably yearning for more, I won't keep you in suspense any longer. Keep reading for details on more useful @functions.

@MAX

Imagine that you started a worksheet and entered monthly sales figures for all of the sales people in your organization. It might look something like the list in Figure 7-3. You want to give an award to the top salesperson of the month. You could scan through the numbers and try to figure out which number is the highest, or you can use the @MAX function to find out automatically.

In the example shown, the formula @MAX(B3..B20) was entered into cell D4, and the cell displays the maximum sales figure.

@MIN

If you need to locate the lowest sales volume — to determine which under-achiever gets to hear your motivational spiel — you can use the @MIN function. The following formula is very similar to the formula used in Figure 7-3:

```
@MIN(B3..B20)
```

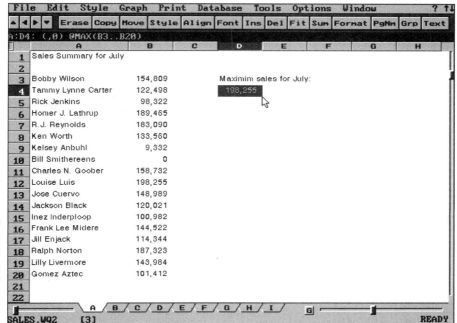

Figure 7-3:
The @MAX
function
tells you the
highest
sales figure.

@COUNT

This function returns the number of non-blank cells in a block. It can save you the trouble of counting things manually. Here's an example:

```
@COUNT(A1.A8192)
```

This formula returns the number of cells in the entire first column that have any information in them.

> **Note**: One hitch with this formula: Don't put this particular formula in column A; otherwise, it counts itself and results in a *circular reference* — which is what happens when a formula refers to the cell that the formula is in.

@ROUND

This function rounds its numeric argument and displays the result. If cell A1 contains 12.67, you can round this value to the nearest integer and display the result (13) in cell B1 by entering the following formula in B1:

```
@ROUND(A1,0)
```

Notice that this function needs two arguments. The first argument is the cell that you want to round; the second argument tells Quattro Pro how many decimal places you want to round it to. In this case, the second argument is 0, which means round it with no decimal places. If you used @ROUND(A1,1), the formula returns 12.7 (rounded to one decimal place).

> *Note*: You can also change the numeric format of a cell so it doesn't display decimal places, yet changing a number's format doesn't change the number itself. The @ROUND function, on the other hand, produces a result that is, in fact, the rounded version of its argument.

Using @Functions with Text

Besides using @functions with numbers, many @functions work with text stored in cells. Using @functions with text is sometimes useful for cleaning up labels and names stored in a spreadsheet. Keep reading for some examples.

@LENGTH

This function displays the length of a string. The formula @LENGTH("Telephone") returns 9 because there are nine letters in the argument (the word *telephone*). And of course, this function also works with cell references. If cell A1 contains the text *Bill Clinton,* you could write a formula such as @LENGTH(A1), which would return 12 since there are 12 characters in the string (spaces count as characters).

@UPPER

The @UPPER function converts its argument to all uppercase letters. For example, @UPPER("san diego") displays *SAN DIEGO.*

@LOWER

This works just like the @UPPER function, except in reverse. It returns its argument in lowercase. @LOWER("San Diego") displays *san diego.*

@PROPER

This function converts a string argument to proper case (the first letter of each word is capitalized). Therefore, @PROPER("SAN DIEGO") displays *San Diego.*

@REPEAT

This function reproduces its first argument as many times as you specify in its second argument. For example, @REPEAT("Ha",3) returns *HaHaHa*.

Want more text @functions?

There are many other functions that work with text strings. If you find yourself with a bunch of labels that you need to manipulate, check out Appendix A for more nifty @functions.

Using Date and Time @Functions

If you need to enter dates directly into your worksheet, make sure you read the sidebar "How about a date?" But you can also use the @DATE function to put a date into a cell. Here's a description of @DATE, and some other useful date @functions.

@DATE

This function takes three arguments: a year, a month, and a day. @DATE(92,12,25) displays 33963 — which is a date serial number. To make this number show up as a date, use the **Style**⇨**Numeric Format**⇨**Date** command, and specify one of the five date format options.

@TODAY

This function doesn't need an argument. It simply returns the serial number that corresponds to the current date. Make sure your computer's internal clock is set properly; otherwise, this function returns the wrong date.

Procedures for setting your computer's clock to the correct date and time vary with different computer manufacturers. Consult your hardware manual for instructions on how to do this — or bribe your office computer guru to do it for you.

@TIME

This function takes three arguments: an hour, a minute, and a second. @TIME(17,30,0) corresponds to 5:30 p.m. (30 minutes and zero seconds into the 17th hour of the day). If you enter this function into a cell, Quattro Pro displays .7292824074. To see it as a readable time, use the **Style**⇨**Numeric Format**⇨**Date**⇨**Time** command and choose one of the four time formats provided.

How about a date?

If you're an adventurous type, you may have discovered that Quattro Pro doesn't know what to do when you enter a date into a cell. Try this at home — enter the following date into a cell:

12/25/92

Quattro Pro displays .005217 — definitely not Christmas.

Okay, try this one:

12-25-92

This time, you get −105.

The problem is that Quattro Pro thinks these are formulas and proceeds to divide the numbers in the first case and subtract them in the second. Does this mean that you can't use dates in Quattro Pro? Not by a long shot. Read on.

Quattro Pro, like all other spreadsheets, has a special way of dealing with dates. It uses a serial number system in which each number corresponds to a day. The serial number system starts with March 1, 1800 (−36,463) and goes up to December 31, 2099 (73,050). This is 300 years worth of dates — enough for even the most aggressive budget projection. You can enter any number in that range into a cell, format it as a date, and Quattro Pro displays the date.

To format a date serial number so that it looks like a date, use the Style⇨Numeric Format⇨Date command, and select one of the date format options. You may have to make the column wider to display the date (or you may end up with a cell full of asterisks).

Unless you like memorizing numbers, you'll find it easier to use one of the other techniques for entering dates:

✔ **Preformatting:** Use the Database⇨Data Entry⇨Dates Only command to tell Quattro Pro that you want to enter dates into cells. Once you do this, you can use command date formats such as 4/23/93, and Quattro Pro interprets them as dates, not formulas.

✔ **@DATE function:** Use this function to simplify entering dates. See the text for more details.

You got the time?

Quattro Pro can not only deal with dates, but it can also handle time. It does so by extending the date serial number concept to include decimal values. Here's what I mean. The date serial number 33963 corresponds to December 25, 1992. If you tack on a decimal point, you can also work with times during that day.

For example, 33963.5 corresponds to 12:00 noon (half-way through Christmas day, 1992). 33963.1 corresponds to 2:24 a.m. (one-tenth of the way through the day). Since there are 86,400 seconds in a day, one second works out to be .000011574074074 in this serial number format. One minute, on the other hand equates to .0006944444. And one hour is .041666667. Therefore, to express 1:00 a.m. on December 25, 1992, you could enter a date/time serial number of 33969.041666667.

If all of these numbers have your head reeling, don't fret. Using the @TIME function makes it painless.

Using @Functions in Formulas

So far, the example formulas I've shown have pretty much consisted only of @functions. You can, however, use @functions with more complicated formulas. Here's an example:

```
@SUM(A1..A10)+@SUM(C1..C10)
```

Here, you're simply taking the sum of the numbers in the block A1..A10 and adding the result to the sum of the numbers in block C1..C10. Another way of looking at it is that you're taking the sum of the block A1..C10 — but skipping block B1..B10. Therefore, the following formula would produce the same result:

```
@SUM(A1..C10)-@SUM(B1..B10)
```

You can also work with dates and times. For some reason, you might want to know the number of days between August 3, 1990 and July 16, 1992. Here's the formula to do it:

```
@DATE(92,7,16)-@DATE(90,8,3)
```

As an alternative, you might prefer to put the date @functions in separate cells (such as A1 and A2) and then use a simpler formula such as +A2-A1 to do the subtraction. That way, you can easily change the one or both of the dates without having to mess with the formula. In other words, it makes the formula more general — typically a good thing to do in a spreadsheet.

The nesting instinct

Fact is, you can create some *very* complex formulas using @functions. You can even use @functions as arguments for other @functions. This is known as *nested @functions*.

Refer to Figure 7-4 for an example. This figure has values in column A and formulas in Column B. The formula in cell B3 is @ROUND(A3,0), which rounds the value in A3 to no decimal places. This same formula is in the cells below. But the formula you're interested in (the one that uses a nested @function) is in cell D13:

```
@ROUND(@SUM(A3..A9),0)
```

Here, I'm using the @SUM function as the first argument for the @ROUND function. Quattro Pro tackles this formula as follows: First, it evaluates the @SUM function and stores the answer in its memory. Then it uses this answer as the first argument for the @ROUND function and combines it with the second argument for the @ROUND function (which is 0). It then displays the final answer in cell D13.

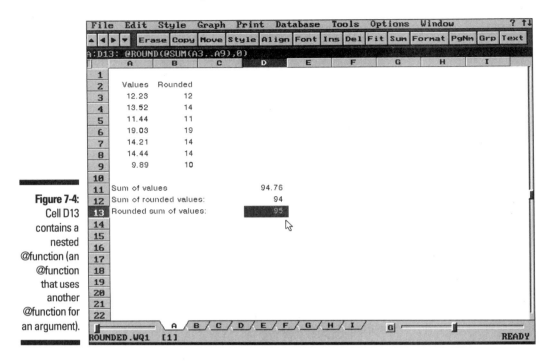

Figure 7-4:
Cell D13
contains a
nested
@function (an
@function
that uses
another
@function for
an argument).

Note: Interestingly, rounding off the sum of the values does not produce the same result as summing the rounded off values. If you don't believe this, examine the figure again and take a look at the formulas in D11 and D12.

Testing conditions

One of the more useful @functions is the @IF function. It requires three arguments:

- ✔ A condition to test

- ✔ What to display if the condition is true

- ✔ What to display if the condition is false

Here's an example:

@IF(A1>0,"Positive","Negative or zero")

Notice that the three arguments are separated by commas. The first argument is the condition. It checks A1>0, which means *Is the number in cell A1 greater than zero?* If it is, then the formula displays the word *Positive.* If the value in cell A1 isn't greater than zero, the formula displays *Negative or zero.* (By the way, notice that I put the text arguments in parentheses so Quattro Pro wouldn't interpret them as named cells or blocks.)

Here's another twist on this same concept that uses nested @IF functions. This time, the formula returns one of three results: Positive, Negative, or Zero:

> @IF(A1>0,"Positive",@IF(A1<0,"Negative","Zero"))

Quattro Pro first tests to see if A1 is greater than zero. If so, it returns *Positive* and is done with it. If A1 is not greater than zero, Quattro Pro goes to the third part of the first @IF argument and discovers another @IF function there — which it proceeds to evaluate. This second (nested) @IF function checks to see whether A1 is less than zero. If so, it returns *Negative.* If not, it returns the third argument of the (second) @IF function, the string *Zero.*

If you understand how this works, congratulations. You're well on your way to being a better-than-adequate Quattro Pro user!

Random acts

There may come a time when you need a random number — it usually happens when you least expect it. If so, Quattro Pro can help out. The @RAND function returns a random number between 0 and 1 every time the worksheet is recalculated or every time you enter something else into the worksheet. This @function doesn't use an argument.

Most of the time, you won't want a random number between 0 and 1. Rather, you'll want more meaningful random numbers, such as a random integer between 1 and 6 (to simulate the roll of a die). The trick is to use the @RAND function in a formula that does some calculations with the random number.

If the lower limit for the random number is in cell A1 and the upper limit is in cell A2, the following formula returns a different random integer in its cell every time the worksheet is calculated:

```
@INT(@RAND/(1/(A2-A1+1)))+A1
```

The @INT function, by the way, converts its argument to an integer — a number with no decimal points. In this case, its argument happens to be a formula that uses the @RAND function.

The nice thing about formulas is that you don't really have to understand how they work to use them. You can often adapt other people's successful formulas. Chapter 16 demonstrates this many times.

Naming Cells and Blocks

This topic isn't absolutely essential for Quattro Pro users, but you may find that it makes your life easier. I'm talking about giving names to single cells and blocks. You can give a meaningful name to any cell or block. After you do so, you can use that name wherever you would normally use a cell or block reference.

An example (naming cells)

Imagine that you named cell F2 *num_employees*. You chose this name because the value in this cell is the total number of employees. (Using meaningful names is helpful but not a requirement. Quattro Pro wouldn't mind if you named this cell *qxplrmt7z9*.) At some other place in the worksheet, you need to use the number of employees in a formula. For example, you might have total salaries and want to figure out the average salary. If you have another cell (cell M12) named *total_salary*, you could then write the formula as

    +total_salary/num_employees

rather than

    +M12/F2

Obviously, the first formula is much easier to read. If you look at the formula, you have a pretty good idea of what it does.

Another example (naming blocks)

You can also give a name to an entire block. For example, if block G1..G12 is named *expenses*, you could then write a formula like this:

    @SUM(expenses)

rather than

    @SUM(G1..G12)

Then if you're out sick one day and people need to work on one of your worksheets, they'll know immediately that this formula is dealing with expenses. Otherwise, they'd have to scroll around and try to figure out what G1..G12 has in it.

How to name cells and blocks

It's not difficult to give a name to a cell or block. Here's a step-by-step procedure for giving the name *interest* to cell C9:

1. Move the cell pointer to C9.

2. Select the Edit⇨Names⇨Create command. Quattro Pro displays the box shown in Figure 7-5.

3. Type **interest** and press Enter. Quattro Pro responds with the message
   `Enter block: C9`.

4. Accept the single cell (C9) Quattro Pro proposes by pressing Enter.

   (If you're naming an entire block, simply use the mouse or arrow keys to extend the cell selection to select the block you're naming.)

After you complete this procedure, you can use the name *interest* anywhere you would normally use a reference to cell C9.

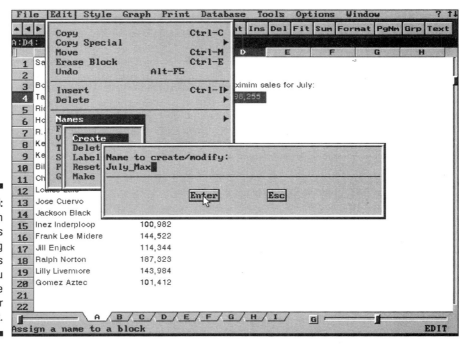

Figure 7-5:
Your screen looks something like this when you give a name to a cell or block.

Here are a few things to keep in mind about naming cells and blocks:

- ✔ Names can be up to 15 characters long.

- ✔ You can't use math operators or spaces in your names. For example a name like int+princ is not valid because it has a plus operator in it.

- ✔ Avoid creating names that look like a cell address. For example, a block named *ab1* can be confused with cell AB1. Quattro Pro lets you do this, but it is a very bad practice.

- ✔ If you already have one or more names in your worksheet, Quattro Pro displays a list of these names after you issue the **Edit**⇨**Names**⇨**Create** command. You can choose a name from this list to change the cell or block that it refers to.

- ✔ You can name a bunch of single cells using labels that are next to them, and do it with a single command. Use the **Edit**⇨**Names**⇨**Labels** command for this (and tell Quattro Pro where the labels are in relation to the cells that you want to name).

- ✔ You can quickly move the cell pointer to a named block by pressing F5, followed by F3. This displays a list of all named blocks. Select the one you want and press Enter; you're there in a flash.

- ✔ If you want to get rid of a block or cell name that you no longer need, use the **Edit**⇨**Names**⇨**Delete** command and select the name you want to delete from the list.

- ✔ To get rid of all cell or block names, use the **Edit**⇨**Names**⇨**Reset** command. This is a rather drastic move, so Quattro Pro makes you verify your intentions.

Note: When you delete or reset cell or block names, Quattro Pro substitutes the actual cell or block addresses in any formulas which used these names.

- ✔ If you have lots of block names and have trouble keeping them straight, use the **Edit**⇨**Names**⇨**Make Table** command to insert a table of names and their blocks into a blank area of your worksheet. You can then print this block for a handy reference.

- ✔ There's no direct way to change the name of a cell or block. You have to delete the old name and then create the new one.

Chapter 8
Changing Things without Messing Up

A woman by the name of Lenore
Did her work and then walked out the door.
But the boss wanted a change
So she had to rearrange
All the numbers she entered before.

● ●

In This Chapter

▶ Copying cells and blocks of cells (or making many from one)

▶ Moving cells and blocks of cells

▶ Changing column widths to avoid the asterisks problem

▶ Inserting and deleting rows and columns

▶ Turning horizontal data into vertical data — and vice versa

▶ Sorting a block of data — and all kinds of options you have

● ●

If you're like most people, you'll find that you spend a large part of your spreadsheeting time changing things that you've already done. This is normal and not necessarily a sign of an indecisive personality disorder. However, you'll soon discover that when you make changes to a worksheet, it's really easy to make something that used to work work no longer. Therefore, it's in your best interest to understand what goes on behind the scenes when you copy and move things — especially things that contain formulas. That's why this chapter has more than its share of Warning icons.

Types of Changes You Can Make

So what do I mean by making changes to a worksheet? Here are some examples:

✔ You spent five minutes creating a killer formula that does magic with a column of numbers. You have 20 more columns that need the same formula applied to them. Solution? Copy the formula so that it works for the other blocks of cells.

✔ You have a nice table of numbers, but for some reason it's about 50 rows below where you want it. So you need to move the table up to a more reasonable location in the worksheet.

✔ You're just about ready to turn in your department budget and realize that you forgot to enter a budget item (Dog Collars) that should go right between the Cosmetic Surgery category and the Explosive Devices category. So you need to insert a new row.

✔ Your boss informs you that you can't budget for monthly pool parties. So you need to zap the entire Pool Party row in your budget worksheet.

✔ You've got a great worksheet, but the numbers are all crammed together and hard to read. You need to make some of the columns wider.

✔ You've got a bunch of labels entered in a column — and you realize that you should have put them in a row. You need to transpose these labels and don't feel like typing them in again.

✔ You just spent two hours entering all of your sales figures in alphabetical order by sales rep names. Then you discover that they need to be in descending order by sales amount. Unless you like to redo your work, you need to sort this block of cells.

Relative and Absolute References (For Adult Viewing Only)

Well, now it's time to have that talk. You know — the one I've been putting off, the one I've been avoiding, the one you weren't ready for until now: it's time you understood the difference between relative and absolute references. Understanding and appreciating the differences between these two types of references is one of the most fundamental and rewarding experiences you'll ever have as a spreadsheet user. In fact, you will never be able to comfortably copy or move formulas without understanding these differences, and I don't want you hearing this stuff on the street.

It's all relative

Up until now, all of the cell references you've used in formulas have been *relative*. If you copy a formula that has relative references, the copies of the formula change. Here's an example. Assume the following formula is in cell A3:

```
+A1+A2
```

If you copy this formula to the cell next door (B3), the formula in cell B3 reads

```
+B1+B2
```

In other words, copying the formula changed the cells in a relative manner. No matter where you copy the formula, it always computes the sum of the two cells directly above it.

By default, all cell references are relative.

Absolutely absolute

But what if you want the copy of the formula to return the sum of A1 and A2? In this case, you want to use *absolute* references. The same formula with absolute references would be

```
+$A$1+$A$2
```

Using dollar signs tells Quattro Pro that the cell reference is absolute — that it will always refer to those specific cells, even if you copy the formula.

A dollar sign in a cell reference means that that part of the reference is absolute and, therefore, won't change when you copy or move the formula.

Why use absolute references?

The best way to understand why to use absolute references is to go through an example. Figure 8-1 shows a worksheet designed to calculate sales tax on certain amounts. The sales tax rate is in cell B1. Column A has labels, column B has amounts, and column C has formulas that calculate the sales tax on the amount in column B.

The formula in cell C4 is

```
+B4*$B$1
```

The first cell reference (B4) is a normal relative cell reference, but the second cell address ($B$1) is an absolute reference that, in this example, refers to the tax rate. When you copy this formula down the column, the first part changes to reflect the price in the cell to the left, but the copied formula *always* refers to cell B1 — which is just what you want. For example, when copied to cell C5, the formula reads

```
+C4*$B$1
```

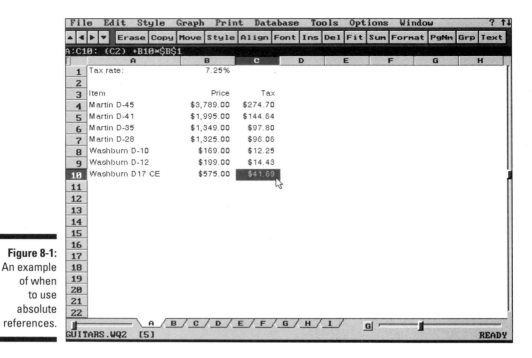

Figure 8-1:
An example
of when
to use
absolute
references.

If you use a relative reference (B1) instead of the absolute reference ($B$1), the copied formula is

```
+C4*B2
```

This formula returns the wrong answer.

It gets even more complicated

If you think you understand the difference between relative and absolute cell references, let me throw some more things at you.

References can also be mixed. That is, one part can be relative and the other can be absolute. Here's an example of a mixed cell reference:

```
+A$1
```

In this case, copying the formula always results in a reference to row 1, since that part of the formula is absolute. The column part changes in a relative manner.

When you get into Version 5's 3-D notebooks, you can also get involved with absolute and relative page references. To help clarify things (or muddy the waters completely), Table 8-1 lists all possible types of cell references.

Table 8-1	Type of Cell References
Example Reference	*Type of References*
A:A1	All relative
A:$A1	Page and row relative, column absolute
A:A$1	Page and column relative, row absolute
A:$A$1	Page relative, row and column absolute
$A:A1	Page absolute, row and column relative
$A:$A1	Page and column absolute, row relative
$A:A$1	Page and row absolute, column relative
$A:$A$1	All absolute

When you're editing a cell, press F4 to cycle through all of the possible absolute/relative combinations of the cell references that you're editing.

Copying Things with Abandon

In 3rd grade, copying was a no-no — the forbidden salvation of a pop-quiz or a difficult lesson. You never wanted to copy and never planned to. Yet despite your good intentions, you practiced looking to the far left and right without moving your head, considered yourself accomplished when you conquered that slight stiff-necked movement that gave you away every time, and secretly took pride in being able to see over the forearm stretched strategically across the coveted answers. You never admitted it, always denied it, and more than once protested that you were "just trying to see how far she was."

Well, rejoice! In Quattro Pro, the stigma of copying is gone. You can, with arms outstretched and voice booming, proclaim to the world, "I can copy!" and be proud of it.

One of the things people do most often when using a spreadsheet is to copy information. Here are your three options when copying:

✔ Copy a single cell to another cell

✔ Copy a single cell to a block of cells (making multiple copies of one cell)

✔ Copy a whole block of cells to another area

When you make a copy of a cell or block, the original cell or block remains the same — you're simply making a replica of it and sticking it somewhere else.

When you copy information to an area that already contains data, Quattro Pro overwrites the cells with the new copied information — without warning you about it. So if you have some important stuff on your worksheet, be careful when you copy.

Why copy?

The most obvious reason to copy a cell or a block of cells is so that you don't have to type the information again. Copying is also useful for duplicating formulas — and it does some interesting things, as I'll explain below.

Copying a cell to a cell

Here's how to copy the contents of cell A1 to B1:

1. Move the cell pointer to A1.

2. Issue the Edit⇨Copy command.

Rather than go through the Edit⇨Copy menu, you can simply press Ctrl-C to begin the copying process.

Quattro Pro displays the message `Source block of cells.`

3. Since you've already selected the block (which just happens to be a single cell), press Enter to accept the suggestion.

Quattro Pro displays the message `Destination for cells.`

4. Use the arrow keys to move the cell pointer to the cell that you want to copy to (in this case, right next door at cell B1), and press Enter. Mission accomplished.

If cell A1 contained a value or a label, the worksheet displays the same thing in cell B1. If A1 contained a formula, cell B1 has a copy of the formula.

Copying a cell to a block

Copying a single cell to a block of cells works exactly the same as copying to a single cell. The only difference is that you'll be making multiple copies of the original cell (with only one command). When Quattro Pro asks you where you want to copy the cell (by displaying the `Destination for cells` message), you specify a block rather than a single cell. To specify a block, first move to the first cell in the block and press the period key to anchor it; then move to the last cell in the block and press Enter. Every cell in the destination block will contain what was in the original cell. Figure 8-2 shows a single cell being copied to a block.

Copying a block to a block

Copying a block of cells to another block is very similar to the other copy operations I just described. The only difference is that when Quattro Pro displays the `Source block of cells` message, you specify a block. To do this, move to the first cell in the block and press the period key to anchor it; then move to the last cell in the block and press Enter.

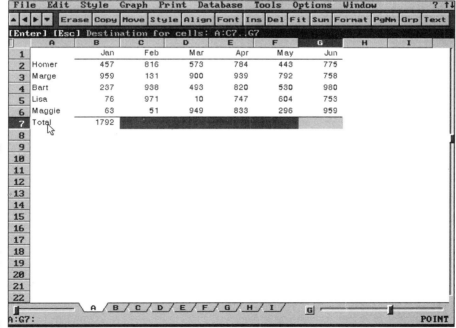

Figure 8-2:
Making many copies of a single cell is a common operation — especially when you're dealing with formulas.

Quattro Pro then asks you where you want to copy the block. Move the cell pointer to the upper left corner of the block where you want the copy to be and press Enter. Notice that you don't have to specify the full block — specifying just the upper left cell is sufficient. When you complete this command, you'll have another copy of the original block.

Copying formulas

You copy formulas exactly like you copy anything else. In other words, you can copy a single formula to another cell, copy a single formula to a block of cells (making multiple copies of it), or copy a block of formulas to another block of cells. If you're a typical spreadsheet user, you'll probably spend a lot of time making copies of formulas.

When you copy a formula, something special happens: all of the cell references in the formula get adjusted. Assume for a minute that cell A3 has the formula -A1-A2. When you copy this formula to cell B3, the formula reads -B1-B2. In other words, the cell references get changed to refer to the same relative cells in its new position.

This might seem contrary to your expectation. If you make a copy of a formula, the copy should be exact, right? Copying a cell that contains -A1-A2 should produce -A1-A2 in the cell that it gets copied to. Well, if you think about it, you usually never want to make an exact copy of a formula. Rather, you want the copied formula to refer to a different set of cells. And that's exactly what Quattro Pro does — automatically.

An exception to this is absolute cell references, which were discussed earlier in this chapter. As you may recall, an absolute cell reference uses dollar signs (for example, -$C$9) to specify that you don't want the cell reference to change when you copy the formula.

When you copy a formula, the cell references are adjusted automatically — unless you use absolute cell references.

If you have a mouse, you can preselect the block that you want to copy. Just click in a cell and drag the cell pointer over the other cells in the block. This eliminates Quattro Pro's `Source block of cells` prompt.

Get'em Up, Move'em Out

When you enter information into a cell, it's not stuck there for life. You can move it anywhere else on the worksheet. And it's not hard to do.

This is the same warning I gave for copying, but it is important enough to repeat. When you move something and the area that you're moving to already contains information, Quattro Pro overwrites the cells with the moved information — without warning. So if you have some important stuff on your worksheet, be careful when moving.

Why move?

Let's say you enter a list of numbers and then discover that you forgot to leave space for a heading at the top of the list. You *could* insert a new row and stick the heading in the new row. But if you have other material in the first row, the inserted row would mess this information up. Therefore, the easiest solution is to move the list of numbers down a row.

You also may want to move things in a worksheet to simply reorganize it. No harm in doing that.

Moving a cell

Here's how to move the contents of a cell from one place to another. Assume that you're moving the contents of cell A1 to its new home in cell B1:

1. Start by moving the cell pointer to the cell that you want to move (cell A1, in this case).

2. Select the Edit⇨Move command. Quattro Pro's message to you will be `Source block of cells`, and it will propose the cell you selected.

   Use Ctrl-M as a shortcut for the Edit⇨Move command.

3. Press Enter to accept Quattro Pro's suggestion of the block to move (just one cell, in this case).

   Quattro Pro then asks you for the destination.

4. Simply move the cell pointer to the new cell location (cell B1) and press Enter again. Done.

The contents of cell A1 are now in cell B1.

Moving a block

Moving a block of cells is very similar to moving one cell. Start by placing the cell pointer at the upper left cell in the block, and then select **Edit⇨Move**. Quattro Pro displays Source block of cells. Use the arrow keys to highlight the complete block you want to move, and then press Enter. Quattro Pro then displays Destination for cells. Move to the upper left corner of the new destination (you don't need to highlight the complete block) and press Enter. The contents of the cells in the original block vanish and appear in their new home.

Moving formulas

You move cells that contain formulas just like you move other cells. But unlike copying formula cells, Quattro Pro does *not* adjust the cell references in the formula. So if you move a cell that has a formula such as -A1-A2, the formula continues to refer to those cells no matter where you move it. If you think about it, you'll realize that this is almost always what you want to happen. If you move a cell with a formula, you almost always want the formula to return exactly the same result (and this is what happens).

When you move cells that contain formulas, the cell references in the formulas do not change.

If you have a mouse, you can preselect the block that you want to move by clicking a cell and dragging the cell pointer over the other cells in the block. Preselecting the block eliminates Quattro Pro's Source block of cells prompt.

The Safe Way to Lose (or Gain) Column Width

When you start a new worksheet, all of the 256 columns are the same width: nine characters. You can make any or all of these columns wider or narrower to accommodate the information you put in. When you change a column width, the entire column changes. In other words, you can't adjust the width of individual cells.

> *Note*: The "nine characters" reference in the preceding paragraph should be taken rather loosely and is valid only if you're running Quattro Pro in

Text mode. In WYSIWYG mode, the actual number of characters that fit into a cell depends on the font you use, the size of the type, and the width of the letters. Nevertheless, cell widths are always given in character units.

Why do it?

There are three main reasons to adjust column widths:

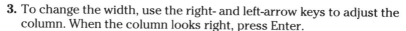

✔ Some or all of the numbers are too wide to fit in the column, and they show up as a series of asterisks, like this: **********.

✔ A long label may not display entirely if the cell to the right has something in it.

✔ You want to make the worksheet look better by spacing things out or moving them together a bit.

Doing it to one column

Here's how to change the width of one column:

1. Move the cell pointer to any cell in the column you want to adjust.

2. Select the **Style➪Column Width** command. Quattro Pro responds with the message `Alter the width of the current column` and displays a number that corresponds to the current column width (see Figure 8-3).

   You can use Ctrl-W as a shortcut way of executing the **Style➪Column Width** command.

3. To change the width, use the right- and left-arrow keys to adjust the column. When the column looks right, press Enter.

   Instead of using the arrow keys, you can simply type in a number. Typing in the number is handy if you want to make the column very large and don't want to bang away on the right-arrow key.

To set a column back to its normal width, use the **Style➪Reset Width** command.

Changing a group of columns

If you have several columns next to each other and you want to make all of these columns the same width, you can do it in one fell swoop. Use the **Style➪Block Size➪Set Width** command. At the `Enter block of columns` prompt, highlight the columns you want to change by moving the cell pointer to

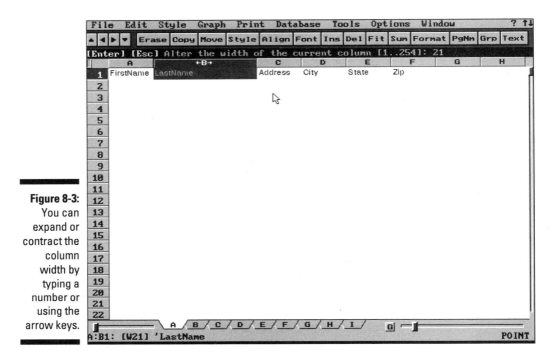

Figure 8-3:
You can
expand or
contract the
column
width by
typing a
number or
using the
arrow keys.

select them, and press Enter to tell Quattro Pro that you're finished selecting columns. Then use the arrow keys to make the adjustment. Press Enter to lock the new column widths.

Automatic column widths

There's yet another way to change column widths — this one is automatic because Quattro Pro adjusts the column to accommodate the largest entry in the column.

Global column widths

In its natural state, every column in a Quattro Pro worksheet is nine characters wide in Text mode. If you ever find yourself wanting narrower or wider columns on an entire worksheet, you don't have to go through the normal steps to set the column widths. Use the **Options⇨Formats⇨Global** Width command to change every column with one command. Once you change the global column width, using the **Style⇨Reset Width** command resets the column to the *new* global default — the one you set.

Use the **Style**⇨**Block Size**⇨**Auto Width** command to accomplish this. But be careful because this command adjusts columns based on labels as well as numbers. So if you have a 30-character title, for example, in a cell that spills over to adjacent cells, this command makes the column 30 characters wide (which is probably not what you want).

You're Out! Erasing Cells and Blocks

Getting rid of the contents of a cell — or a whole group of cells — is easy. This is known as *erasing, deleting, wiping out, nuking, killing, zapping,* and all sorts of other terms. Regardless of what you call it, after you do it, the information is gone.

The command to erase cells or blocks is **Edit**⇨**Erase Block**. When Quattro Pro displays the `Block to be modified` message, simply select the block whose contents you want to get rid of by using the arrow keys or your mouse, and press Enter.

To erase a single cell, just move the cell pointer to the offending cell and press the Del key.

Erasing the contents of cells can be rather drastic. Fortunately, if you discover that you accidentally zapped the wrong cells, you can recover from your error by immediately issuing the **Edit**⇨**Undo** command (or pressing Alt-F5). But this works only if the Undo feature is enabled. Use **Options**⇨**Other**⇨**Undo** to check or change the status of Undo.

Congratulations! It's a Row

You can insert new rows and columns into your worksheet. Actually, the number of rows and columns always remains the same. Inserting a row simply scoots everything down, and inserting a new column scoots everything over to the right.

Why do it?

It's not uncommon to discover that you need to insert something between two other cells. You might have a list of products and prices, for example, and discover that you left one out. One approach is to move part of the block down one row to make room for the new entry. A faster method is to simply insert a new row, which pushes everything down and makes room for your forgotten stuff.

If you insert a new row or column, you have to be careful that it doesn't mess up other areas of your worksheet. For example, you might have a table of numbers somewhere in your worksheet that's not visible on your screen. If you insert a new row or column without thinking, your table of numbers may end up with a blank row or column in it.

Adding new rows

Here's how to add a new row to your worksheet:

1. Move the cell pointer to the row that will be just below the new row.

2. Issue the Edit⇨Insert⇨Rows command and press Enter.

If you want to add more than one row, simply extend the selection in response to Quattro Pro's `Enter row insert block` message.

Adding new columns

You add one or more columns just like you add rows. The only difference is that you use the Edit⇨Insert⇨Columns command.

If adding an entire row or column would mess up another area of your worksheet, you can use the Edit⇨Insert⇨Row **Block** or Edit⇨Insert⇨Column **Block** command to insert new cells rather than a complete row or column. Simply select the block into which you want to insert. This will push everything down or to the right.

Use caution when inserting and deleting rows and columns

It may sound like a pretty dumb warning, but you need to remember that deleting a row or column does just that — it deletes an entire row or column. Lots of users tend to focus on just one part of their spreadsheet and forget that there are other parts out of view. They go about inserting and deleting rows and columns and are surprised to discover that another area of their worksheet is messed up. So let's be careful out there, okay?

When They Leave The Nest: Getting Rid of Rows and Columns

Since you can add rows and columns, you ought to be able to take them away, right? Quattro Pro lets you remove as many rows and columns as you like. However, the total number of rows and columns always remains the same. If you remove a row, for example, all of the other rows move up one slot and Quattro inserts another row at the bottom. For example, if you remove row 2, everything in it goes away, and what used to be row 3 is now row 2. The former row 4 becomes row 3, and so on.

A similar thing happens when you remove a column. Removing a column moves all of the other columns to the left (and Quattro Pro inserts a new column at the end).

Why do it?

If you discover that the information in a row or column is not needed, you can get rid of it quickly by deleting the entire row or column. This is a much faster alternative to deleting the block and then moving everything else around to fill up the gap.

Eliminating rows

To get rid of a row, move the cell pointer to any cell in the row to be extinguished and use the **Edit➪Delete➪Rows** command. To delete more than one row, simply extend the selection when Quattro Pro prompts you with `Enter block of rows to delete`.

Deleting columns

You can get rid of entire columns the same the same way you delete rows — except that you use the **Edit➪Delete➪Columns** command.

If you don't want to get rid of an entire row or column, use the **Edit➪Delete➪Row Block** or **Edit➪Delete➪Column Block** command. This gets rid of the selection you specify and moves everything around to fill up the hole.

Hiding things

Quattro Pro lets you hide columns or individual cells. When something is hidden, it's still in the worksheet and can be referred to in formulas — it just doesn't appear on-screen.

Hiding is often handy when you are printing and don't want particular information to be printed. Simply hide the unwanted columns or cells and commence printing.

To hide one or more columns, use the **Style**⇨**Hide Column**⇨**Hide** command, and then select the columns to hide. To hide individual cells or a block of cells, use the **Style**⇨**Numeric Format**⇨**Hidden** command. To unhide cells hidden in this manner, just format them with some other numeric formatting.

When you use point mode (when you're copying something, for example), Quattro Pro temporarily displays all of the hidden columns while you do your pointing.

Don't delete a row or column that contains the end of a block used in a formula. For example, assume you have a formula that reads: @SUM(A1..A10). If you delete row 1 or row 10, this formula becomes invalid and displays ERR. You can, however, delete any of the rows in the middle of the block without messing up the formula. If you delete row 2, for instance, the formula changes to read @SUM(A1..A9). A similar problem happens when you use named blocks (discussed in Chapter 7). If you delete a row or column that contains a named cell (or contains an end cell of a named block), Quattro Pro deletes the name. Consequently, any formulas that use these names become invalid.

Transposing Rows and Columns

Transposing means changing the orientation. If you have numbers in a single column, you can transpose them so they appear in a single row — and vice versa.

Why do it?

You transpose, or switch, cell entries in rows and columns if you discover that information in the worksheet is in the wrong orientation — vertical when it should be horizontal, for example, or horizontal when it should be vertical. Figure 8-4 shows a block of cells before and after being transposed.

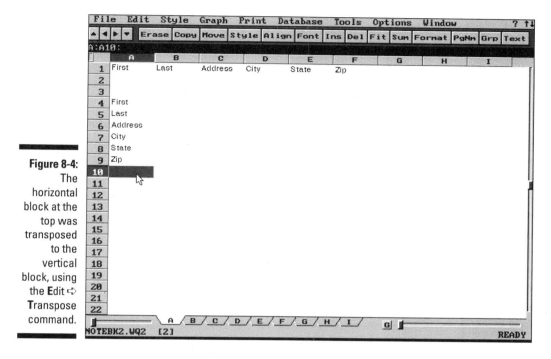

Figure 8-4:
The
horizontal
block at the
top was
transposed
to the
vertical
block, using
the Edit ⇨
Transpose
command.

How to do it

Use the Edit⇨Transpose command. In response to the Source block of
cells prompt, highlight the block that you want to transpose and press Enter.
Quattro Pro then displays Destination for cells. Simply move the cell
pointer to the first cell in the block where you want the cells to be (you don't
need to specify the entire block).

If the area you specify to hold the transposed data already contains information, Quattro Pro overwrites it without warning you.

Sorting Blocks of Cells

When you *sort*, you rearrange the contents of a block of cells in such a way that
the order of the rows changes. Sorting is a very common operation among
spreadsheet people.

Why do it?

There are lots of reasons why you would want to sort a block of data. You may have entered data haphazardly and now need to print it in a particular order. Or you may want to sort your data to make certain information easier to find. Or you may want to rank a group of numbers. Figures 8-5 and 8-6 show a block of data before and after being sorted. The class roster and grades in Figure 8-5 are not sorted in any particular order. The roster in Figure 8-5, however, is sorted by grade so that all As appear together, Bs appear together, and so on.

How to do it

To sort spreadsheet information, follow these steps:

1. Issue the **Database**⇨**Sort** command. This leads to another menu, shown in Figure 8-7.

2. Tell Quattro Pro which block of cells you want to sort by selecting the **B**lock option on this menu.

3. Select the block and press Enter.

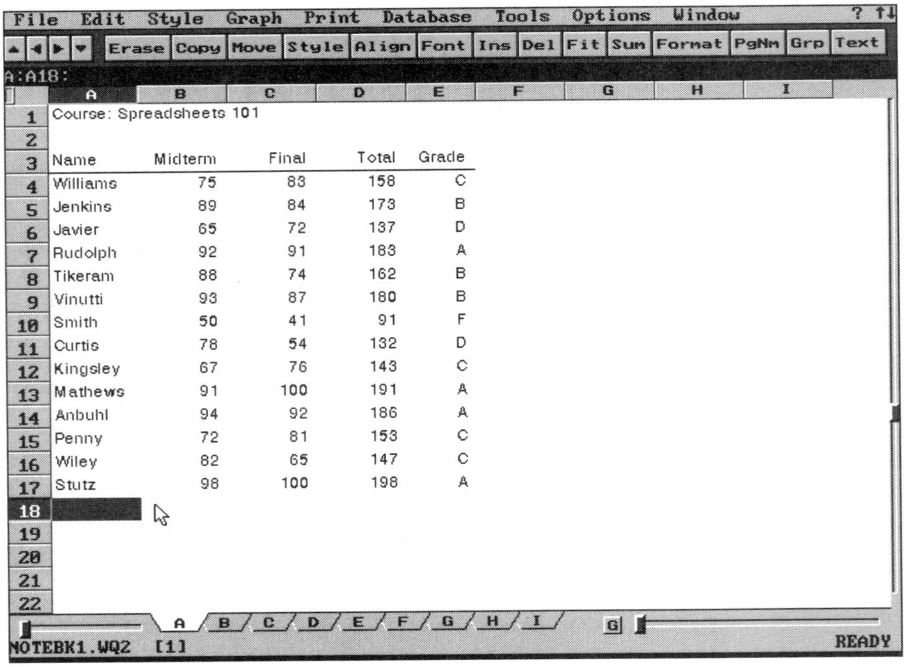

File	Edit	Style	Graph	Print	Database	Tools	Options	Window	? ↑↓

| ▲ ◀ ▶ ▼ | Erase | Copy | Move | Style | Align | Font | Ins | Del | Fit | Sum | Format | PgNm | Grp | Text |

A:A18:

	A	B	C	D	E	F	G	H	I
1	Course: Spreadsheets 101								
2									
3	Name	Midterm	Final	Total	Grade				
4	Williams	75	83	158	C				
5	Jenkins	89	84	173	B				
6	Javier	65	72	137	D				
7	Rudolph	92	91	183	A				
8	Tikeram	88	74	162	B				
9	Vinutti	93	87	180	B				
10	Smith	50	41	91	F				
11	Curtis	78	54	132	D				
12	Kingsley	67	76	143	C				
13	Mathews	91	100	191	A				
14	Anbuhl	94	92	186	A				
15	Penny	72	81	153	C				
16	Wiley	82	65	147	C				
17	Stutz	98	100	198	A				
18									
19									
20									
21									
22									

A / B / C / D / E / F / G / H / I /   G

NOTEBK1.WQ2 [1]   READY

Figure 8-5:
An unsorted
class roster.

```
 File  Edit  Style  Graph  Print  Database  Tools  Options  Window        ? ↑↓
 ▲ ◄ ► ▼  Erase Copy Move Style Align Font Ins Del Fit Sum Format PgNm Grp Text
A:A18:
         A         B         C         D         E        F       G       H       I
  1  Course: Spreadsheets 101
  2
  3  Name      Midterm      Final     Total    Grade
  4  Stutz        98        100       198        A
  5  Mathews      91        100       191        A
  6  Anbuhl       94         92       186        A
  7  Rudolph      92         91       183        A
  8  Jenkins      89         84       173        B
  9  Vinutti      93         87       180        B
 10  Tikeram      88         74       162        B
 11  Williams     75         83       158        C
 12  Wiley        82         65       147        C
 13  Penny        72         81       153        C
 14  Kingsley     67         76       143        C
 15  Javier       65         72       137        D
 16  Curtis       78         54       132        D
 17  Smith        50         41        91        F
 18
 19
 20
 21
 22
         A / B / C / D / E / F / G / H / I /      G
NOTEBK1.WQ2  [1]                                              READY
```

Figure 8-6:
A class roster sorted by grade.

You return to the previous menu (but the selected block appears in the menu).

4. Specify your sort key or keys. A *sort key* is the column on which the sorting will occur. Select **1**st Key from the menu and move the cell pointer to any cell in the column that you want to sort on.

5. Press Enter.

Quattro Pro displays a box in which you specify whether you want to sort in ascending order (A to Z, lowest to highest, smallest to largest) or descending order (Z to A, highest to lowest, largest to smallest).

6. Press A for ascending order or D for descending order and press Enter. You return to the preceding menu.

At this point, you can specify more sort keys. Additional sort keys are used to handle ties. This determines how the rows get sorted if a column in the 1st sort key contains duplicate values. If you're sorting by ZIP code, for example, an additional sort key would determine what happens with rows that have the same ZIP code. If so, Quattro Pro goes to the 2nd sort key to resolve the tie. If there's a tie in the 2nd sort key, it uses the 3rd sort key, and so on. Most of the time, one sort key is enough.

7. Select **G**o from the menu.

Quattro Pro sorts the information, and you're done.

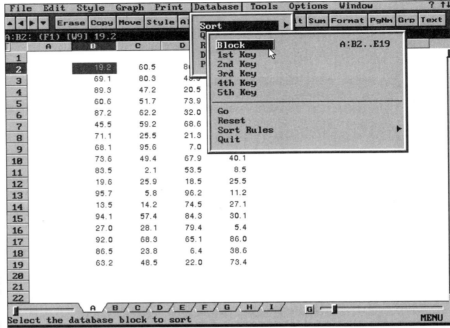

Figure 8-7:
You use this
menu to sort
a block of
cells.

More on sorting

The **Database**⇨**Sort** command has several other options. If you plan on doing lots of sorting, you should understand what else you can do.

Sorting columns

In the vast majority of cases, people sort rows, not columns. However, Quattro Pro lets you sort a block by columns. To do so, issue the **Database**⇨**Sort** command and select the **Sort Rules** command from the menu. Then select the **Sort Rows/Columns** Command and specify **Columns**.

Resetting a sort

When you do a sort, Quattro Pro remembers the settings you give it. The next time you issue the **Database**⇨**Sort** command, Quattro Pro attempts to use exactly the same block and sort keys that you specified earlier. To make Quattro Pro forget your previous sort specs, issue the **Database**⇨**Sort** command, and then select the **Reset** from the menu.

What to watch out for when sorting

One of the most common mistakes people make with spreadsheets is that they mess up when sorting. They don't select the entire block as the sort block. Suppose, for example, that you have a block that consists of three columns: Name, Age, and Salary. If you want to sort the block in alphabetical order using Name as the sort key, it's critically important that you select all three col-umns when you specify the sort block. If you only select the column with the names, only the names will be sorted. This means that everyone will have a different age and salary. In other words, the data is messed up royally, and all the work you put into entering this information will be for naught.

Letters first?

Normally, Quattro Pro considers letters to be "less than" numbers when it sorts. In other words, if the entries in your sort key column contain both values and labels, Quattro Pro puts the labels before the values. If you want to change this, issue the **Database**⇨**Sort** command and select **S**ort Rules from the menu. Then select **N**umbers Before Labels and specify **Y**es.

Dealing with upper- and lowercase

When sorting, there are two ways to handle upper- and lowercase. The normal method is to consider that all uppercase letters come before all lowercase letters. This is called *ASCII order*. If you want all of the *A*s (both upper- and lowercase) to be sorted before all the *B*s, you need to change the method to *dictionary order*. Issue the **Database**⇨**Sort** command and select **S**ort Rules from the menu. Then select **L**abel Order and then **D**ictionary. Notice that the status line provides a message to remind you of what each option does.

"ALRIGHT, WHICH ONE OF YOU CLOWNS IS RESPONSIBLE FOR THURSDAY'S DOWN TIME?"

Chapter 9
How to Keep from Losing Your Work

There was a young lady from the Nile
Whose desk was just one big pile.
She found the solution
And made a steadfast resolution
To store it away in a file.

In This Chapter

▶ All about files, disks, saving worksheets, and related topics

▶ Why computer users lose their work, and how you can prevent such things from happening to you

▶ The importance of saving frequently and making backup copies of important files

▶ How to save Quattro Pro files so that other programs can use them

If you work with computers, sooner or later you will lose some work. True fact. Happens to everybody. Once the cursing subsides, you'll simply have to bite the bullet and repeat things that you've already done.

There *are* some things you can do to minimize the heartbreak of data loss. But if you like to live on the edge and don't mind wasting time re-doing hours of work that disappeared down the toilet, feel free to skip this chapter.

Using Files with Quattro Pro:
The Adventure Begins

When you start Quattro Pro, you are actually loading the program from your hard disk into your computer's memory. Quattro Pro stays on the hard disk and loads a copy of itself into memory. Actually, the complete program isn't loaded into memory — only the most important parts. This leaves enough memory available so that there's room for you to work on a worksheet. As you use Quattro Pro, it may need other parts. It loads these parts from the hard disk in the background, so you don't even notice what's going on.

When you start working on a new worksheet, you're simply storing things in your computer's memory. Therefore, if you turn off your PC, your work is gone for good. In order to keep your work from being simply a memory, you need to save the worksheet that's in memory to a file on a disk. The first time you attempt to save a worksheet to disk, you need to tell Quattro Pro what filename to use. After that, it knows which filename to use.

Files and Windows

Quattro Pro has a nice feature that lets you work with more than one file at a time — something you can only fully appreciate if you've used a spreadsheet that limits you to one worksheet at a time. Working with more than one worksheet at a time can be very handy because you don't have to close one worksheet when you want to work on another. Those who tend to juggle a bunch of things at once particularly like this capability. (Is there anyone who *doesn't* juggle a bunch of things at once?)

Disk vs. Memory

One thing I've noticed over the years is that new computer users often get confused about memory and disks. This isn't surprising since both of these things are places to store data. Here's the difference:

Memory: This is a part of your computer that stores things that you are currently working on. It also goes by the name of *RAM* (Random-Access Memory). Memory is very fleeting — a flick of the power switch and it's wiped out immediately.

Computers vary in the amount of memory they have installed. Nowadays, most computers have at least one megabyte (1MB) of RAM, and systems with 8 to 16MB are common. When you're working on a program with a lot of data, you may get an "out of memory" error. This means that your system doesn't have enough memory to handle what you want to do. It *doesn't* mean that your disk is filled up.

Disks: A disk stores information more or less permanently. If you turn off the power to your PC, the information stored on disk remains there. Disks come in a variety of sizes, which correspond to how much information they can hold. Your computer has a built-in hard disk (which holds a lot) and can also use removable floppy disks (which hold less and which may or may not actually be floppy). Most computers have a hard disk of at least 40MB, but most new systems have at least 200MB of hard disk storage.

If you have a lot of programs and data files stored on your hard disk, you may at some time get a "disk full" message. This means that your disk is so full that it can't hold any more information (this has nothing to do with the amount of memory in your computer). To free up some disk space, you need to erase from the disk files that you no longer need.

Every worksheet that you have open appears in its own window, and you can activate windows, move windows around, resize them, and so on. You must be in Text mode (not WYSIWYG mode) to work with windows in this way. See the next section for more information on dealing with Quattro Pro's worksheet windows.

Figure 9-1 shows several worksheets, each in a separate window, arranged so that you can see what's in them and jump between them.

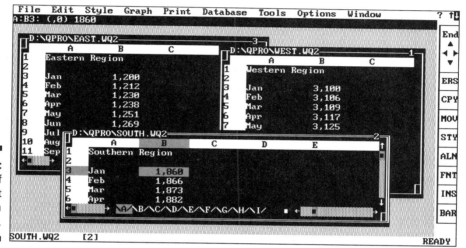

Figure 9-1:
A bunch of worksheet windows in Text mode.

If you're in WYSIWYG mode, you can still work with more than one worksheet, but you can't display the worksheets in separate movable and resizable windows. You have to be in Text mode to do this.

Looking through windows (Moving and resizing)

Normally, the worksheet that you're working on fills the entire screen. But you can also turn it into a window that you can move and resize (unless you're in WYSIWYG mode). Only one window at a time can be the active window, and the active window is on top of the stack of windows.

For Keyboarders: You toggle the active window between window view and full screen view (*zoomed*) by pressing Alt-F6. To move the active window, first select the **W**indow⇨**M**ove/Size command (or press Ctrl-R), and then use the arrow keys to move the window around on-screen. To change the size of the active window, use the same command, but hold down the Shift key while you press the arrow keys. In either case, press Enter to get out of this Move/Size mode.

For Mouseketeers: Moving and resizing windows is much easier if you have a mouse . To toggle between full screen and window view, click on the two arrows at the upper right of the screen (right next to the question mark). To move a window, click on any of its borders and drag it to the desired position. To resize a window, click on the little rectangle at the lower right of the window and drag the mouse until the window is the size you want.

Dealing with windows

If you have several windows open, the screen can get a bit cluttered, and some windows may even be hidden behind others. Quattro Pro provides two commands to clean these windows up (sometimes known as the Windex commands): the **S**tack command and the **T**ile command.

The **Window**⮑**Stack** command arranges all the windows in a tidy stack so that you can see the worksheet names (see Figure 9-2). This command only works in Text mode.

The **Window**⮑**Stack** command has no effect in WYSIWYG mode.

The **Window**⮑**Tile** command (or Ctrl-T) fills the screen with all of the windows showing, with no overlaps (see Figure 9-3).

Figure 9-2:
Stacking all
of the open
worksheet
windows
with the
Window⮑Stack
command
puts them in
a neat pile.
This works
only in Text
mode.

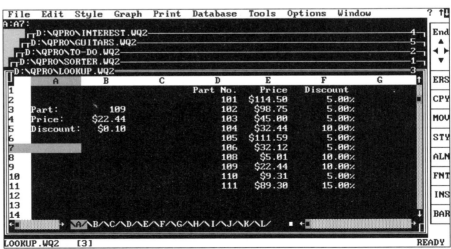

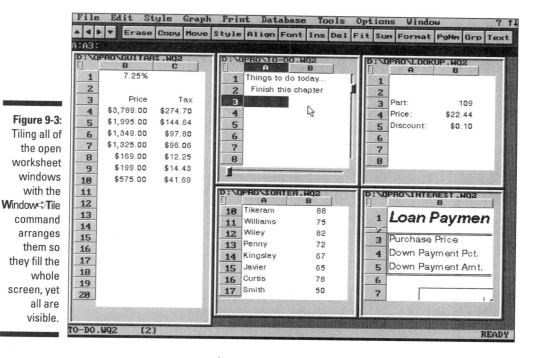

Figure 9-3:
Tiling all of the open worksheet windows with the Window⇨Tile command arranges them so they fill the whole screen, yet all are visible.

If you have so many windows open that you have trouble finding the one that you want, use the **Window⇨Pick** command (or press Alt-0) to choose a window from a list of all windows. Notice that each window has a number displayed towards the right in its top border. You can use this number, along with the Alt key to activate a specific window, that is, bring it to the top of the stack. For example, to activate the worksheet in window #4, press Alt-4.

File Commands

When you're working in Quattro Pro, everything you do that has anything to do with files is done through — you guessed it — the File menu. For your convenience, Figure 9-4 shows the commands on this menu. Some of these commands are absolutely essential (you can't work without them), and others are less than essential (though they may make your life a bit easier).

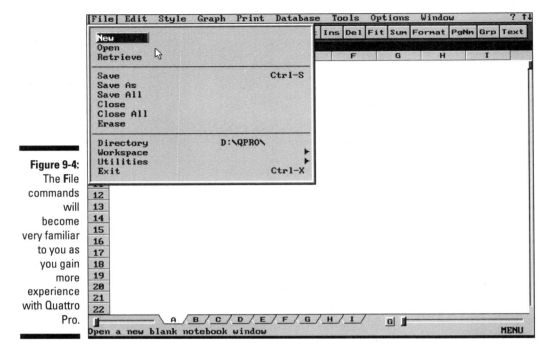

Figure 9-4:
The File
commands
will
become
very familiar
to you as
you gain
more
experience
with Quattro
Pro.

Essential File Commands

Here's a summary of what the important File commands do and when you would use them.

File⇨New

This command creates a new blank worksheet in memory (but doesn't save this worksheet to disk). If you're already working on a worksheet, this command starts a new worksheet (and the first worksheet remains open).

File⇨Open

This command lets you bring a previously saved worksheet from disk into memory. If you're already working on a worksheet, this command brings another worksheet into memory (and the first worksheet remains open).

File⇨Retrieve

This command replaces the current worksheet with another worksheet, which has been saved to disk. If the current worksheet has not been saved, Quattro Pro asks whether you want to save the current worksheet before the program destroys the copy in memory.

File⇨Save

This command saves the worksheet in memory to a file on disk. If you saved the file before, the program uses the same name. If it's a new worksheet without a name, Quattro Pro asks you for a name to use for the file. Ctrl-S is a shortcut for this command.

File names can be no longer than eight characters (with no spaces). Also, there are a few characters that are verboten in file names — backslash (\), plus sign (+), colon (:), and a few others. If you try to use one of these characters, Quattro Pro complains and makes you change it.

File⇨Save As

This command saves the worksheet in memory to a file on disk — and you have to provide a name. This command is useful if you want to save a worksheet in memory to a different drive, directory, or with a different filename. Saving to a different filename is useful if you want to keep the old version of your worksheet but also want to save changes you've made to it. You also use this command when you want to save a Quattro Pro file in a different file format so that other programs can read the data.

File⇨Close

This command removes the current worksheet from memory. If you haven't saved the worksheet, Quattro Pro asks whether you want to save it.

File⇨Exit

Use this command when you are finished with Quattro Pro. If you have any unsaved work, Quattro Pro lets you know and gives you the opportunity to save your work to disk before quitting. Ctrl-X is a shortcut for this command.

Non-Essential File Commands

Here's a description of other file commands. You may never need to use these commands because they do pretty much the same thing as the file commands discussed earlier. Some of these commands are shortcuts you can use when you're working with several different files at one time.

File⇨Save All

This command saves all worksheets in memory to separate files on disk. If any of the worksheets don't yet have a name, Quattro Pro asks you for a name.

Foreign files

If you have a VHS video cassette player, you probably know that you can't play old beta video cassettes in your machine. Besides being different physical sizes, the tapes are two different formats. Even if you took the tape out of a beta cartridge and spooled it onto a VHS cartridge, your VHS machine couldn't understand it. Similarly, if you save a file from Quattro Pro, you normally can't use it in your word processor because the programs use different file formats. If you tried to load a Quattro Pro worksheet file into dBASE, for example, dBASE would complain because it can't recognize the information.

Note the word *normally* in the preceding paragraph. Actually, there is a way to save Quattro Pro files so that other software programs can use the information. The trick is to save the file in a format other than Quattro Pro's format. In other words, you'll save it in a foreign file format—one that the other program can understand. You do this with the File⇨Save **A**s command. You also have to specify the appropriate file extension (described below) so that Quattro Pro will know what format you want.

There's also a way to read foreign files into Quattro Pro. When you use the File⇨Open or File⇨**R**etrieve command, simply specify the foreign filename in full (including the extension).

Quattro Pro is pretty adept at bringing in foreign files and translating its stuff into other file formats. Some of the more popular file formats and the appropriate extensions for each are listed below:

Software Program	Extension
Paradox database program	.DB
dBASE database program	.DBF, .DB2, .DB4
Lotus 1-2-3 Release 2.x	.WK1
Lotus 1-2-3 Release 1A	.WKS
Lotus 1-2-3 Release 3.x	.WK3
Lotus Symphony Release 2	.WR1

The list above is not exhaustive. You can get a complete list of the extensions Quattro Pro can use by pressing F1 (for Help) and then selecting the 1-2-3 topic, followed by the Files topic, and then the Translating Files topic. You'll end up with a screen that shows all of the extensions you can use and also see other handy tidbits of information.

File⇨Close All

This command removes all of the worksheets from memory. If any of the worksheets haven't been saved, Quattro Pro asks whether you want to save them.

File⇨Erase

This command erases the contents of the current worksheet from memory. The command does not affect the copy (if any) on disk. Use this command if you totally mess your worksheet up and want to start over. If you haven't saved the worksheet, Quattro Pro asks whether you want to lose your changes.

It's a good practice to consider Quattro Pro's messages seriously, but don't get in the habit of saving everything just because it hasn't been saved. For example, if you totally destroyed your current worksheet and want to start over, you would use the File⇨Erase command. Quattro Pro asks whether you want to save the worksheet before it is erased from memory. In this case, you *don't* want to save it. If you *do* save it, you will overwrite the previous version (if any) on disk — which may be a good version. I've seen this happen many times, and there's nothing you can do about it after the fact. So watch out, okay?

File⇨Directory

This command lets you specify a directory on a disk. The directory that you choose determines the files that are displayed with the File⇨Open and File⇨Retrieve commands and also determines where files are saved with the File⇨Save and File⇨Save As commands. In most cases, you don't need to fiddle with this command.

File⇨Workspace

This command lets you save the current configuration of worksheets and window positions. If you're working with a group of worksheets and later want to pick up where you left off, use this command. This command doesn't actually save the files — only the position of the windows.

File⇨Utilities

This command lets you access DOS, run the file compression program, or open Quattro Pro's File Manager in a separate window. Most users can go their whole life without getting into this menu, but the File Manager in particular can be useful — so useful that I'm going to devote the next section to it.

Managing Files with Quattro Pro

Note: Quattro Pro's File Manager is not really part of the spreadsheet program. It's more like a bonus feature that you can use or not use. If you're just starting out, you may want to put off learning about the File Manager until after you become more familiar with the more important parts of Quattro Pro.

If there's one thing that almost all beginning computer users have trouble with, it's managing files on their hard drive. Most people don't take the time to learn the cryptic DOS commands that are normally used to copy files, rename files, erase files, and so on. Fortunately, there are a number of easy-to-use programs that make doing all of this file stuff much easier. These programs include Symantec's Norton Commander, XTree Corporation's XTree, and lots of others.

But if you own Quattro Pro, you already have a fairly adept file manager free of charge (and you may not even realize it!). You get into this file manager with the File⬩Utilities⬩File Manager command. Issuing this command opens up a new window, shown in Figure 9-5. Unless your hard drive contains exactly the same files as mine, your File Manager window will look different. Entering the File Manager also gives you a new menu at the top of the screen, and the SpeedBar is not available.

This window has three "panes" (although one of them is optional):

Control pane: This is where you specify things like the disk drive you want to see, the directory, and even a filter (that you use to show files of a certain type — *.* means show all files, for example). You can change any of these items to change the files displayed below in the file list pane.

File list pane: This is where the files are displayed, using the information in the control pane. The file list pane shows each file's extension, its size (in bytes), the date it was last saved, and the time it was last saved.

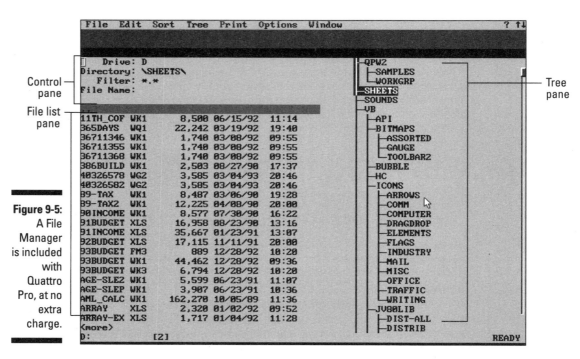

Control pane — File list pane —

Tree pane

Figure 9-5:
A File Manager is included with Quattro Pro, at no extra charge.

Tree pane: This pane only appears when you select the **Tree⇨Open** command from the File Manager menu. It shows a graphical listing of the directories on the disk that's being displayed. When you move the highlight in this pane (with any of the arrow keys or your mouse), the files in that directory appear in the file list pane.

You move among these panes with the Tab and Shift-Tab keys or with the mouse. Once you're in one of these panes, you can use the up-arrow and down-arrow keys to move within a pane.

The File Manager makes locating files that you want to load into Quattro Pro very easy. Normally, you start in the tree pane and select the appropriate directory. As you arrow your way through the directories, the file list pane shows the files that meet the filter criterion in the control pane. When you spot the file you want, move to the file list pane, highlight the file, and press Enter.

You can tag files in the middle window to open a bunch at one time. Highlight the file, and then tag or untag it with Shift-F7.

Although you might find the File Manager useful for opening files, it's also handy for copying, moving, and renaming files (you perform these actions via the **Edit** menu). The File Manager has lots of other neat things in it. If you want to find out more, press F1 (Help) while the File Manager window is active.

The File Manager window stays open and is treated like any other Quattro Pro window. If you're in Text mode, you can move it and resize it. If it gets in your way, close it by using the **File⇨Close** command.

It's very easy to delete files on disk, using the File Manager, so be careful that you don't erase something that's important. Quattro Pro makes you verify your intentions when you choose the File Manager's **Edit⇨Erase** command, but it can't tell you whether the file is important or not. When in doubt about erasing a file, don't erase it.

Protecting Your Work

There are two things you can do to be on the safe side when using Quattro Pro (or any computer program, for that matter):

- ✔ **Frequently save your work into a file.** I've seen far too many people spend the whole day working on a worksheet without saving it until they're ready to go home. In most cases, you won't get into any trouble. But look at it this way: Saving a file takes but a few seconds, but re-creating eight hours of lost work takes eight hours.

✔ **Make a backup copy of your important files**. Most people who back up their work religiously do so because they've been burned in the past (present author included). Hard disks aren't perfect, and one bad byte (if it's the right bad byte) can make the entire disk unreadable. If a file has any value to you at all, make a copy of it on a floppy disk and keep the disk in a safe place. Don't leave it next to your computer; if the building burns down during the night, the smoldering, melted backup floppy won't do you much good.

Saving files

Every time you save your file (with the File⇨Save command), Quattro Pro replaces the file on disk with the updated information from memory. Therefore, it's a good idea to save your work at least every half hour. Otherwise, an unexpected power outage or an ungainly coworker who kicks the plug out of the wall could destroy every thing you did since the last time you saved.

Backing up a file

If you're just starting out, maybe you don't have a clue as to how to make a backup copy of an important file. Here are step-by-step instructions for making an extra (backup) copy of a worksheet. You'll need to have a formatted floppy disk that has enough available space to hold the worksheet file.

This procedure uses the File⇨Save As command to save your file to a floppy disk rather than your hard disk. This procedure is best used when you're finished with a file and are ready to close it.

1. Save your worksheet as you normally do with the File⇨Save command. Presumably, you save your worksheets on your hard drive.

2. Make sure you have your backup floppy disk inserted in your floppy disk drive.

3. Select File⇨Save As.

   Quattro Pro displays a pop-up message asking you what name to use for the worksheet.

4. Press Esc three times to clear the filename that Quattro Pro proposes.

5. If the floppy is in drive A, type **A:** followed immediately by the filename. If your floppy is in drive B, type **B:** followed by the filename. (Use the same name as Quattro Pro proposed earlier, but you can leave off the three-letter extension.) An example of how this might look is shown in Figure 9-6.

6. Press Enter.

Quattro Pro lets you know if there's a problem. Otherwise, the pop-up box disappears, and your worksheet is saved to the floppy disk you specified.

7. Select File➪**Close** to close the worksheet.

You now have two copies of this worksheet: one on your hard drive and a backup copy on a floppy. Store the floppy disk in a safe place. When you need to work on this file again, open the copy on your hard disk (not the backup copy on the floppy disk).

Note: This is just one way to make a backup of your worksheet. You can also use Quattro Pro's File Manager, the normal DOS COPY command, or you can use the features in programs such as XTree, Norton Commander, or other file manager software. Regardless of how you do it, making a backup of important files is an excellent habit to get into.

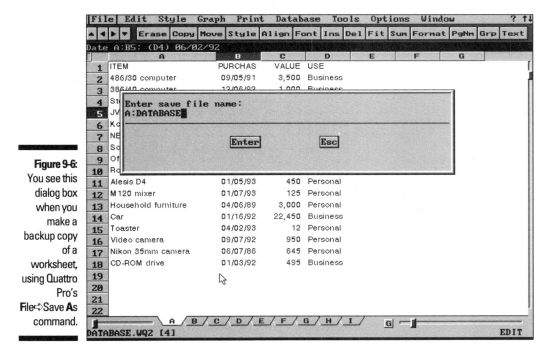

Figure 9-6:
You see this dialog box when you make a backup copy of a worksheet, using Quattro Pro's File➪Save **As** command.

Chapter 10
Hard Copy (As in Printing, Not the TV Show)

A fellow I know named Draper
Wanted his work to be more than a vapor
The books made him bored
So he finally implored,
"How do I get this sucker on paper?"

In This Chapter

▶ Why printing can be a pain in the drain

▶ A crash course on printer types and how to figure out which type you have

▶ How to print your work

▶ How to have more control over how worksheets are printed

Most of the time, you'll want to get a hard copy of the results of your efforts. You basically have two choices: Use a Polaroid camera to photograph your computer monitor or send the worksheet to your printer. Most people choose the latter option because Polaroid prints are too small.

Why Printing Is a Pain

Dealing with printers can be one of the most frustrating parts of working with computers. Here's why:

✔ Your printer is never good enough for what you want to do. Sure, it looked enticing in the store: the flirtation of 300 dpi, of printing six pages per minute, and all those built-in fonts. But the courtship was too quick, and you jumped too soon. The day after you buy a new printer, the manufacturer comes out with a newer, sleeker, faster model that's several hundred dollars cheaper.

✔ The paper jams at the most inopportune times. Never start printing a 30-page job and go to lunch. Printers know when you leave, they know how important the job is, and they know that you can't stay past five o'clock. And they jam the paper three minutes after you're gone.

✔ Printers have minds of their own. When you want to print in Helvetica typeface, your printer may decide Courier is more appropriate.

✔ Printers can hear. Just as your boss yells, "I need that report now, you dolt!" the ribbon dries up, or the toner cartridge bites the dust.

✔ When you install new software, your printer doesn't appear on the list of choices. And the 700-page printer manual is printed in Japanese.

✔ Nobody really knows what all those little buttons and lights are for.

Types of Printers

It's usually a good idea to know what type of printer you have. It's also a good idea to know the name of your printer. Most printers have a name printed somewhere on them, but what *type* of printer you have may not be so obvious. Refer to Figure 10-1 for assistance.

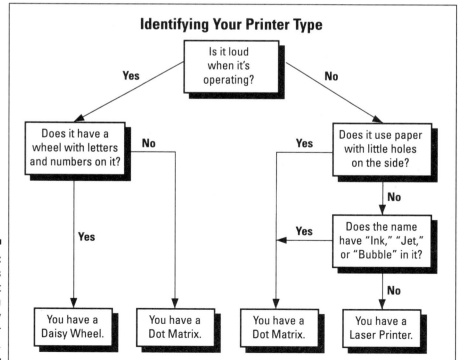

Figure 10-1: This flowchart can help you properly identify your printer.

Here's a quick run-down on the pros and cons of each printer type.

Laser printers: Laser printers are the best. They are fast, quiet, easy to work with, and do great graphics. Laser printers range in price from about $600 up to several thousands of dollars. They differ in print speed and maximum print resolution (300 dots per inch or very high resolution 600 dots per inch). This class of printers is now considered the standard printer.

Inkjet printers: The output from inkjet printers can be very good — nearly as good as output from a laser printer, but inkjet printing is much cheaper. Since the ink is gently sprayed on the paper, these printers are very quiet. Some models even print in color.

Dot-matrix printers: Dot-matrix printers come in a variety of styles, ranging in price from cheap to expensive. Their output quality can be bad to pretty good. These days, the main advantage of using dot-matrix printers is that they can print multi-part forms (which lasers and ink jets can't handle). These printers are also very noisy. Dot-matrix printers should come with a free Sony Walkman to drown out the clatter — but they don't.

Daisy wheel printers: You rarely see these printers anymore. They do their thing much like a typewriter — a wheel of letters and numbers slams up against a ribbon and creates the image on paper. They are very slow, extremely noisy, and can't do graphics. Because of this, they are nearly obsolete (good riddance).

Everything You Always Wanted to Know about Printing but Were Afraid to Ask

In a perfect world, you would simply issue the **Print** command, and all your work would instantly appear on paper just as you expect. Sorry to burst your bubble jet, but this isn't a perfect world (at least it wasn't when I wrote this chapter).

In real life, you have to tell Quattro Pro what block of cells you want to print. And if you want to do anything slightly out of the ordinary (such as print sideways on a page or use different margins), you also have to specify those options. In other words, printing can sometimes be a multi-step process. But you'll learn what you need to know in the following pages.

Printing in Quattro Pro is done through the **Print** menu, shown in Figure 10-2.

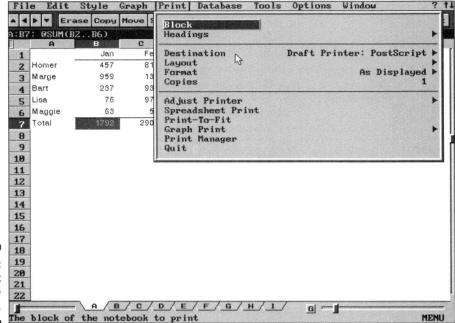

Figure 10-2:
You print
from the
Print menu.

Here are the basic steps involved in printing. These steps are explained in more detail in the sections that follow:

1. Before you start printing, you need to make sure that your printer is installed and connected properly. It also has to be on and have paper in it.

2. Make sure your worksheet is how you want it to be. If you see the CALC indicator at the bottom of the screen, press F9 to recalculate and bring your formulas up to date.

3. Select **Print⇨Block**. Quattro Pro displays the prompt The block of the notebook to print in the input line.

4. Highlight the range that you want to print. Press period to anchor the cell pointer, and then use the normal navigation keys or your mouse to select the print block. Then press Enter.

5. At this point, you can issue the **Print⇨Layout** command to change some things about how the printout will look. I talk about this in the section "The page layout."

6. Issue the **Print⇨Spreadsheet Print** command. Quattro Pro displays a message telling you that it's printing. If you change your mind, you can press Ctrl-Break to abort the printing.

As I mentioned, the steps above are the basic steps. The rest of this chapter discusses the options you have when printing.

Specifying the print block

Before you print, you have to tell Quattro Pro what you want to print. Even if you want to print everything on your worksheet, you still have to tell Quattro Pro. The command to specify the print block is **Print**⇨**Block**. After you select this command, you simply point out the range to print by highlighting it and then pressing Enter.

If you have a mouse, you can preselect the print block before you issue the **Print**⇨**Block** command. Do this by clicking and dragging over the cells.

The destination

The destination determines where the printed output goes. Although you usually print to the printer, you can also print to a disk file or to the screen (that is, print preview). You tell Quattro Pro your print destination by using the **Print**⇨**Destination** command (see Figure 10-3). When the Print menu drops down, the current destination is shown. If it's the destination you want, you can skip this step.

For normal text printing (without fancy fonts, line drawing, shading, and so on), select the **Print**⇨**Destination**⇨**Draft Printer** command.

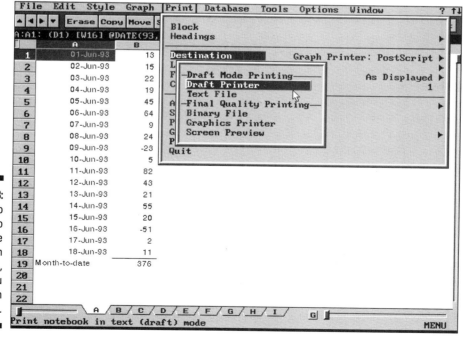

Figure 10-3: Quattro Pro needs to know the destination for printing, which you indicate in this menu.

Getting a sneak preview

Sometimes, printing can take a long time since Quattro Pro does a lot of work behind the scenes. It's not uncommon to wait five minutes for your printed output, only to discover that it didn't come out right. One way around this is to preview your work before you send it off to the printer. Previewing is fast, and it can save you time (not to mention paper).

To preview your work, you must change the destination from the printer to the screen. Do this by selecting **Print**⇨**Destination**⇨**Screen Pre-** view. To actually see the preview, select **Print**⇨**Spreadsheet Print**. Almost immediately, you'll see a miniature version of your printed output appear before your very eyes (it'll look something like the accompanying figure). You have lots of control while viewing the preview since the preview window has its own menu. Commands on this menu let you zoom in or zoom out, display the next or previous page, and do several other things. To get out of the preview window, press Esc.

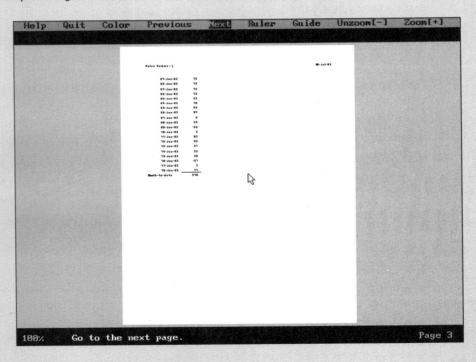

For the highest quality printing (with fancy fonts, borders, shading, and so on), select the **Print**⟿**Destination**⟿**Graphics Printer** command.

The page layout

You have quite a bit of flexibility in how your output will look. When you issue the **Print**⟿**Layout** command, you get the handy dialog box shown in Figure 10-4. This dialog box lets you change various settings in one central location. When you change settings here, it's a good idea to use the print preview feature before printing to make sure it works. See the sidebar "Getting a sneak preview" for details.

I explain these settings in the following sections.

Header text and Footer text

If you want something to appear at the top or bottom of every page you print, you need to know about headers and footers. Headers appear at the top of every page, and footers appear at the bottom of every page. If you have trouble keeping this straight, think of an upright human body. The head is at the top, and the foot is at the bottom.

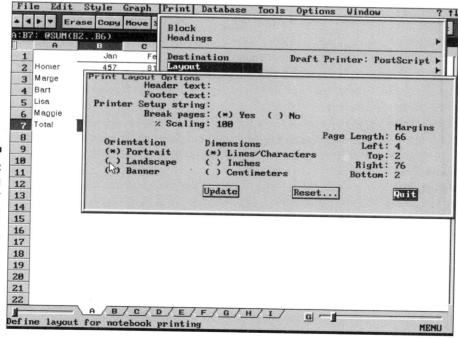

Figure 10-4:
This dialog box is your one-stop shopping place for determining how your printed output will look.

Why use headers or footers? Well, some people like to identify what the printout is all about. For example, your 3rd Quarter Tardiness Report could have a header that reads *3rd Quarter Tardiness Report.* You can also use a header or footer to insert page numbers or the date the report was printed.

Printer Setup string

This is another confusing issue carried forth from the early days of Lotus 1-2-3. This setting is completely irrelevant if you're printing in WYSIWYG mode. A *setup string* is basically a set of cryptic codes that only your printer (and one or two computer geeks) understands. Even worse, every printer understands different setup codes. For example, you can insert a setup string to make your output come out in a smaller typeface. I could waste many pages discussing this stuff, but I know only about three people would ever find it useful. There's an excellent chance that you will never be concerned with setup strings. If you are, however, consult with someone who knows about such things (and make sure you have your printer's reference manual close at hand).

Break pages

How can you print a large worksheet without using page breaks, you might ask. Actually, this option is only relevant if you're printing to a disk file. For example, you might want to print a table of numbers to a file so that you can read the file into your word processor.

Setting this option to No tells Quattro Pro not to insert big blank spaces between what would normally be pages. If you print to a file, you normally set this to No (unless you want those would-be page breaks to appear as blank lines in your file).

% Scaling

This option is handy for those cases in which you want to fit your report on one page — but you end up with one or two extra lines on page 2. You can scale the output down by some percentage so that all text fits in the space you want.

To let Quattro Pro automatically determine the scaling, use the **Print⇨Print-To-Fit** command.

Orientation

These terms refer to how the information is printed on the paper: normally or upright (*portrait*), sideways (*landscape*), or continuous across several pages (*banner*). These are some strange terms, and I have no idea where they came from. But everybody uses them, so get with the program, okay?

Dimensions

This setting lets you choose how you want to measure margins and page size. Normally, Quattro Pro uses Lines/Characters, but you can choose inches or centimeters if you want to specify margins in these units. For example, if your company has a policy that all reports must have one-inch margins on all sides, select the Inches option here and specify 1 for the margins.

Margins

Margins are the white spaces around the perimeter of the page. You change the margin settings here. Margins, by default, are measured in characters and lines, but you can change the measurement system with the Dimensions option.

Other printing particulars

The following sections tell how to do various things that people like to do when printing (and often have trouble with). For example, you'll learn how to insert page numbers, print the current date, and a few other things.

Inserting page numbers

To add page numbers to your printouts, follow these steps:

1. Select **Print⇨Layout**.

2. Move the pointer to the Header text or Footer text field and press Enter (or simply press H for **H**eader text or F for **F**ooter text).

3. Type a pound sign (#).

   To center the page number, precede the pound sign with a vertical bar character (|#). To right-justify the page number, precede the pound sign with two vertical bars (| |#).

4. Choose Update to update the settings.

5. Press Enter to return to the Print menu.

You can also combine the page number with text. For example, if you insert |Page # in the Footer field, *Page xx* prints at to bottom of each page (centered).

When Quattro Pro sees a pound sign (#) in the Header text or Footer text fields, it substitutes the current page number of the printout.

Inserting the date

To add the current date to your printouts, follow these steps:

1. Select **Print⇨Layout**.

2. Move the pointer to the Header text or Footer text field and press Enter (or simply press H for **Header** text or F for **Footer** text).

3. Type an at sign (@).

   To center the date, precede the at sign with a vertical bar character (|@). To right-justify the date, precede the at sign with two vertical bars (||@).

4. Choose **Update** to update the settings.

5. Press Enter to return to the **Print** menu.

When Quattro Pro sees an at sign (@) in the Header text or Footer text fields, it prints the current date on the printout.

You can combine dates and page numbers in headers and footers. The example below, inserted in the Footer field, prints the date at the bottom left of each page and the page number at the bottom right of each page:

```
Printed: @||Page #
```

Row and column headings

Sometimes, you might want a couple of rows at the top of your worksheet to print on every page. Or you might want the first column or two to print on every page. This is handy when you have column labels in your worksheet, and you discover that they only print on the first page. Fortunately, Quattro Pro lets you set it up so selected rows and/or columns print on every single page.

Assume that the first row of your worksheet has column labels, and the second row is filled with underline characters. And you want these two rows to print at the top of every page. You need to specify a top heading.

1. Start by moving the cell pointer to any cell in the first row.

2. Select **Print⇨Headings⇨Top** Heading.

   Quattro Pro responds with a message asking you to select the rows that will print across the top of each page.

3. Press period to anchor the current cell, and then press the down arrow once to extend the selection one more row. Press Enter.

4. Now you can specify your print block with the **Print⇨Block** command.

You can also include headings on the left by following the same sort of procedure. So if you have a really wide budget, for example, you can use both row headings and column headings to make the budget categories (left column) and months (top row) appear on every printed page. Without these headings, interpreting anything that's not on page 1 would be very difficult.

To remove print headings, use the **Print⇨Layout⇨Reset⇨Headings** command.

When you use top headings or left headings, do *not* include these rows or columns in your print block. If you do, they print twice on the first page. Everybody makes this mistake at least once, so when you do, don't feel bad about it.

Multiple copies

If you want to print more than one copy, use the **Print⇨Copies** command. You can enter a number up to 1,000 (gee whiz, only 1,000!). Actually, if you need more than a dozen or so copies, you might want to check out the wonderful world of photocopiers.

WYSIWYG Printing

Printing from WYSIWYG mode is not much different from normal printing. The only difference is that you select the **Print⇨Destination⇨Graphics Printer** command before you do your printing. Selecting this command tells Quattro Pro to take advantage of all of the graphics characteristics of your printer when it prints your work. Consequently, your worksheet is printed in the best possible manner.

Printing Graphs

Printing graphs is a whole other story (though not difficult), and I really don't want to get into it here. Check out Chapter 12.

Chapter 11
Notebooks from the 3rd Dimension

Sharon worked in a lab
And had a wonderful gift of gab
But her files were a disaster
Till she met with a master
Who told her about clicking a tab.

In This Chapter

▶ Why 3-D notebooks are a good idea, and what you should know about them

▶ How to give meaningful names to pages

▶ Navigating around a notebook and dealing with 3-D blocks of cells

▶ How to make the best use of Quattro Pro's 3-D notebooks — including instructions for viewing two pages at once

▶ How Group mode can save you lots of time and energy

The most significant new feature added in Quattro Pro 5 is 3-D notebooks. Until this upgrade was released, a Quattro Pro file consisted of a single worksheet with only 2 million and some odd cells. But Version 5 lets you work with 256 of these sheets in a single file, bringing the total number of accessible cells to more than half a billion. Picture a single worksheet with 256 columns and 8,192 rows. Then picture 255 more of these things stacked behind it. That's a Quattro Pro notebook.

> *Note*: If you don't have Quattro Pro Version 5, this chapter won't be of much value to you.

Using 3-D Notebooks: No Glasses Required

The benefit of 3-D notebooks is not the number of cells you have access to. Rather, the notebook structure is a great way to organize your work and break things up into more manageable units.

Many spreadsheet projects can be broken down into several chunks. For example, you might have a chunk that holds your assumptions, several different chunks that hold tables of values, a chunk to store data for graphs, and so on. Back in the days before 3-D, one of the most difficult aspects of dealing with large spreadsheets was figuring out where to put all the various chunks. With a 3-D worksheet, it's simple: Put each chunk on a separate page.

An example of how you might use the notebook feature is in consolidating a bunch of separate worksheets. Suppose you've been given the task of rolling up all the department budgets for your company into a master budget. The best way to approach this job is to put each department budget into a separate notebook page. Then use another page to hold formulas that you create that add up the corresponding items.

Figure 11-1 shows an example of using several notebook pages. Notice that the name of each department appears on the tab. You can jump to a department's budget just by clicking the tab.

There are lots of other ways to make use of these extra pages. Stay tuned, and I'll give you some more ideas later in this chapter. But first, you'll need to know a little background and learn some techniques.

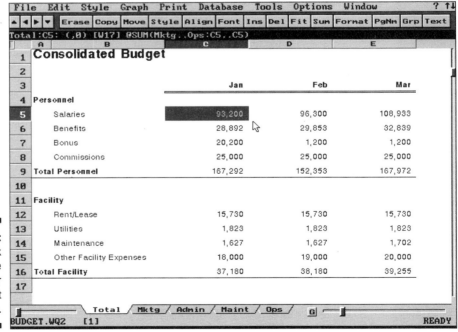

Figure 11-1: Notebook pages are ideal for budget applications.

Reading 1-page worksheets into separate pages

One way to work with different pages in a note-book is to enter the information into each page manually. But what if you already have single-sheet files that you want to combine into a single notebook (one on each page)?

If you need to combine a bunch of 1-page worksheets into a multi-page notebook, you can search the File menu all day and still not figure out how it's done. The trick here is to use the Tools⇨Combine command to combine the information in a file with the current notebook.

First, move to a blank page. And then select Tools⇨Combine⇨Copy⇨File from the menu.

Quattro Pro displays a file list. Choose the file you want, and it will be loaded into the current page of the notebook. If you have several files to load in, move to a blank page and repeat the procedure for each one. Once the files are loaded into separate pages, you can do whatever you want — including writing formulas to add up corresponding cells (that is, consolidate the information).

If all of this seems too complicated, don't forget about the ultimate spreadsheet operation: bribing the office computer guru to give you a hand.

Things to know about 3-D notebooks

Here are a few things to keep in mind when you're working with more than one page in a Quattro Pro file:

- ✔ The pages are normally labeled with letters, starting with A and continuing up to IV. This labeling method is exactly the same way columns are labeled.

- ✔ Each tab displayed at the bottom of the screen represents a page. Although only a few tabs appear at a time, there are actually 256 of these tabs lurking around. The short horizontal scroll bar to the left of the tabs lets you display other tabs. By the way, a person who is looking for one of these notebook tabs is often referred to as a Tab Hunter. (If you don't understand the preceding joke, you're probably under 40 or not a B-movie fan.)

- ✔ You can change the page names to names that are more meaningful to you and reflect the contents of the page.

- ✔ When you refer to cells or blocks on another page, you must precede the cell reference with the page letter (or page name, if it has one).

- ✔ Formulas that use block references can use blocks that cut across pages. For example, @SUM(A..C:A1..C3) adds up a $3 \times 3 \times 3$ cube of cells starting with the upper left cell on the first page and extending through to the cell in the third row and third column of the third page (27 cells in all).

Naming Pages: Albert, Otto, Cedric...

It's really a good idea to give a name to the pages that you use. Naming pages makes it easy for you (or anybody else who may use the worksheet) to remember what's on each page. After all, it's easier to remember that your boss's assumptions are on a page named BOSS than on a page labeled R. You can also use these names in formulas — which makes the formulas more understandable. Calculating a ratio with a formula such as +BOSS:A1/BOSS:A2 makes more sense than +R:A1/R:A2, no?

To give a name to a page, use the **Edit⇨Page⇨Name** command. You'll get the box shown in Figure 11-2. Simply enter a name (up to 15 characters, with no spaces) and press Enter. After you do so, the former letter that appeared in the tab display is replaced by the name you gave it.

You can also use the PgNm button (PAG in Text mode) on the SpeedBar to name a page.

You can continue to use the old page letter, even if you give the page a name. For example, if you give the name *IntroScreen* to the first page, entering a formula like @SUM(INTROSCREEN:A1..A6) returns the same thing as the formula @SUM(A:A1..A6). However, Quattro Pro always replaces a page reference that you enter with its name (if it has one).

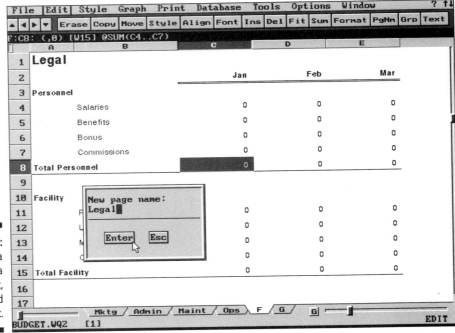

Figure 11-2: Giving a name to a page is fast, easy, and smart.

If you want to change a page name, just use the Edit⇨Page⇨Name command again and enter a different name. To get rid of a page name and return it to its default letter, use Edit⇨Page⇨Name and backspace over the existing name until it's entirely erased.

3-D Blocks

One of the nice things about using 3-D notebooks is that your formulas can "slice through" the pages and refer to cells on different pages. And @functions can use cells across different pages for their arguments. The only thing you have to remember is to precede the cell reference with a page letter (or name). If you don't do this, Quattro Pro assumes that you're referring to the current page.

Single-page references

If you're referring to a block of cells on a page other than the current page, you only need to put the page reference before the first cell in the block. Here's an example:

```
@SUM(B:A1..A12)
```

Notice that the B: page reference is used only before the first cell in the block. You *could* enter the following instead, with the same results:

```
@SUM(B:A1..B:A12)
```

This takes a few nanoseconds longer to type, and you'll find that Quattro Pro removes the second page reference anyway.

Multiple-page references

When you're entering a formula that refers to a 3-D block of cells, you have to put the actual page numbers in — which makes sense, since Quattro Pro would have no idea of what you're trying to do otherwise. For example, to add up all the cells in A:A1..A12, B:A1..A12, and C:A1..A12, you would use this formula:

```
@SUM(A..C:A1..A12)
```

You'll notice that the pages used in the reference appear first and are separated with the normal double dots. Then there's a colon, and the cell references appear. The logical side of you may think that the proper way to enter such a formula is

@SUM(A:A1..C:A12)

In fact, you *can* enter the formula like that — but Quattro Pro converts it to @SUM(A..C:A1..A12) after you enter it.

If you *really* want to include the page reference immediately before each cell reference (as in the preceding example), you can have it your way. Select the **O**ptions➪**S**tartup➪**3**-D Syntax command, and select B for the second alternative.

If you use named pages, the same rule holds: put the page references first and then the cell references. Here's an example of a formula that uses named pages:

@SUM(JANUARY..JUNE:A1..A45)

This formula adds up the cells in A1..A45 across all the pages from the page named *January* to the page named *June* (six pages, 45 cells on each page).

Copying formulas with page references

You probably already know that Quattro Pro adjusts cell references when you copy a formula to a different location on the same page. It stands to reason, then, that Quattro Pro also adjusts cell references when you copy a formula to a different page. In fact, it does all of this in a way that makes perfect sense, and the result is almost always what you intended.

Here's an example. Suppose you have this formula in cell A:A1 (the upper left cell on the first page):

```
@SUM(A..B:A2..A7)
```

This formula refers to a 3-D block of cells on two pages (the current page, plus the next page). If you copy this to the cell directly to the right on the same page (to A:B1), Quattro Pro adjusts the references as follows:

```
@SUM(A..B:B2..B7)
```

If you copy it to the corresponding cell on the next page (B:A1), the references get adjusted like this:

```
@SUM(B..C:A2..A7)
```

The page letters are adjusted, but the relative cell references remain the same.

If you find that dealing with the third dimension is rather confusing, don't despair. It's all very logical, and you'll get the hang of it when you start playing around with multi-page worksheets. If you find it just *too* confusing, just stick with single-page worksheets. After all, people have been using only one page for more than a decade — and they got along just fine.

Where Am I? Lessons in Navigation

Moving around in a 3-D notebook requires a bit more effort since you have a whole other dimension to be concerned with. But again, it's all pretty logical once you get the hang of it.

Activating other pages

Before you can scroll around on a page, you must activate it — or display it on the screen. The easiest way to activate a notebook page is to click on the tab with your mouse. If the tab is not showing, use the little scroll bar to the left of the tabs to scroll the tabs to the left or right until the one you want appears.

You might find it more efficient to use the keyboard to activate a different page. Here are the keys you need to know about:

Ctrl-PgDn   Activates the next page, unless you're on the last page; then it has no effect

Ctrl-PgUp   Activates the previous page, unless you're on the first page; then it has no effect

Ctrl-Home   Moves to the upper left cell of the first page

Ctrl-End   Activates the last page (IV) of the notebook

End, Ctrl-Home   Moves to the last cell with data on the last page with data

A fast way to activate a far off page is to press F5, the "goto" key. Quattro Pro asks you what address you want to go to. Enter a page letter followed by a colon, and you're there in a jif. For example, if you want to activate page M, press F5, type **M:**, and then press Enter. If the page has a name, you can enter the name followed by a colon.

Selecting 3-D blocks

When you're building a formula that uses references on one or more other pages, you can either enter the cell references manually, or you can use pointing techniques similar to those used in a single page.

Here's an example of what I'm talking about. Assume that you are building a formula in cell A:A1 that adds up the range B..F:A1..A1. This is actually rather common, and you would do this if you want to consolidate the numbers in five pages. You could just enter **@SUM(B..F:A1..A1)**, but you might prefer to point to the argument:

1. Move to A:A1 and type **@SUM(** to start the formula.

2. Press Ctrl-PgDn to move to the next page. Then move the cell pointer to B:A1 if it's not already there (watch the formula being built in the input line).

3. Press period to anchor the selection.

4. Press Ctrl-PgDn four more times until you get to page F. Move the cell pointer to F:A1 if it's not already there.

5. Type **)** and press Enter to finish off the formula.

   Quattro Pro brings you back to the cell that holds the formula.

Rather than press Ctrl-PgDn to activate other pages while pointing, you can click on a page tab.

Preselecting 3-D blocks

When you're formatting blocks that extend across different pages, you may prefer to preselect the block before you issue the formatting commands.

When you're dealing with a single page, you can just drag the mouse across the block to preselect it (or you can press Shift-F7 to anchor the cell and use the navigation keys to preselect the block). Preselecting across pages is very similar: just hold down the Shift key while you activate another page either by clicking a tab or pressing Ctrl-PgUp or Ctrl-PgDn.

Moving pages

You can move cells and blocks, so you should be able to move pages too, right? You betcha. That's why Quattro Pro has an **Edit⇨Page⇨Move** command. For example, you might want page R to be the first page in the notebook.

1. Activate the page that you want to move — in this case, page R.

2. Select **Edit**⇨**Page**⇨**Move**. Quattro Pro displays the message `Source block of pages` and suggests the current page. The actual cell reference displayed in this message is not important — only the page reference matters.

3. If you want to move only the current page, just press Enter. If you want to move several contiguous pages, press Ctrl-PgDn or Ctrl-PgUp to select more pages before you press Enter.

   As you do so, Quattro Pro changes the display to show the page letters (or names) of the pages you're selecting.

   Quattro Pro then displays the message `Destination for pages` and the current page reference.

4. Use the Ctrl-PgUp or Ctrl-PgDn keys to activate the page that you want to move it to, and press Enter. You can also click on a page tab to select the destination page.

   Quattro Pro inserts the page or pages directly before the page you select in this step.

When you move a page, all of the subsequent pages are pushed forward. For example, if you move page Z to page A, page A becomes page B. The names of pages that have names do not change; they're just pushed back. This is exactly what you want to happen, and Quattro Pro automatically adjusts all of the references in your formulas.

Two for the Price of One

Normally, you can see only one page at a time. But if you want to see or work with two pages from a worksheet, you can split the screen into two panes with the **Window**⇨**Options**⇨**Horizontal** or **Window**⇨**Options**⇨**Vertical** command.

Start by moving the cell pointer to the place in the worksheet where you want the split to occur. Then issue either one of these commands. The worksheet displays another set of borders, and you can jump between the panes by clicking the mouse button or pressing F6. Better yet, each of these panes can display a different page from the notebook.

Figure 11-3 shows a worksheet that has been split into two horizontal panes. Notice that the top pane is displaying page A, and the bottom pane shows page C, which is the active page.

To clear the split window, use the **Window**⇨**Options**⇨**Clear** command.

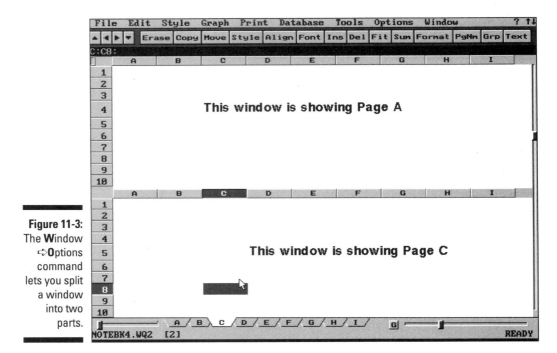

Figure 11-3: The **Window** ⇨**O**ptions command lets you split a window into two parts.

Printing Multiple Pages

If you read Chapter 10, you should already know how to print a worksheet. But what about printing a worksheet that has more than one page?

Easy. All you need to do is specify a 3-D print block with the **Print**⇨**Block** command. Use the PgUp and PgDn keys to point to the block you want to print. That's all there is to it.

If you want each notebook page to start on a new sheet of paper, move to the upper left cell of the print block and select the **Style**⇨**Insert Break** command. Quattro Pro inserts a new row and puts in a double colon character to force a page break.

Group Mode: Once You Try It, You'll Never Go Back

One final topic that deals with 3-D notebooks is Group mode. Group mode lets you define a group of pages, and then you can work on all of the pages at once. When you're in Group mode, the following things change:

- ✔ Any normal 2-D selection you make turns into a 3-D selection that includes all of the other pages in the group.

- ✔ Some changes you make on one page of the group affect all other pages of the group. These changes include applying formatting, changing column widths and row heights, copying and moving cells and blocks, and inserting and deleting rows and columns.

In Group mode, simple entries that you make into a worksheet are *not* entered into all of the pages in the group. However, you *can* put an entry into all pages by using Ctrl-Enter instead of Enter when you enter a value or label into a cell. For example, if you want to put a formula into cell A12 of all the pages in a group, enter the formula into one page and press Ctrl-Enter.

You can have more than one group defined within a worksheet, but each page can only belong to one group at a time.

Creating groups

To create a group, use the Edit⇨Group⇨Create command. If you have any groups defined, Quattro Pro displays the list. To create a new group, enter a name for it and specify the first page and the last page (using the page letters or names).

Entering and leaving Group mode

When you have at least one group defined, you can enter Group mode by selecting Edit⇨Group⇨Mode⇨Enable. From that point on, anything you do in a page that belongs to a group happens to the other pages in that group. For example, suppose that you want to change column widths or cell formatting. Do it to one page in a group, and all other pages in the group follow suit. Obviously, this can be a real time-saver — and also make your work look more consistent.

To get out of Group mode, choose Edit⇨Group⇨Mode⇨Disable.

You can toggle between Group mode and non-Group mode by clicking on the G button that's directly to the right of the page tab display at the bottom of the screen. (In Text mode, this button appears as a small white square.) The tab display also changes to show you which pages are part of a group. Yet another way to toggle between these modes is to press Ctrl-F5.

Ideas for Using Notebook Pages

I'll close this chapter with a bunch of miscellaneous ideas about using 3-D notebooks. Maybe you can use some of them, or maybe you'll come up with some better ideas on your own.

- **Consolidate department budgets.** This is a very common use for note-books, and I showed an example earlier in the chapter.

- **Store results for different time periods.** If you track things in a spread-sheet — such as sales, orders, and new customers, for example — you might want to organize your work by time periods. For example, you could have a separate page for each month or each quarter, enabling you to quickly locate what you want and still use formulas to get grand totals and summaries.

- **Document your work.** If you're working on a fairly complex worksheet, it's not a bad idea to use a separate page to make notes to yourself to remind you of things like what you did, why you did it, and how you did it. And if you're really industrious, you could even keep sort of a historical log that describes the changes you made to it over time.

- **Keep macros in a separate page.** If you're into macros, you'll find that it makes a lot of sense to keep your macros on a separate page so that they'll be out of the way of your data and easy to find when you need to make a change or try to figure out why a macro isn't working right.

- **Put graphs on separate pages.** If your worksheet has several graphs, you can insert each one onto a separate notebook page and give each page a descriptive name. Then when your boss barges in and wants to see the production chart for July, you can just click on the appropriate tab. He'll think you're very organized and give you a raise.

- **Use a notebook in place of separate files.** If you're working on a project that uses, say, five different one-page worksheets, you might find it more practical to keep them all in a single notebook (each on a separate page). That way, when it's time to work on the project, you can just load the one file and everything you need will be handy.

- **Store different scenarios.** Lots of people use a spreadsheet to do "what-if" analysis. 3-D notebooks make this easier. For example, you can copy an entire page of a worksheet to other pages. Then make a few changes in the assumptions for each copy and give the pages names such as *BestCase*, *WorstCase*, *LikelyCase*, *JoesScenario*, and so on.

Part III:

Things to Impress the Easily Impressed

The 5th Wave By Rich Tennant

"...AND TALK ABOUT MEMORY! THIS BABY'S GOT SO MUCH MEMORY, IT COMES WITH EXTRA DOCUMENTATION, A HARD DISK—AND A SENSE OF GUILT! I MEAN I'M TALKIN MEMORY!"

In This Part...

These chapters get into some other aspects of Quattro Pro that aren't essential for everyone, but some people find them really slick and impressive. For example, you'll learn the ins and outs of WYSIWYG mode, discover how to make graphs, and learn what all those weird SpeedBar buttons do. And I'll also tell you how to bring information from other files into Quattro Pro — and save yourself lots of time and effort (maybe).

Chapter 12
To GUI or Not to GUI

There once was a man who was kind,
But he couldn't quite make up his mind.
Between graphics and text
He was truly perplexed,
So he drank a few beers to unwind.

In This Chapter

▶ An overview of Quattro Pro's WYSIWYG mode

▶ Why you may or may not want to use WYSIWYG

▶ How to do some basic WYSIWYG things.

In the past, character-based software was all that was available. But graphical user interfaces (or GUIs — pronounced "gooies") are all the rage these days. Most new software is written for Microsoft Windows, which is a GUI. But other non-GUI products are also taking on GUI faces. Quattro Pro is an example of a software program that's basically character-based but has a GUI option called WYSIWYG mode.

If you want to improve the way your worksheets look on-screen and paper, you'll be interested in WYSIWYG mode. As you may recall, WYSIWYG stands for "what you see is what you get." This means that you can do all sorts of fancy formatting things on-screen — and the printed document output will look just like the on-screen document.

On the other hand, if you're already running in WYSIWYG mode, you may want to know about Text mode. As you'll see, both modes have their advantages and disadvantages. The choice of display modes is yours.

> ***Note***: You may think this book has a distinct "pro-GUI" slant to it since almost all of the figures show screen shots in WYSIWYG mode. Using WYSIWYG mode in the figures is certainly not to imply that WYSIWYG mode is better than Text mode. I made the screen shots in WYSIWYG mode mainly because they look better than Text mode. But here's the truth: When I use Quattro Pro, I almost always use it in Text mode — until it's time to format the worksheet for printing. Then I switch over to WYSIWYG mode so I can see exactly how my worksheet will look when it's printed.

The Case for WYSIWYG

Figure 12-1 shows a worksheet with formatting applied. If you're out to impress someone with a presentation, this type of output would typically get more attention than plain old garden variety text, don't you think? The rest of this section provides some more reasons why you might want to use WYSIWYG mode.

The screen looks better

Practically everyone would rather look at Quattro Pro's WYSIWYG screen than its Text mode screen. In particular, I hate the way the tabs look on the bottom of the Text mode screen, and everything is far too cluttered for my tastes. The WYSIWYG screen, with its sculpted look, is simply more appealing.

Fewer surprises

If you find that you have to print your work several times before it comes out right, you'll like that WYSIWYG mode can eliminate much of this since, well, what you see is what you get. (On the other hand, if you have to print your

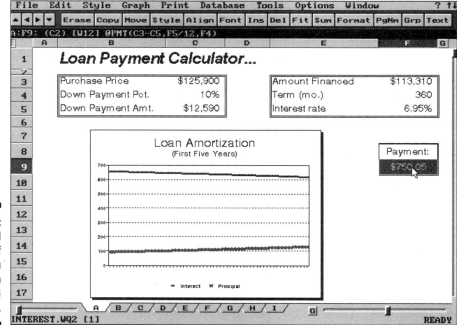

Figure 12-1:
Just a small sample of what you can do in WYSIWYG mode.

work more than once, you probably haven't discovered the screen preview feature. Select **Print**⇨**Destination**⇨**Screen Preview** to avoid repetitive printing and unnecessary trips to the printer.)

Graphs in worksheets

Another neat thing about WYSIWYG mode is that you can stick graphs right in your worksheet. You can do this in Text mode, but the graph simply shows up on the screen as a colored placeholder.

The Case against WYSIWYG

There ain't no such thing as a free lunch, and if you choose to use WYSIWYG, you'll pay a certain price. WYSIWYG comes free with Quattro Pro, so the price I'm referring to is not monetary.

It may not work on older computers

WYSIWYG requires a computer with a graphics card running EGA or better graphics. While almost all PCs sold in the past few years meet these criteria, there are lots of older systems still in use that don't have graphics cards. If your computer can't display graphics, it can't run Quattro Pro in WYSIWYG mode — it's that simple.

It slows you down

The main reason *not* to use WYSIWYG is that it slows things down quite a bit. Quattro Pro running in Text mode is fast and snappy. Move the cursor keys and select menu commands, and Quattro Pro responds instantly (even on fairly slow computers). But get into WYSIWYG mode and you might suspect Quattro Pro is on Quaaludes. Unless you have a super-fast computer, you'll notice that things take a little longer and the characteristic responsiveness is gone.

You may not need it

Another reason not to use WYSIWYG is because you don't need the fancy formatting. Let's face it, not everyone needs to produce impressive documents, and sometimes simple things are the best.

No movable windows

Using WYSIWYG means that you give up the ability to display worksheets in their own movable and resizable windows. If being able to move and resize windows appeals to you, understand that WYSIWYG just can't handle the extra strain involved with handling multiple windows. You can still work with multiple worksheets, but your only option to view more than one at a time is to tile them.

More stuff to learn

Finally, using WYSIWYG means learning some additional commands. If you're already feeling overwhelmed with Quattro Pro, you may be better off tackling WYSIWYG at a later date (pencil in July 12, 1998).

You can perform all of the WYSIWYG formatting tasks even if you work in Text mode — you just can't see the results on-screen. When you print your worksheet, all of the enhancements will be printed just as if you were using WYSIWYG mode. Note that before printing you have to set the print destination to a graphics printer, using the **Print**⇨**Destination**⇨**Graphics Printer** command. Just about any printer in use nowadays (except daisy wheel printers) are graphics printers.

More about WYSIWYG and Text Mode

If you've gotten to this point, you probably fell for the arguments I presented above in favor of WYSIWYG. So here's what you need to know.

Getting into WYSIWYG mode

By default, your system is set up so that you enter WYSIWYG mode automatically whenever you start Quattro Pro. However, someone may have switched you to Text mode. If you're in Text mode, you can enter WYSIWYG mode in either of two ways:

✔ Look at the SpeedBar on the right side of the screen (you won't see it if you don't have a mouse installed). If there's a button labeled WYS, click on it. If that button isn't there, click on the button labeled BAR to bring up the other SpeedBar. Then click the WYS button.

✔ Select **Options**⇨**Display Mode**⇨**B: WYSIWYG** from the menu.

In either case, your screen will be transformed before your very eyes, and things will look a lot different than they did before (sort of like the transition from black & white to color in *The Wizard of Oz*).

When you switch to WYSIWYG mode, you'll notice the following differences:

- ✔ The screen looks much nicer — it has a cool "sculpted look" to it.

- ✔ The page tabs look like real page tabs.

- ✔ The SpeedBar is at the top of your screen, not at the right, and the SpeedBar buttons actually look like buttons.

- ✔ The scroll bars (for mousers) are in a different color and don't take up as much screen real estate.

- ✔ Different formatting that you apply to cells and blocks (fonts, colors, line, shading) actually appears on-screen.

If you don't like the colors used in WYSIWYG, change them by using the Options➪Colors➪Spreadsheet➪WYSIWYG Colors command. You have control over the color of just about every part of the screen. (And it doesn't take long to come up with a color scheme that's absolutely hideous.) By the way, if you want to see your new color choices the next time you start Quattro Pro, you have to use the Options➪Update command before you exit Quattro Pro.

Getting into Text mode

If you're in WYSIWYG mode, enter Text mode in either of two ways:

- ✔ Look at the SpeedBar on the top of the screen (you won't see it if you don't have a mouse installed). Click on the Text button.

- ✔ Select Options➪Display Mode➪A: 80X25 from the menu.

When you select Options➪Display Mode, Quattro Pro presents a list of display mode options. Be careful here. If you select a mode that is not supported by your video card, your system could go into limbo (that is, crash), and you'll lose your work and have to restart your PC.

You can switch freely back and forth between Text mode and WYSIWYG mode. The work you did in WYSIWYG mode is not lost.

How to Do WYSIWYG Things

Applying formatting in WYSIWYG mode is actually pretty easy; all it takes is a little practice, and then you'll feel right at home.

> *Note*: You can also do this formatting in Text mode. But since you can't see the effects of your formatting commands in Text mode, you can sometimes be in for a real surprise when you print. Therefore, it's a good idea to do this type of formatting (as opposed to numeric formatting) in WYSIWYG mode.

Change fonts and colors

One of the simplest things you can do to spiff up a worksheet is to change the fonts used. By *font,* I mean a combination of a typeface and a type size. You change fonts using the **Style**⇨**Font** command. This command brings up the menu shown in Figure 12-2. This menu also lets you adjust the color of the text and determine whether the text's bold, italic, or underlined. To get rid of all of these formatting things, select **Reset**.

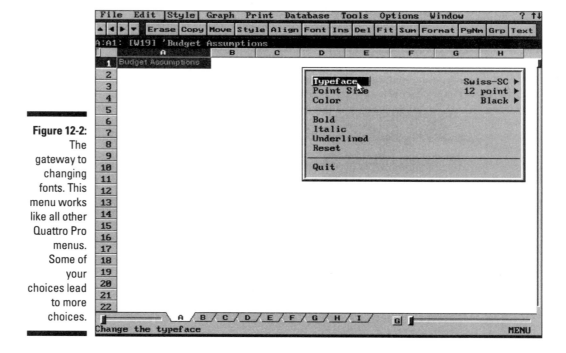

Figure 12-2:
The gateway to changing fonts. This menu works like all other Quattro Pro menus. Some of your choices lead to more choices.

Do it with style

You may notice some additional commands under the **S**tyle menu — specifically the **U**se Style and the **D**efine Style commands. These can be very handy, but many people find the concept hard to grasp. If you've ever used the style feature in a word processor, you can appreciate Quattro Pro's version.

Basically, a style is something that you define — although Quattro Pro includes several built-in styles that you may find handy, including numeric formatting styles (see the accompanying figure). Each style can include settings for the font, line drawing, shading, alignment, data entry mode, and numeric format (but it doesn't have to include *all* of these). Once you define a style, you can apply it to a cell or block, and it immediately takes on all of the attributes you defined for it.

As you might guess, applying a style with a single command is *much* faster than doing all the individual formatting. A side benefit is that your worksheets will look more consistent by using styles. The real benefit of using styles, however, is that you can change the definition for a style,

and everything that is tagged with that style changes automatically. The downside is that you have to spend a bit of time defining the styles. But on the balance, you can save yourself lots of time by understanding styles.

The **S**tyle⇨**D**efine Style command is where you start out. This command lets you create, erase, remove, load, and save your custom styles. The easiest way is to format a cell the way you want, and then select **S**tyle⇨**D**efine Style⇨**C**reate. Then enter a name for the style (such as **Heading**). Quattro Pro uses the existing formatting for the style definition. Once you define a style, you apply it to a cell or block by issuing the **S**tyle⇨**U**se Style command. The selected cell or block immediately takes on the attributes for the style you select. If you want to change the way all of the blocks tagged with a particular style look, use the **S**tyle⇨**D**efine Style⇨**C**reate command and modify the style. Everything with that style changes to reflect the new formatting.

By the way, each worksheet can have up to 120 styles, so you can go hog wild if you're so inclined.

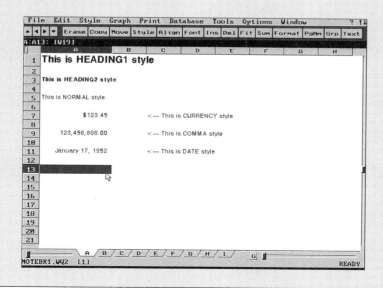

Use line drawing

Another common formatting procedure is to use lines. Putting lines (or borders) around a table, for example, makes the table stand out and usually easier to read. All line drawing is done with the **Style**⇨Line Drawing command. This command leads to the Line Drawing menu. When you select where you want the lines to go, you get another menu, shown in Figure 12-3.

This menu takes a bit of getting used to since there are lots of options, and it doesn't go away when you think it should (you have to select **Quit** to get out of line drawing mode). But again, the key to getting what you want is to play around with the menu options until you understand what's going on.

Selecting **U**nderlined from the Font menu is not the same as using the **Style**⇨Line Drawing command to insert a bottom border (described later). Underlining is done on all of the text in a cell, even if the text spills over into the next cell. A border, on the other hand, extends only as far as the cell boundary. If text runs into adjoining cells, it will not have the border under it.

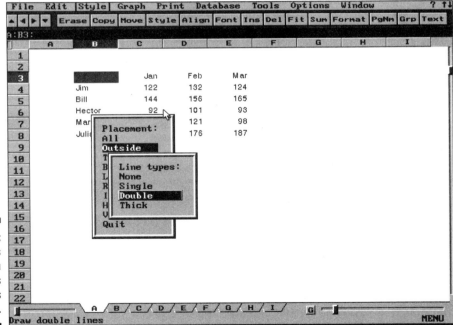

Figure 12-3:
Here's
where you
put lines
around cells
and blocks.

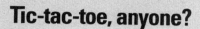

Tic-tac-toe, anyone?

To create a tic-tac-toe game, start by selecting a 3-row x 3-column block. Use **S**tyle⇨**F**ont⇨**P**oint **S**ize⇨**48** Point. Then with the same block selected, choose the **S**tyle⇨**L**ineDrawing⇨**I**nside⇨**D**ouble command. Find someone with comparable intelligence and play the game (cov-ering all the rules is beyond the scope of this book). To start a new game, use the **E**dit⇨**E**rase **B**lock command to get rid of the *X*s and *O*s. The following figure shows an example of an exciting game in progress. Who says spreadsheets can't be exciting?

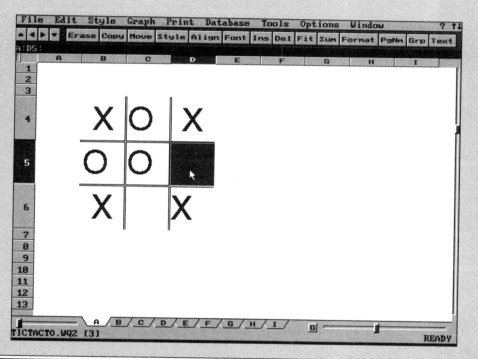

Shady characters

Another way to make specific cells or blocks pop out is to use shading in the background. This is particularly effective for the row and column titles in tables of numbers that you create. You can apply either of two types of shading: gray or black. By the way, text in a cell with a gray shaded background doesn't look all that great on the screen, but it looks much better when it's printed.

Shading cells can also be used to create very thick lines. The key is to apply black shading to a column or row of cells and then adjust the column width and row heights to make it look like a thick border (adjust row heights with the Style⇨Block Size⇨Height command). Figure 12-4 shows an example of how you can use shading.

Graphs

There may be times when you want to show the numbers that are used to create a graph. Quattro Pro lets you stick a graph anywhere in a worksheet. In Text mode, the graph shows up as a colored block on-screen (but prints okay). In WYSIWYG mode, the graph actually looks like a graph on-screen (and also prints okay). Figure 12-5 shows a graph that I stuck next to the numbers it uses.

To insert a graph into a worksheet, you must first create the graph. Then use the Graph⇨Insert command to put the graph where you want it. Chapter 13 gets into all the gory details.

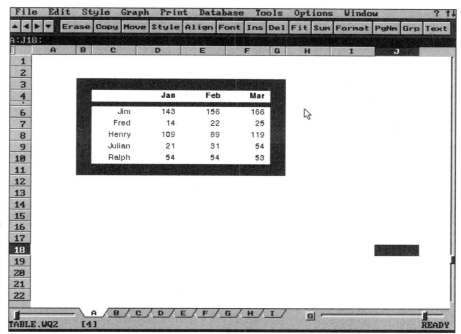

Figure 12-4:
You can use the shading attributes to create thick borders.

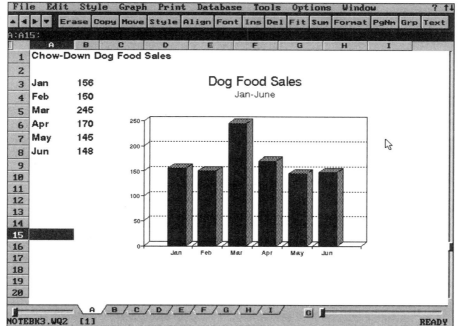

Figure 12-5:
In WYSIWYG mode, inserted graphs appear in all their natural splendor.

Chapter 13
Making Pretty Pictures Out of Numbers

Bruce majored in liberal arts
But for a living sold used auto parts.
His boss wanted to know
How the business would grow,
So Bruce gave him some nice looking charts.

● ●

In This Chapter

▶ How to transform numbers into graphs (magic not required)

▶ What types of graphs you can make

▶ How to make your graphs even more lively and exciting

▶ How to print your graphic creations and save them in separate files so you can recycle them into other applications

▶ Oodles of sample graphs to spark your imagination

● ●

Most people who know about such things consider Quattro Pro to be one of the best spreadsheets available when it comes to making graphs. You can, indeed, create some impressive-looking graphs with this product. It's easy to make simple charts, and if you spend some time playing around, it won't take long to discover how to customize the simple charts to your liking and make them good enough to enter in the county fair.

This chapter tells you enough so that you can create nice looking graphs. It touches on some of the more advanced features, but you're pretty much on your own if you care to tread into the territory known as graph annotation. You might find making graphs kind of fun and won't mind killing some time exploring what you can do. It's the one aspect of Quattro Pro that allows your creative juices to flow (or trickle, as the case may be).

Why a Graph?

Good question. You already know how to put numbers in a spreadsheet, manipulate them with formulas, format them so they look good, and print the results for the world to see. But the reality is that most people can't make sense out of a table of numbers. They would rather see it presented visually — in a graph (also known as a chart). Interestingly enough, as people rise in the corporate hierarchy, they often have a lower tolerance for numbers and prefer to see graphs. That's why these critters are so popular in boardroom presentations.

But even if your work isn't destined for the corporate boardroom, you'll find that creating a graph from a series of numbers can sometimes put the information all into perspective; maybe you'll even be able to spot trends or relationships that you wouldn't have noticed otherwise. So take my word for it, graphs are good.

The Anatomy of a Graph

Figure 13-1 shows a graph I created in Quattro Pro, with all of the major parts labeled. I'll be referring to various parts of a graph throughout this chapter, so you may want to familiarize yourself with these terms.

Graphs typically plot one thing against another. In the example, the graph displays a dog food company's monthly sales over a six-month period. It also shows the monthly sales goal. The dark bars represent actual sales, and the hatched bars represent the goal. Every bar in this graph has a corresponding value in a cell in the worksheet.

The graph shows that sales exceeded the goal for the first three months (and March was an exceptionally good month). But during the second quarter, things started to go downhill, and the monthly goals were not attained.

Things to Know about Graphs

Before jumping into the wonderful world of graphs, take a few minutes to digest the following factoids:

- Except for a text-only graph (which is a special case), Quattro Pro's graphs need to use numbers that are stored in a worksheet.

- When you change any of the numbers used in a graph, the graph automatically changes to reflect the new numbers.

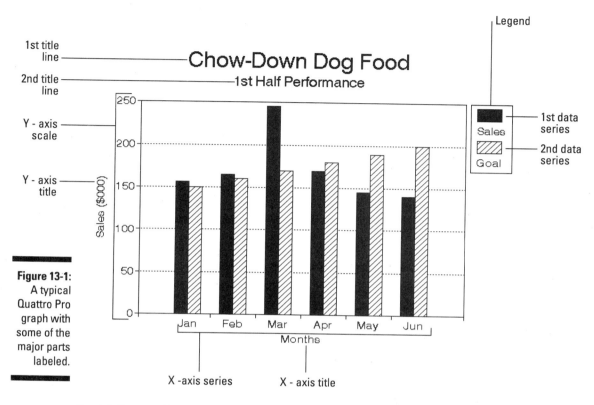

Figure 13-1:
A typical
Quattro Pro
graph with
some of the
major parts
labeled.

✔ A Quattro Pro graph can show as many as six different series of numbers in a single graph.

✔ You can choose from a long list of graph types: bar graphs, line graphs, pie graphs, and more. And a single graph can have both lines and bars. Unless you tell it otherwise, Quattro Pro displays numbers in a graph as stacked bars.

✔ You don't have to have a legend if you don't want one. (A *legend* explains what each color or line stands for.)

✔ You have almost complete control over the colors used, the hatch patterns, line widths, line markers, fonts used for titles and labels, and so on.

✔ When you display a graph, your screen changes: the worksheet disappears, and the graph fills up your whole screen. Pressing any key returns you to the worksheet.

✔ You can insert a graph right into your worksheet. This lets you print a graph along with the data the graph uses. You need to be in WYSIWYG mode in order to see the inserted graph on your screen (but not to print it).

✔ A worksheet can have any number of graphs stored in it. If you use more than one graph, you have to give the graphs names.

✔ You can use the special graph annotation mode to add other things to a graph — additional text, lines, arrows, boxes, and so on.

You must have a graphics card installed in your computer in order to view graphs on the screen. But even if you don't have a graphics card, you can still create and print graphs — but I don't recommend it. Working with graphs without seeing the result is like working on a paint-by-numbers painting in the dark.

How to Create a Graph

If you've never made a graph before, here's a once-in-a-lifetime opportunity to do so. And you don't even have to know what you're doing — just follow the step-by-step instructions below. You'll end up with a reasonably attractive graph and maybe even learn a few things in the process.

Before you make a graph, you need some numbers. Use the numbers shown in the worksheet in Figure 13-2. This worksheet shows the average annual rainfall in my hometown. If you're following along at home, take a minute to create a new worksheet and make it look like the one in the figure.

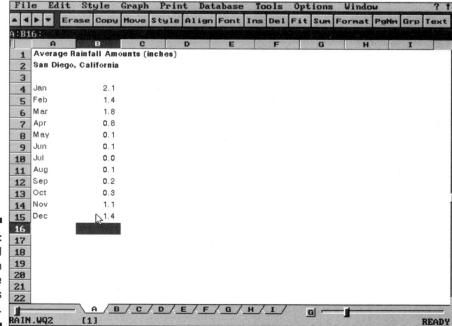

Figure 13-2:
You will transform these numbers into a graph.

After you enter the numbers into a worksheet, the first step in the graph-making process is to tell Quattro what data you want to graph. In this case, you need to point out two blocks of cells: the labels for the x-axis and the values for the first data series.

1. Issue the **Graph⇨Series** command. Quattro Pro displays another menu.

2. Select the **X-Axis** series option from the menu. This option puts you in point mode.

3. Highlight the month names and press Enter.

4. Select **1st Series** from the menu (you'll be in point mode again). Highlight the rainfall amounts in column B and press Enter.

5. Select **Quit** to get rid of this menu.

6. Select the **View** option from the menu that's left on-screen.

   Quattro Pro displays the graph (see Figure 13-3).

7. When you're finished admiring your work, press any key to return to the Graph menu.

8. Before you quit, you will want to give the graph a name. Select **Name** from the menu, and then select **Create**.

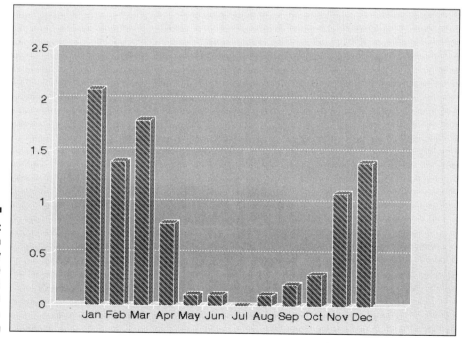

Figure 13-3:
The graph created by Quattro Pro with just a few simple commands.

9. Enter a name for this creation (**SDRain**, for example) and press Enter. (Graph names can be up to 15 characters in length, with no spaces.)

10. Choose **Quit** or press Escape to get back to the worksheet.

If you're only going to have one graph in your worksheet, you don't need to give it a name. Quattro Pro can remember the settings for one graph and calls it the *current graph*. If you plan to have more than one graph in your worksheet, you must give each graph a name. It's a good idea to use descriptive names, such as *1stQExpenses* or *DogFoodSales*, rather than generic names like *1stGraph* or *AnotherOne*.

Adding titles

The graph isn't bad, but the person who sees this graph will have no idea what information it's showing. Therefore, you will add some titles.

1. You need to call the graph back up. Select **Graph**⇨**Name**⇨**Display**.

   Quattro Pro shows a list of all named graphs (there should be only one — the one you just created).

2. Press Enter to activate the *SDRain* graph. Quattro Pro displays the graph so that you can make sure you got the right one. Since there's only one graph in this worksheet, this step isn't really necessary (but it's good practice for you).

3. Press any key to get back to the **Graph** menu.

4. Select the **Text** option. This option lets you add labels. You want to add a title to the graph. The graph's title can use two lines, but you'll just use the first line.

5. Select the **1st Line** option, and then enter a title. Type something like **San Diego Average Rainfall**, and press Enter.

6. It's pretty obvious that the x-axis refers to months, but it may not be clear what the y-axis represents. Therefore, select the **Y-Title** option, type **Inches**, and press Enter.

7. Choose **Quit** to close this menu.

8. To take a look at what you did, select the **View** option from the menu. The titles add a lot, and this graph is shaping up. Now the graph should look like the one shown in Figure 13-4.

9. Press any key to get rid of the graph, and then press Esc until you're out of the graph menus.

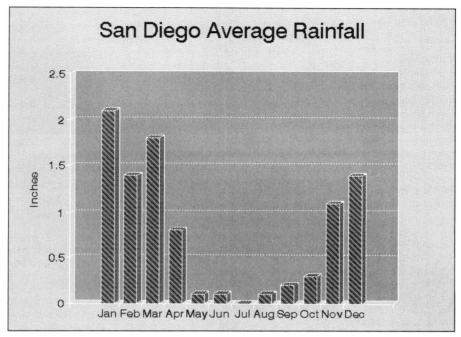

Figure 13-4:
The graph
after you
add some
labels.

Customizing graphs

You may be content with the graph as it is. But maybe you don't like the colors
it uses, or you would prefer a different type of pattern in the bars. You can
change a few things, using the dialog box shown in Figure 13-5.

1. Select **Graph**⇨**Customize Series** to bring up the rather intimidating dialog
   box shown in Figure 13-5.

   You move through this screen with the arrow keys or by pressing the
   highlighted letters. If you have a mouse, you can just click on the area you
   want to change.

2. Check the top of this box and make sure the asterisk is next to 1 (for the
   first series).

3. Press C for **Color**, and you'll be able to select a color from the list shown.

4. Choose **B**lue. Notice that pressing B selects **B**lack. Therefore, use the
   arrow keys to move to **B**lue and press Enter.

   The option **B**lue should have an asterisk next to it.

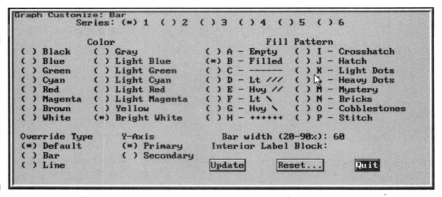

Figure 13-5:
This dialog box, which isn't as bad as it looks, lets you customize your graph series.

5. Press F for **F**ill Pattern and select one of the options, labeled A through P. Choose option **B** - Filled, which is completely filled (solid).

6. If you want to see what you've done, you *could* escape out of this menu and then select **V**iew. But there's an easier way: just press F10.

   You can press F10 any time you're working on a graph for a quick peek. This works from within any of the graph menus.

   Your graph should now look like the graph in Figure 13-6.

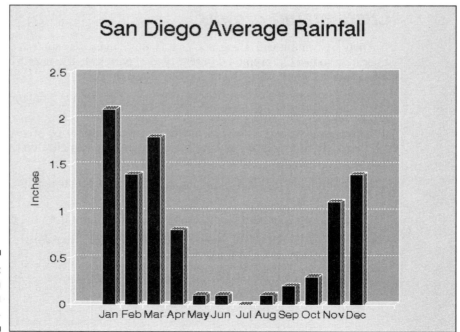

Figure 13-6:
The graph after you customize it.

7. When you're satisfied with your customization, choose **Quit**. You return to the Graph menu.

8. Escape out of this menu and return to the worksheet.

Updating the name

Now that the graph is created, you need to update the changes. As it stands, Quattro Pro still associates the name *SDRain* with the original, unmodified graph. Therefore, you need to tell Quattro Pro to save the new customized version.

1. Select **Graph⇨Name⇨Create** and enter **SDRain2** as the title.

    You now have two graphs stored in this worksheet: the original graph with no titles (named *SDRain*) and the customized one (named *SDRain2*).

2. Escape out of the menu.

3. Select **Graph⇨Name⇨Display**, and you can see the two named graphs. Pick one of the graphs and press Enter to view it.

Changing the numbers

At this point, both of these graphs are tied to the data in the worksheet. Try this:

1. Change one of the numbers in the worksheet. Do something outrageous. Make the March rainfall 12 inches.

2. Select **Graph⇨Name⇨Display**, and choose *SDRain2*.

    Notice that the graph has changed and now uses the new number. Also notice that the y-axis scale has changed to accommodate this wider range of values in the series.

Linking the graph to the worksheet is a handy feature. If you need to make a last-minute change in one or more numbers, you don't have to create a new graph if the graph is linked to the worksheet because Quattro Pro updates the graph automatically.

Changing the graph type

The graphs you've been viewing so far have been bar charts. Now convert the SDRain2 graph to a line graph.

1. Select **Graph**⇨**Name**⇨**Display** and choose SDRain2.

2. Press a key to return to the menu.

3. Choose the **G**raph Type option and select Line from the menu that pops up.

4. Press F10 to view the graph. *Voila!* From bars to a line.

The graph with the new look appears in Figure 13-7.

You might want to play around with this, and select some other graph types to see what you get. (Notice that several of the graph types won't work because they require more data series or a different type of data series. Quattro Pro beeps at you and tells you why it can't display a particular type of graph.)

If you make any changes to your graph, you must use the **Graph**⇨**Name**⇨**Create** command to save your changes. Most of the time, you'll just use the graph's current name (unless you want to save different versions of the graph).

If you don't like having to remember to use the **Graph**⇨**Name**⇨**Create** command all the time, issue the **Graph**⇨**Name**⇨**Autosave Edits** command and select the **Y**es option. When Autosave Edits is active, Quattro Pro automatically saves your changes, using the graph's name. Pretty handy stuff.

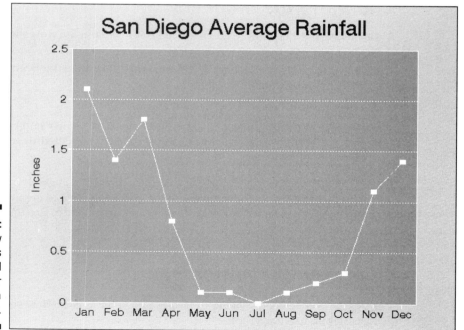

Figure 13-7:
A few keystrokes converted the bar graph into a line graph.

And Now, the Easy Way to Make Graphs

In some cases, you can let Quattro Pro assign the series for you automatically. Doing this lets you create a graph very quickly and with minimal finagling. Take a look at the worksheet in Figure 13-8. This would make a pretty spiffy graph, don't you think? You could use the **Graph⇨Series** command and assign the X-Axis series, the 1st Series, and the 2nd Series. And then you could use the **Graph⇨Text⇨Legends** commands to add text so that you can tell which series is which. Quite a few steps.

Here's an easier way. Select **Graph⇨Fast Graph** (or simply press Ctrl-G in READY mode). Quattro Pro prompts you with the message `Enter Fast-Graph block`. Use the arrow keys (or mouse) to highlight all the data, including the legend text, and press Enter. The graph appears before your very eyes. You can then use all the other Graph commands to fix the graph up to your liking (change the graph type, modify colors, and so on).

A few paragraphs ago, I said you can use this technique in *some* cases. The only time you *can't* use the Fast Graph method is when the single block you select contains data that you don't want to graph (blanks are okay). So in other words, you can almost always use this quick and easy method to make graphs. But if you need to change these graphs, you have to plod your way through all the Graph menu commands.

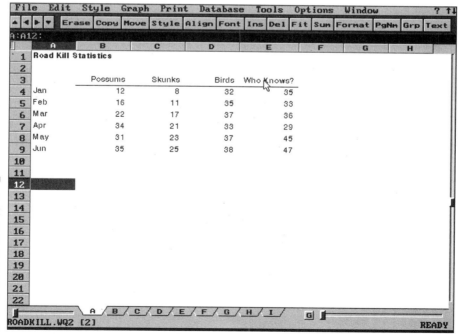

Figure 13-8: Data that practically begs to be turned into a graph with the Fast Graph command.

More about Graphs

If you made it through the preceding exercises, you now know enough about graphs to create one on your own, if necessary. Here's some extra stuff you might be interested in.

A legend in your own time

If a graph has only one series, it's usually pretty obvious what the series represents. The viewer can usually figure it out by the graph's title or by examining the x-axis label. But when you have two or more series in a graph, you'll need some way to identify them. The normal way to do this is to use a legend.

You work with legends with the **Graph**⇨**Text**⇨**Legends** command. This command leads to another menu, shown in Figure 13-9.

To add a legend, select **Graph**⇨**Text**⇨**Legends**, choose the series, and enter the legend text for that series. Repeat this for each series that the graph uses. Choose the **Position** option in this menu to tell Quattro Pro where to put the legend. Your choices are at the bottom of the graph (**B**ottom), to the right of the graph (**R**ight), or nowhere (**N**one).

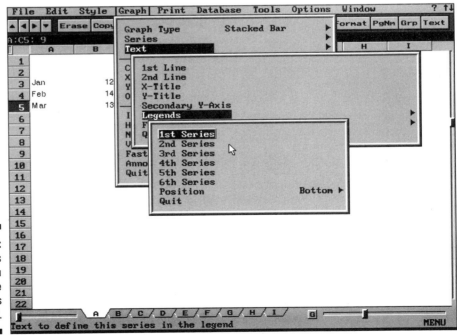

Figure 13-9: Here's where you manipulate the graph's legend.

TIP

If you use the fast graph (Ctrl-G) method to create your graph, you can include the legend text directly before the first entry in each data series. Quattro Pro uses this text in the legend.

Graph annotation

If you really want to have some fun with graphs, you can learn how to annotate them. Annotating a graph means adding your own stuff to it — text, lines,

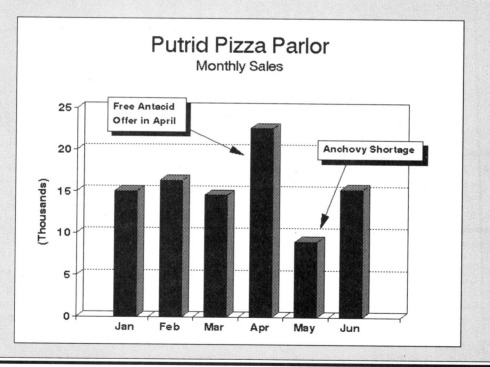

A graph with arrows and comments

I used the **Graph⇨Annotate** command to add arrows and comments to the graph in the following figure. You add text in the Annotator window, using the T (text) icon. You have a lot of control over how the text looks, including what type of box to put it in.

arrows, boxes, circles, and so on. For example, you can insert some explanatory text with an arrow pointing to a particularly good (or bad) data point on the graph. Or you can insert a picture or two to make your graph even more interesting.

To annotate a graph, you must first create the graph, using the normal methods. Then you use the **Graph⇨Name⇨Display** command to make sure you selected the right graph. Then select **Graph⇨Annotate**; a special annotation screen, something like the one shown in Figure 13-10, appears. (By the way, a mouse comes in real handy when you annotate a graph.)

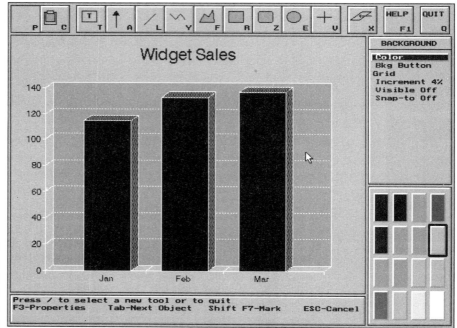

Figure 13-10:
The graph
annotation
screen.

Discussing all of these commands is beyond the scope of this book, but if you've ever used a presentation graphics software package, you should get up to speed pretty quickly. It's kind of fun to play around with, and F1 gives you lots of on-screen instructions. I suggest you dig right in, do some clicking, and see what happens. But don't do your experimenting on the only copy of a graph that your boss needs later in the afternoon.

The right graph type

Quattro Pro lets you choose from 15 graph types. Each of these can be customized quite a bit, so you really have more flexibility than you'll probably ever need. How do you know what type of graph to create? Don't ask me.

There are no hard and fast rules on choosing graph types, but I do have some advice: Use the graph type that gets your message across in the simplest way possible. You normally don't want the graph itself to overwhelm the message (unless, perhaps, the message is so bad that you want to divert attention elsewhere). Typically, line graphs are useful for data in which the x-axis has some type of numerical progression — such as months, years, or quarters. If the x-axis consists of mere labels like *Western, Eastern,* and *Northern,* a bar chart is a better choice.

The bottom line? Experiment with different graph types until you get one that seems to work. And now that you're on your way to becoming a graph aficionado, you'll probably pay more attention to other graphs that you see in your work. These are always a good source for ideas.

Inserting a graph into a worksheet

You might like to stick your graph right in your worksheet, next to the numbers it uses. This is useful for some reports in which the reader needs to know the actual numbers that are used in a graph. Quattro Pro makes this very easy to do.

1. Create and name a graph as you normally would.

2. Select the **Graph⇨Insert** command, highlight the named graph that you want to insert, and press Enter.

   Quattro Pro responds with the message `Enter block to insert graph.`

3. Highlight the block of cells in the worksheet where you want the graph to appear, and press Enter.

   If you're in WYSIWYG mode, you'll see the graph displayed in all its glory (see Figure 13-11). If you're working in Text mode, you'll see a colored block that represents the graph.

To remove a graph that you inserted in a worksheet, use the **Graph⇨Hide** command and select the name of the graph that you previously inserted. The graph disappears from the worksheet but remains attached to the worksheet's data. You can still display the graph and work on it.

Graphs that are inserted in your worksheet are still live graphs. In other words, if you make changes to your numbers, the graphs are updated automatically.

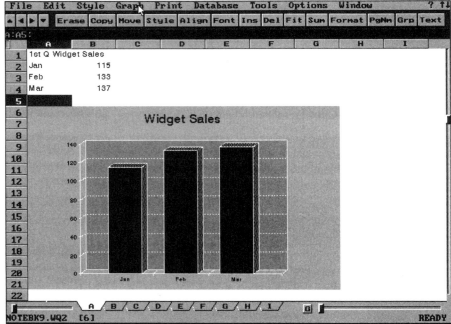

Figure 13-11:
A graph
inserted
right into a
worksheet
with the
Graph⇨Insert
command.

Printing graphs

Graphs look best on the screen since they show up in living color (assuming you have a color monitor, of course). But most of the time, you'll need to print a graph on paper so that you can share it with someone who likes to see such things.

If a graph is inserted on your worksheet, you can include the graph in your print block, and it will print. Make sure you select a graphics printer with the **Print⇨Destination⇨Graphics Printer** command. Chapter 10 covers all of this printing business in detail.

Saving a graph to a separate file

There may be times that you want to use a graph in some other application. For example, you might want to put a Quattro Pro graph into your company newsletter (which you probably produce using some type of desktop publishing program). To do this, you must save the graph to a file in a format that your other software can handle.

1. Create and name the graph as you normally would.

2. Select the **Print**⇨**Graph Print** command. Quattro Pro displays another menu.

3. From this new menu, choose **Write Graph File**. Yet another menu appears.

4. From this last menu, choose a file format that your other software can use. You're on your own here since I don't know what other software you're using.

5. Provide a filename to hold the graph.

If the other software supports both EPS and PCX formats, use EPS because you usually get better results with EPS, which is scalable rather than bitmapped. With a scalable font, you can stretch or shrink the graph, and it will still look good. Choosing EPS format is just a general rule of thumb, and if you're after optimal quality, experiment with the various formats and see which produces the best results in your application.

A Gala Gallery of Gorgeous Graphs

I'll close this chapter with a bunch of graphs I created in Quattro Pro. You may be able to get some ideas from these.

A text graph

The graph in Figure 13-12 doesn't use any numbers from the worksheet. Rather, I used the **Graph**⇨**Graph Type** command to designate it as a text graph and then used the **Graph**⇨**Annotate** command to add all the accouterments you see. The map is a bit of clip art that's included with Quattro Pro. (In the Annotator window, click on the C (clipboard) icon and then select the **Paste From** command.) The image I used is in the WORLDMAP.CLP file (I had to shrink it considerably). Most of the CLP images can be broken apart. In this case, I deleted everything in the image but North and South America.

A 3-D bar graph

The graph in Figure 13-13 shows a different slant on bar graphs. This graph consists of three series of data. The graph type is called Bar (3D).

Figure 13-12:
Graphs don't always have to represent numbers. This one is a text graph.

A rotated column graph

Bar graphs don't always have to start from the ground and work their way up. The graph in Figure 13-14 shows a rotated bar graph.

A mixed graph

When is a bar graph not a bar graph? When it also includes lines. The graph in Figure 13-15 is usually called a *mixed graph.* This graph began life as an ordinary 3-D bar chart. Then I used the **Graph**⇨**Customize Series** command, selected Series 2, and designated Series 2 as Line in the **O**verride Type section.

A stacked bar graph

I originally wanted to create two pie graphs next to each other to compare the sales breakdown by product in two years. Since Quattro Pro doesn't let you put two pie graphs in a single graph, I used a stacked bar graph to get a similar effect (shown in Figure 13-16). Both of the two data series had values that added to 100 percent.

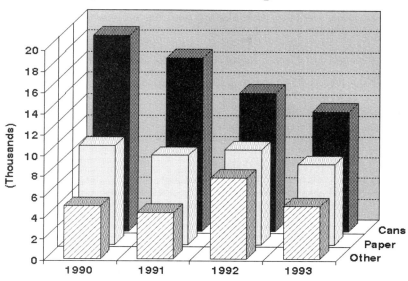

Figure 13-13:
Three-dimensional charts can add some pizzazz to an otherwise boring topic.

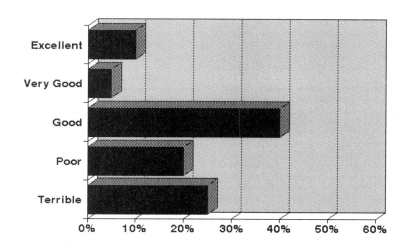

Figure 13-14:
A rotated bar chart.

A graph with two y-axes

Notice that the mixed graph (bars and a line) in Figure 13-17 has two different scales. The bars, which belong with the left y-axis, show the monthly sales. The line, which goes with the right y-axis, shows the percent of sales goal reached. If I used the same scale for both series, the line would not have even showed up since all of the values are less than 1.2 (120 percent).

An XY graph

The graph in Figure 13-18 is an XY graph (sometimes known as a *scattergram*). The heights are in the X-Series and the weights are in Series-1. Each dot represents one person and shows the person's height and weight. As you can see, there's an upward linear trend: taller people generally weigh more than shorter folks. I also used the **Graph⇨Annotate** command to make a comment about the person who belongs to one of the dots.

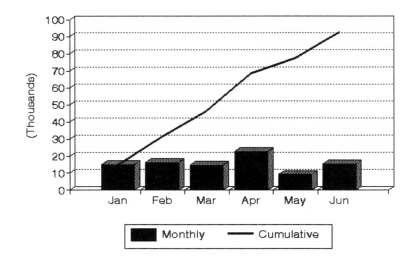

Figure 13-15:
This mixed
graph has
bars and a
line (hence
the name).

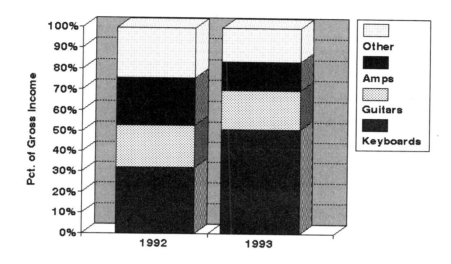

Polyphonic Paradise Music Stores
Where We Get Our Income

Figure 13-16:
A stacked
bar graph
can
substitute
for two or
more pie
graphs.

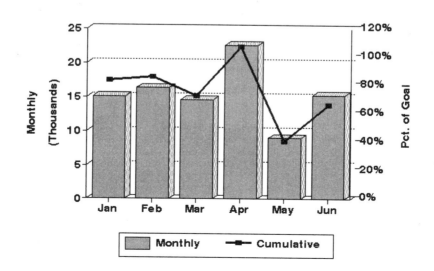

Sales Summary
First Six Months

Figure 13-17:
Using two
y-axes is
useful when
the data
series have
drastically
different
scales.

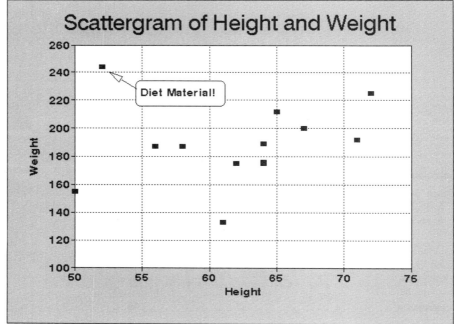

Figure 13-18:
An XY graph
can show
whether
your data
has any
discernible
trend.

A stock market graph

Stock market analysts love this sort of thing. The graph in Figure 13-19 shows stock performance over a period of time. For each day, the graph shows the opening price, closing price, the daily high, and the daily low — a lotta information for one graph.

A 3-D ribbon graph

Figure 13-20 shows another twist on 3-D graphics — this one's called Ribbon (3D).

A bubble graph

You probably won't have a daily need for bubble graphs (although some people do take daily bubble *baths*). The bubble graph in Figure 13-21 actually shows three pieces of information for each of four sales regions: the number of sales made (x-axis), the amount of the sales made (y-axis), and the average sales amount (represented by the size of the bubbles).

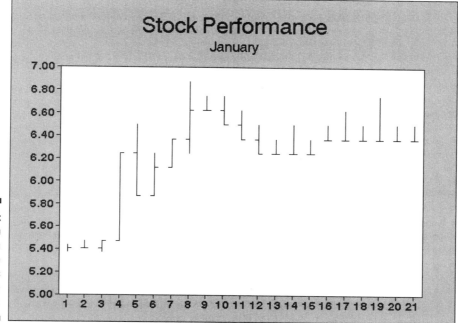

Figure 13-19:
This graph
shows at a
glance the
month's
performance
of this stock.

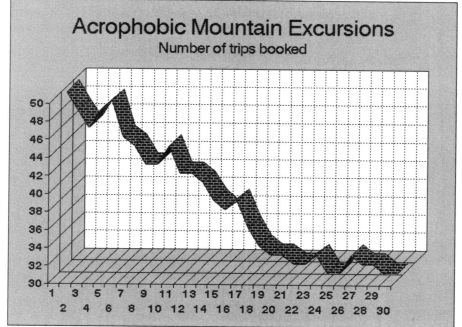

Figure 13-20:
A ribbon
graph is
another 3-D
variation
offered by
Quattro Pro.

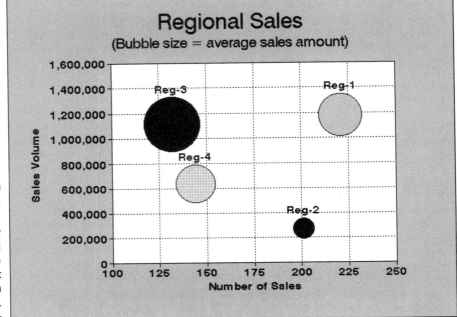

Figure 13-21: Someday, you may have a need for a bubble graph — but then again you may not.

Chapter 14
Belly Up to the SpeedBar

There once was a woman named Faye
Who liked using the menus okay
But nodded in the affirmative
When showed an alternative
That was only a mouse click away.

In This Chapter

▶ All about the SpeedBar — what it is, why it exists, and how to use it

▶ How the SpeedBar takes on a dual personality

▶ Lots of ways to speed up your work

You should know by now that Quattro Pro's menus let you do lots of things with your worksheet. But you may also know that the menus can sometimes get confusing. Some menus seem like they go on forever. To help you, several menu commands have shortcut keys that you can use to avoid menus. For example, Ctrl-C is the shortcut for the Edit⇨Copy command. Borland realizes that their menus are complicated, so they also include a SpeedBar.

Quattro Pro is smart enough to know if you have a mouse connected to your computer and the mouse software is loaded into memory. If it can't find a mouse, it doesn't even bother to display the SpeedBar since a mouse is required to use the SpeedBar.

> *Note*: If you don't have a mouse, this chapter won't do much for you — except maybe make you want to get a mouse.

What's a SpeedBar?

A few years ago, software was much more difficult to use. Then at some point, software developers realized that users tend to use some commands much more often than others. It occurred to them that maybe they could help out us poor users by providing faster access to these commonly used commands. Hence, the SpeedBar was born.

A SpeedBar by any other name

Borland uses the term SpeedBar for its mousable on-screen shortcuts. Other software companies refer to this same sort of thing by other names. If you use products by Microsoft, you'll run across the name *Toolbar* to describe their version of the SpeedBar. Lotus calls them *SmartIcons*. Regardless of what they're called, these things are worth knowing about.

Here's an example of how you might use the SpeedBar.

Let's say you have a block, A1..A10, that you want to copy to B1..C10. You can use the SpeedBar to perform this task.

1. Use the mouse to select the block A1..A10.

2. Click the Copy (or CPY) SpeedBar button. Quattro Pro responds with the message `Destination for cells`.

3. Click in cell B1 and drag over to C1.

4. Click the word [ENTER] in the input line.

This method is faster than using the Edit⇨Copy menu command and even faster than the Ctrl-C shortcut. I guess that's why they call it a SpeedBar, eh?

Zooming through the SpeedBar

If you went through the preceding exercise, you already know how to use the SpeedBar. But if you skipped that section, here's a recap.

1. Figure out what you want to do. If it involves a block, you can eliminate a step by preselecting the block with the mouse before you use the SpeedBar.

2. Find the correct SpeedBar button (assuming one's available to do the job).

3. Click it.

4. Finish off the command.

Any questions?

WYSIWYG vs. Text Mode SpeedBars

The SpeedBar you see varies, depending on whether you're in Text mode or WYSIWYG mode. In Text mode, the SpeedBar is shown along the right side of the screen (see Figure 14-1). The screen isn't tall enough to show all the buttons, so you can toggle between two sets by clicking the BAR button.

In WYSIWYG mode, the SpeedBar makes its home at the top of your screen, right under the menu bar (see Figure 14-2). Since the screen is wider than it is tall, the entire SpeedBar fits, and there's no need for a BAR button. For the most part, the button names aren't abbreviated, like they are in Text mode.

Different SpeedBars

Quattro Pro actually has two different SpeedBars. One is displayed when you're in READY mode. But this one is replaced by another SpeedBar when you're editing a cell (in EDIT mode). This section simply provides a summary of the buttons found on both SpeedBars.

The READY mode SpeedBar

For the most part, clicking a button on the READY mode SpeedBar is equivalent to issuing a command from the menu. But the SpeedBar also has buttons that you can use to move the cell pointer. Table 14-1 summarizes all of the SpeedBar

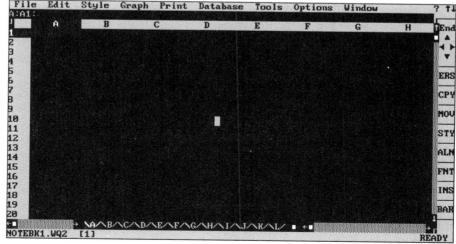

Figure 14-1: In Text mode, the SpeedBar shows up on the right edge of your screen.

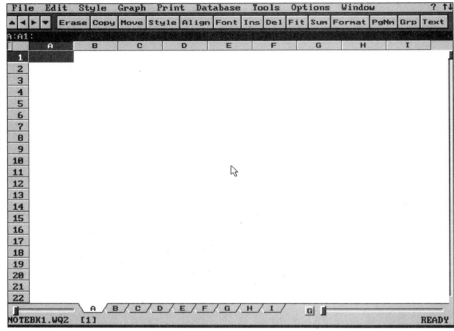

Figure 14-2:
The
WYSIWYG
mode
SpeedBar
appears at
the top of
your screen.

buttons by telling you what commands they execute. (However, the best way to learn about SpeedBar buttons is to play around with them — not to read this table.)

Table 14-1 A Quick Summary of the READY Mode SpeedBar Buttons

WYSIWYG Mode	Text Mode	What It Does
▲ ◄ ► ▼	End ▲ ◄ ► ▼	Moves the cell pointer from one edge of a block of data to another (just as if you press the End key followed by an arrow key)
Erase	ERS	Issues the Edit⇨Erase Block command
Copy	CPY	Issues the Edit⇨Copy command
Move	MOV	Issues the Edit⇨Move command
Style	STY	Issues the Style⇨Use Style command
Align	ALN	Issues the Style⇨Alignment command
Font	FNT	Issues the Style⇨Font command
Ins	INS	Issues the Edit⇨Insert command
Del	DEL	Issues the EditÍDelete command

WYSIWYG Mode	Text mode	What It Does
Fit	FIT	Issues the **Style**⇨**B**lock Size⇨**A**uto Width command
Sum	SUM	Builds a formula that adds up a block of values (See "SpeedSum: A special case" sidebar for more information.)
Format	FMT	Issues the **Style**⇨**N**umeric Format command
PgNm	PAG	Issues the **Edit**⇨**P**age⇨**N**ame command (not available in Version 4)
Text	N/A	Changes to Text mode
Grp	GRP	Toggles in and out of Group mode (not available in Version 4)
N/A	WYS	Changes to WYSIWYG mode
N/A	BAR	Displays the other part of the SpeedBar in Text mode

The EDIT mode SpeedBar

Whenever you get into EDIT mode (by pressing F2 or by clicking in the input line), Quattro Pro quickly changes the READY mode SpeedBar into the EDIT mode SpeedBar. This happens so fast that you may not have even noticed that the SpeedBar is different when you're editing a cell.

The EDIT mode SpeedBar has buttons that are relevant to editing cells and building formulas. Unlike the READY mode SpeedBar, these buttons don't have menu command equivalents. Some of the buttons substitute for shortcut keys, and others simply insert common characters that you would normally enter from the keyboard. The point, I guess, is to allow people to build formulas using

---

SpeedSum: A special case

One of the handiest SpeedBar buttons of all is the SUM, which has no menu command equivalent. This button actually builds a formula that adds up a block of values — and it does so by using some intelligence. In other words, Quattro Pro makes its best guess as to what cells you want to add (based on the position of the cell pointer) and

creates the formula for you with a single click of the SUM button.

Since something like 90 percent of all spreadsheet formulas use the @SUM function, this SpeedBar button can save you lots of time.

only the mouse (no keyboard). Personally, I think this is a rather slow way to go, but I guess not everyone's in a hurry when it comes to creating formulas.

Table 14-2 summarizes what these buttons are used for.

Table 14-2 A Quick Summary of the EDIT Mode SpeedBar Buttons

WYSIWYG Mode	Text Mode	What It Does
▲ ◀ ▶ ▼	End ▲ ◀ ▶ ▼	Clicking on the up or down arrow moves the cell pointer to the top or bottom edge (or row) of a block of data (like pressing End, up arrow or End, down arrow; not really very useful when you're editing a cell). Clicking on the left or right arrow moves the insertion point one character to the left or right in the input line.
Name	NAM	Shows list of named blocks (like F3)
Abs	ABS	Toggles cell reference between absolute and relative (like F4)
Calc	CAL	Calculates the formula on the input line and turns it into a value (like F9)
Macro	MAC	Displays menu-equivalent macro categories (like Shift-F3)
@	@	Shows a list of @functions (like Alt-F3)
+	+	Enters a plus sign
-	-	Enters a minus sign
N/A	BAR	Shows the other part of the SpeedBar in Text mode
*	*	Enters an asterisk (multiplication sign)
/	/	Enters a slash (division sign)
(	(	Enters an opening parenthesis
,	,	Enters a comma
)	)	Enters a closing parenthesis

When the EDIT mode SpeedBar is showing, Quattro Pro also places two words in the input line: [ENTER] and [ESC]. You can click these words as a way to avoid having to return your hands to the keyboard. Press Enter to finish editing and store the edited contents in the cell. Pressing Esc cancels any edits you made and lets you keep the original cell contents.

You may not realize it, but the SpeedBar buttons I've been talking about in this chapter can be changed. When you click one of these buttons, it's actually executing a macro (I talk about macros in Chapter 18). If you're really ambitious, you can customize the SpeedBar so you can have the buttons do exactly what you want them to do. Since there is limited space for the buttons, you have to replace an existing button with a new button. The key to customizing the SpeedBar is the **O**ptions⇨Speed**B**ar command. This leads to another menu that lets you select which of the two SpeedBars you want to modify. The process isn't difficult, but you *do* have to know about simple macros. Chapter 18 tells you enough so that you'll be able to create you own SpeedBar buttons.

Chapter 15
Getting Numbers from Other Places

There once was a man who cut lumber
Who awoke from a very deep slumber.
He dreamed that his hand
Simply typed a command
And like magic, he brought in every number.

In This Chapter

▶ Why you might need to get numbers from somewhere else

▶ A brief discourse on the various types of computer files

▶ How to bring numbers and text into Quattro Pro, even if they're not in Quattro Pro files

▶ What to do with stuff once you get it into Quattro Pro

Let me relate a scenario that happens thousands of times a day throughout corporate America. Your boss asks you to summarize some sales figures. You buzz sales management, and they tell you that their data is in DUMBASE — a weird database program that's not compatible with any other program known to man. They can, however, give you a printed copy of the raw data if you like. Consequently, you're forced to spend the next six hours re-entering numbers into Quattro Pro. And as a final blow, your boss tells you the next day that she doesn't need the summary after all.

Here's something to keep in mind: If data is in a computer, there's an excellent chance that you can get it into Quattro Pro without having to manually retype it. But to do this, you have to know a little bit about how data is stored and a few things about what Quattro Pro can do. And that just happens to be the topic of this chapter.

> *Note:* If the idea of fooling around with data from other sources is a bit too intimidating for you, don't despair. Virtually every office has at least one person who understands this stuff. So you may want to take the easy way out and bribe this person. If that works, you can skip this chapter completely (unless, of course, you want to learn something).

Why Use Other Data?

There are two reasons why you might want to bring data into Quattro Pro from some other source:

- ✔ You don't want to have to enter it manually.

- ✔ You have lots of idle staff sitting around who could enter the data manually, but you can't risk making data entry errors.

So what I'm talking about in this chapter is *importing data* — more specifically importing ASCII, or text, files. If you don't know what a text file is, read on.

Quattro Pro can directly import (and export) quite a few different standard data file formats. If the data you want is in one of these supported file formats, you're in good shape. I talk about these file formats in Chapter 9.

Types of Files

Computers use several types of files. Here are some common examples:

- ✔ **Program files:** Files that contain executable programs. Quattro Pro itself is contained in a file called Q.EXE.

- ✔ **Data files:** Files that programs use to store information that the user is working on. With Quattro Pro, users work with worksheets, which are stored in data files with a WQ2 extension (WQ1 for Version 4). These data files are stored in such a way that other programs can make no sense out of them at all unless you properly convert the file.

- ✔ **Text files:** Files that contain information in ASCII format. This is a fancy term that means that the files are readable by human beings. You don't need any special software to read what's in a text file. You can even use the TYPE command from the DOS prompt to display a text file.

More about Text Files

You can think of text files as the lowest common denominator of file formats. These files contain only words and numbers and absolutely no formatting information. If you're working in your word processor, the word processor saves your files in a format that maintains all of the formatting you specify file, only the words get saved. So if you read this text file back into your word processor, you have to repeat all of the formatting you did earlier.

A similar thing happens with Quattro Pro. Its WQ2 files contain all of the formulas and formatting that you worked so hard on, as well as the values and labels. If you save your Quattro Pro work as a text file, only the labels, values, and *results* of formulas get saved; the formatting is not saved. However, the advantage of saving your Quattro Pro file as a text file is that other programs can then use this information.

Most software programs can read and write text files. Therefore, if two programs can't read each other's files, you can use a text file as an intermediary. But you lose any formatting information (or formulas, in the case of a spreadsheet).

Text files come in three delicious flavors:

- ✔ **Plain.** This is just normal text with a "carriage return" at the end of each line. If the file contains row-and-column oriented data, the data usually lines up vertically into distinct fixed-length fields.

- ✔ **Comma-delimited.** These are also known as *comma-separated-value* (CSV) files because they uses commas to separate fields of information. Furthermore, if the field contains text, the text is usually enclosed in quotation marks.

- ✔ **Tab-delimited.** These files have their fields separated by tabs. Text fields may or may not be in quotes.

Quattro Pro can read all three of these file types. If you're importing a plain text file, you usually have to do some additional work to break the data contained in the lines into separate cells. Most of the time, comma-delimited and tab-delimited text files can be read into Quattro Pro with minimal hassles.

Before trying to import a text file into Quattro Pro, you might want to take a look at the file from the DOS prompt. You can use the File⇨Utilities⇨DOS Shell command to get to DOS temporarily from Quattro Pro. Then use the TYPE command to display the text file on your screen. If the file is named BADCHECK.TXT and is on drive A, you would use this command from the DOS prompt:

```
TYPE A:BADCHECK.TXT
```

The file will scroll by quickly, but you can stop it with the Pause key. If you see a bunch of strange Greek-like characters scroll by, the file is probably not a text file. If you can read the stuff, you've got yourself a text file.

How to read text files in Quattro Pro

The first step is to make sure you have access to the text file that you want to import. If you're getting the file from someone else, tell him or her that you would prefer to have the file in comma-delimited or tab-delimited format. If that's not possible, request a fixed-field format. If that's not possible, take whatever you can get, and then do the following:

1. Copy the file into a directory that you can access from Quattro Pro (or you can simply read the file off the floppy disk that it came on).

2. Issue Tools⇨Import, the menu command you use to import text files. This command leads to another menu, shown in Figure 15-1.

Before you issue the Tools⇨Import command, make sure that the cell pointer is in an empty area of your worksheet because the imported data writes over anything that's already there — beginning with the cell where the cell pointer is. To be on the safe side, start out with a blank worksheet.

What you do next depends on the type of file you're importing.

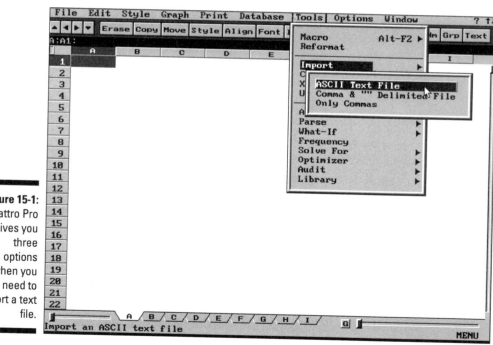

Figure 15-1: Quattro Pro gives you three options when you need to import a text file.

Delimited files

If your file is delimited by either commas or tabs, choose the second or third option (the Comma & " " Delimited File option or the Only Commas option). If you know that labels don't have quotes, use the Only Commas choice.

Next, Quattro Pro displays a box from which you select the file you want. Quattro Pro likes to think all text files have a PRN extension (even though most of them don't); therefore, Quattro Pro only displays files with PRN extensions. If you know the name of the file, you can just type it in. Otherwise, enter ***.*** to display all files, and then locate the file to import.

When you highlight the name of the text file, press Enter; Quattro Pro reads the data and puts the numbers and labels into the cells. Then you can do whatever you want with the data, just as if you entered it yourself. Consider leaving work early, since you possibly saved hours of time by importing rather than re-keying.

Plain (non-delimited) text files

If the text file isn't delimited with tabs or commas, the task is a little more difficult. You need to use the ASCII Text File command, and specify the file name.

Quattro Pro reads the file and puts each line into one cell. In other words, it doesn't split numbers out into separate cells. Although it may *look* good on-screen, if you examine the imported data closely, you'll find that everything in a row is actually only in one cell (a single label). Figure 15-2 shows an example of this. The next step is to *parse* these labels to get the information into separate cells.

If you're running Quattro Pro in WYSIWYG mode, it's a good idea to switch from WYSIWYG to Text mode before you start parsing labels. In WYSIWYG mode, not all characters are the same width — which can make it difficult to see how columns really line up. In Text mode, on the other hand, every character has the same width. I take my own advice, and that's why some of the figures in this chapter are Text mode.

Parsing labels

Parsing labels simply means picking out the information contained in a label (usually a long label) and sticking each value in a separate column in the same row. You do this with the Tools⇨Parse command.

```
 File   Edit   Style   Graph   Print   Database   Tools   Options   Window        ? ↑↓
A:A7:  'Herbert Tarrington   214704      03-31-93      $12,000   Part
       A          B          C          D          E          F          G          H      End
1  EMPLOYEE NAME          EMP NUM    DATE HIRED   SALARY     STATUS                          ▲
2  Michael Nester         214699     03-04-93     $21,000    Full                          ◄ ►
3  Julie G. Whiz          214700     03-11-93     $43,500    Full                            ▼
4  Marvin Garden          214701     03-12-93     $25,000    Full
5  Fannie Packard         214702     03-19-93     $31,200    Full                          ERS
6  Richard R. Poor        214703     03-30-93     $65,900    Full
7  Herbert Tarrington     214704     03-31-93     $12,000    Part                          CPY
8
9                                                                                          MOV
10
11                                                                                          STY
12
13                                                                                          ALN
14
15                                                                                          FNT
16
17                                                                                          INS
18
19                                                                                          BAR
20
   → \A/\B/\C/\D/\E/\F/\G/\H/\I/\J/\K/\L/ ■ ←
NOTEBK1.WQ2   [1]                                                              READY
```

Figure 15-2: Notice the input line. The information in each row is actually contained in a single cell.

You need to use the **Tools**⇨**Parse** command only if you use the **Tools**⇨**Import**⇨**ASCII Text File** command. If your imported data is already in separate columns, parsing is not necessary.

I'll be the first to admit that this parsing business can be confusing — especially if the imported text is not laid out in nice, even columns. I'll go through a step-by-step example and try to clarify things in the process.

An Example? No thanks, I'll parse on this one

This example involves a text file that was generated by a company's human resources department. This company stores all of its personnel information in a mainframe computer that's tied in to payroll. You need to analyze all of the company's new hires for March. The mainframe can't produce files that Quattro Pro can read, but it can print to a file. Therefore, human resources ran the report and sent the output to a file rather than to their printer. This produced a plain text file, NEWHIRES.TXT, which is shown in Figure 15-3. (Obviously, a file this short is hardly worth the effort. I'm using this miniature file to illustrate how to parse.)

You must import this file into Quattro Pro and then parse it into its parts so that you can analyze it.

1. Start with a new, blank worksheet and put the cell pointer in cell A1.

2. Select **Tools**⇨**Import**⇨**ASCII Text File**. Quattro Pro displays a box that lets you select a file.

```
D:\QPRO>type newhires.txt
EMPLOYEE NAME        EMP NUM   DATE HIRED   SALARY    STATUS
Michael Nester       214699    03-04-93     $21,000   Full
Julie G. Whiz        214700    03-11-93     $43,500   Full
Marvin Garden        214701    03-12-93     $25,000   Full
Fannie Packard       214702    03-19-93     $31,200   Full
Richard R. Poor      214703    03-30-93     $65,900   Full
Herbert Tarrington   214704    03-31-93     $12,000   Part


D:\QPRO>
```

Figure 15-3:
Examining
the text file
from DOS.

3. Since Quattro Pro only shows files with a PRN extension, enter ***.TXT** to force the program to display files with a TXT extension. Choose the NEWHIRES.TXT file and press Enter.

Quattro Pro reads this file and puts each line in a separate cell in column A. Since this file has seven lines, the range A1..A7 now contains long labels.

4. The next step is to parse it. Since the first row has titles and is not representative of the rest of the data, move the cell pointer to cell A2.

5. Select Tools➪Parse. Quattro Pro displays another menu, shown in Figure 15-4.

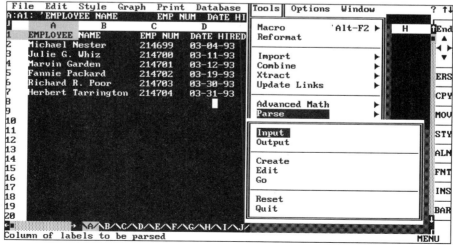

Figure 15-4:
These
commands
are used to
parse a text
file into
separate
cells.

6. Select **O**utput and highlight the single cell A10. This is where the parsed data will start.

7. Select **C**reate to have Quattro Pro create a special format line that describes how the data is laid out.

Notice that it puts this format line in cell A2 and moves everything else down one line.

8. Examine the format line. Quattro Pro is trying to make each name into two separate labels. You don't want this, so you edit the format line.

9. Select **E**dit, and Quattro Pro puts you in EDIT mode so that you can adjust the format line. Move to the part that reads *L, and replace these two characters with >>. Press Enter.

10. Now you need to tell Quattro Pro what to parse. Select **I**nput, highlight the range A2..A8, and press Enter.

11. Finally, select **G**o to start the parsing.

Quattro Pro goes to work, parsing the labels and putting the results in the output range specified. The worksheet now looks like Figure 15-5. All you need to do is adjust the width of column A so that the complete names appear and then delete the rows at the top since they're no longer needed.

Figure 15-5:
After parsing
the labels,
the data
appears in
separate
cells.

```
 File   Edit   Style   Graph   Print   Database   Tools   Options   Window        ? ↑↓
A:A2: [W19]  !L>>>>>>>>>>>>>>>>******U>>>>>***L>>>>>>>>****U>>>>>**L>>>
J                  A              B          C         D          E        F        ⬛End
1  EMPLOYEE NAME                EMP NUM   DATE HIRED  SALARY     STATUS              ▲
2  L>>>>>>>>>>>>>>>******U>>>>>***L>>>>>>>****U>>>>>**L>>>                        ◄ ►
3  Michael Nester              214699    03-04-93    $21,000    Full                ▼
4  Julie G. Whiz               214700    03-11-93    $43,500    Full
5  Marvin Garden               214701    03-12-93    $25,000    Full              ERS
6  Fannie Packard              214702    03-19-93    $31,200    Full
7  Richard R. Poor             214703    03-30-93    $65,900    Full              CPY
8  Herbert Tarrington          214704    03-31-93    $12,000    Part
9                                                                                MOV
10
11 Michael Nester              214699 03-04-93       21000 Full                   STY
12 Julie G. Whiz               214700 03-11-93       43500 Full
13 Marvin Garden               214701 03-12-93       25000 Full                   ALN
14 Fannie Packard              214702 03-19-93       31200 Full
15 Richard R. Poor             214703 03-30-93       65900 Full                   FNT
16 Herbert Tarrington          214704 03-31-93       12000 Part
17                                                                                INS
18
19                                              ⸮                                 BAR
20
   ↵ \A\B\C\D\E\F\G\H\I\J\K\L\  ■ ◄
NOTEBK1.WQ2   [1]                                                               READY
```

Part IV:

Faking It

The 5th Wave   By Rich Tennant

"I'M SORRY, BUT MR. HALLORAN IS BEING CHASED BY SIX MIDGETS WITH POISON BOOMERANGS THROUGH A MAZE IN THE DUNGEON OF A CASTLE. IF HE FINDS HIS WAY OUT AND GETS PAST THE MINOTAUR, HE'LL CALL YOU RIGHT BACK; OTHERWISE TRY AGAIN THURSDAY."

In This Part...

This group of chapters addresses features that are often considered advanced (databases and macros). Don't spend too much time mastering the topics in these chapters. I include enough information so that you can fool people into thinking you actually understand databases, formulas, and macros. In this section, I also include a chapter with a bunch of nifty (and moderately useful) formulas, as well as a chapter that answers the musical question, *How do I?*

Chapter 16
The Lowdown on Databases and Lists

Wanda just loved to be kissed
And enjoyed an occasional tryst.
She had men by the score,
And as they knocked on her door,
She used Quattro to manage her list.

In This Chapter

▶ Why Quattro Pro is good for keeping track of things

▶ The difference between a simple list and a database — and what it means to normal people like you

▶ How to do some basic database and list management tasks

Chances are, you also use a word processing program on your computer. Unlike a spreadsheet, most word processing programs are fairly "dumb." That is, you can't use formulas to do calculations, and working with tables and multi-column lists requires knowing about tab settings and other boring topics.

Here's where I tell you how to use Quattro Pro to keep track of things in lists and how to create and manages these lists.

Databases, Lists; Lists, Databases: What's the Difference?

Before you get too far into this, I'll throw out some definitions. (If these don't help, keep reading — it all sort of makes sense in a few pages.)

> ✔ **Lists.** A collection of items, each in a separate row. Each item may have more than one part (that is, more than one column). The order of the items may or may not be important.

Figure 16-1 shows a list that I developed in Quattro Pro. This particular list has seven items, and each item has two parts. (One of the items actually has three parts, and there's a blank line in the middle.) Notice that the numeric formatting isn't the same for all items — typical of an informal list. There's also a formula that adds up the total.

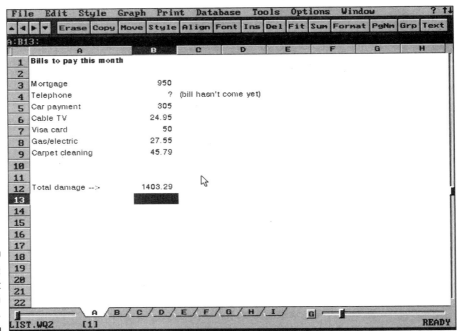

Figure 16-1:
A simple list stored in Quattro Pro.

Creating a simple list is easy — just start entering the stuff you want to keep track of. Feel free to move things around and do whatever makes you happy. There are no rules, so go for it.

✔ **Database.** An organized collection of items. Each item is called a *record*, and each record has more than one part (called *fields*). Furthermore, each field has an official *field name*. It just so happens that, in Quattro Pro, records correspond to a row, and fields correspond to columns.

Figure 16-2 shows a database that I set up in Quattro Pro. This particular database tracks somebody's possessions by purchase date, value, and use (business or personal). This database has 17 records (rows) and four fields (columns). Notice that the first row holds the field names and is not counted as a record.

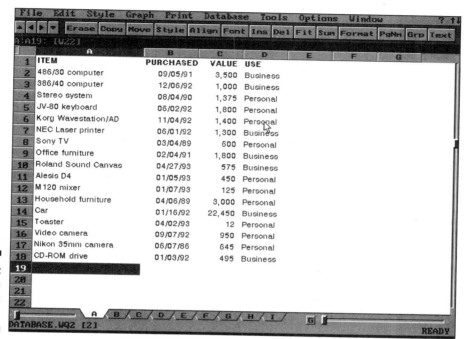

Figure 16-2:
A database
stored in
Quattro Pro.

You've probably already made lists of things in Quattro Pro, and the difference between a list and a database may be rather fuzzy. To make a long story short, a database is basically a more organized list. In the example shown, every record is laid out identically, with the same number of fields and numeric formats.

How Can I Use Thee? Let Me Count the Ways

Because a database is more organized than a plain old list, you can do things with it that would be more difficult (or impossible) to do with a simple list. For example, with a database you can

✔ Find all records that meet some criteria that you specify. In the previous example, I could easily find all items that have a value greater than $1,000, all items that are used for business, all items purchased in 1992, and so on.

✔ Extract all records that meet some criteria and put them in another place (and automatically close up the gaps created in the original database)

✔ Delete all records that meet some criteria

✔ Sort the records by any of the fields (actually, you can sort any block of data — it doesn't have to be a database)

✔ Use database @functions to summarize what's in the database

It's Alive! Creating a Database in the '90s

If you decide that you want to do database things (like search for specific data) and your data is structured enough to qualify as an official database, you need to be aware of just a few things:

✔ Each field in the database must have a name (label), and no two labels can be the same. Also, the field names are limited to 15 characters max, and you can't use spaces in a name.

✔ Don't leave any blank lines between the field names and the actual data.

✔ Use the same type of data in each column. In other words, give some thought to what kind of data each field will hold and don't mix labels and values in a single column.

The next step is to enter your data using methods you already know. You can also import data from other files, using techniques presented in Chapter 15.

If a field (or column) in your database will hold dates, it's a good idea to use the Database⇨Data Entry command and select the Dates Only option. Highlight the column that will hold dates. Doing this lets you enter dates in that field directly, without having to use the cumbersome @DATE function.

Database Drudgery

Most of the work that people do with databases involves searching for the records that meet some criteria. Another word for search is *query* (database people use this term a lot). Quattro Pro has some very definite expectations regarding databases, and to be successful, you have to do things the way Quattro Pro expects them to be done.

For starters, there are three concepts that you need to know about:

✔ **The database block**. This is the database itself, including the field names.

✔ **A criteria table**. This is where you tell Quattro Pro what you want to find (that is, your search criteria).

> ✔ **An output block**. This is where Quattro Pro copies the records that meet your criteria. If you are only locating the records, you don't need to specify an output range.

If you're totally confused, don't despair. I'll discuss these items in more detail.

The database block

Usually, the first step you take when doing searches on a database is to tell Quattro Pro where the database is. This is necessary because you can have more than one database stored in a single worksheet. Use the **Database⇨Query⇨Block** command to indicate what database you want to search. After you select this command, Quattro Pro prompts you with `Enter database block`. Highlight the entire database (including the field names). Make sure you include all of the rows and columns in your database. When it's highlighted, press Enter.

It's an excellent practice (for reasons explained later) to assign names to the cells directly below the field names. Once you specify your database with the **Database⇨Query⇨Block** command, use the **Database⇨Query⇨Assign Name** command to have Quattro Pro create these names for you automatically.

Working with huge databases

This chapter talks about relatively small data-bases — those that easily fit in a worksheet. But what if you need to work with data from a large database that's too big to fit into Quattro Pro? Don't despair. Quattro Pro can come to the rescue once again — as long as the database in question is in Paradox, Reflex, or dBASE format.

The procedure is very similar to what you would do with a normal Quattro Pro database. You have to set up your criteria table and output block (using the field names from the external data-base file). The difference comes when you specify the database. Use the **Database⇨Query⇨Block** command and specify the database *file* as the block. Assume, for example, that you're working with a dBASE file called CLIENTS.DBF. This file is located on your network drive P, in a subdirectory

called DATA. The database file has 10 fields and 5,000 records. Issue the Database⇨Query⇨Block command, and then enter the following instead of pointing out a range:

```
P:\DATA\CLIENTS.DBFA1..J5000
```

In other words, you enter the file's path and file name, followed immediately by a reference to how the data would be referred to if it were in a worksheet. In this case, A1..J5000 specifies a block 10 rows wide (10 fields) and 5,000 rows high (5,000 records).

If your database is very large, you can expect that the database operations will be slower, so be patient.

The criteria table

Many people find the concept of a criteria table confusing and avoid using databases altogether because they can't understand it. You need a criteria table if you want to search for data that meets some criteria that you specify. If you're just using a database to store data and will *never* search for anything, you have no need for a criteria table.

But databases are most useful when you search them, so it's a good idea to learn about criteria tables. Actually, criteria tables are not all that difficult to understand. A criteria table is something that you set up ahead of time and use it to tell Quattro Pro what you're looking for in the database.

A criteria table consists of two parts: The first row of the criteria table holds field names from your database. The rows directly beneath this hold special instructions to Quattro Pro that describe what you're searching for.

Figure 16-3 shows a criteria table set up for use with the database presented earlier in this chapter. The criteria table is highlighted and is in the block A21..D22.

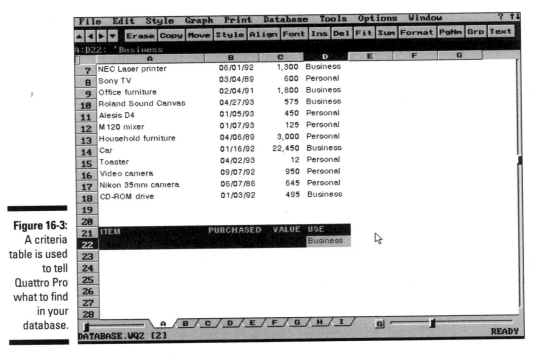

Figure 16-3: A criteria table is used to tell Quattro Pro what to find in your database.

Creating a criteria table

1. Figure out an area to put the criteria table in. Usually, the area directly to the right of the database is a good place. Or if your database isn't going to be increasing in size, you can put it below the database (leaving at least one blank row).

2. Use the familiar Edit⇨Copy command to copy the field names from the first row of your database block to the area you chose for your criteria block.

3. Directly below the field names in your criteria block, enter instructions that tell Quattro Pro what to look for. For example, if you want to locate all records with *Business* in the Use field, simply enter **Business** under the Use field in the criteria table. See the section "Entering search instructions" for more information on how to enter these search instructions.

4. To make things simpler, you may want to give the criteria table a name, using the Edit⇨Names⇨Create command. As you'll see later, Quattro Pro asks you for the criteria table — and it's easier to enter a named block than to point it out. If you do name the criteria table, make sure you name the entire block, including the field names and the row or rows that contain the instructions. This step is optional, but you'll see the advantage later on.

Entering search instructions

Step 3, above, was admittedly rather vague. The instructions that you put under the field names in the criteria block can be of two types:

- ✔ **An exact match.** Use a label or value. If you're looking for all records that have the label *Business* in the Use field, simply put the label *Business* under the Use field in the criteria block.

- ✔ **A condition.** Use a formula. If you're looking for all records that have a value greater than or equal to $1,000, you can use a formula like +C2>=1000. Place this formula under the Value field name in the criteria block.

You can also put instructions under more than one field name in the criteria block. For example, if you want to find all records that are used for business *and* have a value greater than or equal to $1,000, you would put the label Business under the Type field and +C2>=1000 under the Value field name.

And there's more. You can use more than one line of instructions to perform "or" searches. For example, if you want to locate records that have a value greater than or equal to $1,000, *or* have a value less than or equal to $100, you would use two formulas under the Value field name (in separate rows).

As you may expect, there's even more you can do when it comes to entering search instructions. If you don't need an exact match, you can use wildcard characters: ? and *. Quattro Pro interprets ? as "match any single character." Therefore, entering **?ig** as a search instruction locates records that have *fig, big, dig,* and so on in the field. When you enter *, Quattro Pro interprets it as "match any number of characters." Therefore, ***ig** finds records with *twig, big, thingamajig* — and anything else that ends in "ig." Quattro Pro interprets ~ to mean "not." Therefore, if you want to locate all records except those that have *paid* in a field, enter ~**paid** as the search instruction.

If you're constantly changing the instructions in the criteria table to perform different database tasks, consider setting up more than one criteria table. Then when you're ready to do a task, simply specify the appropriate criteria table. Specifying a criteria table is much easier if you give a descriptive name to each criteria table since you can just type in the name rather than point out the block.

The output block

When you do operations on a database, you can either locate the records in the database or extract the records you're interested in to another area called the *output block*. The *output block* is the area that holds copies of the found records.

An output block consists of the field names from your database. Use the Edit⇨Copy command to copy the field names to another area of your worksheet. Then use the **Database**⇨**Query**⇨**Output** Block command to specify this block as the output block.

If you don't need to see all of the fields of your database, set up the output block only with the fields you want.

Doing the Database Thing

Now that you have a semi-firm understanding of the concepts of a database block, criteria table, and output block, you can finally get to the topic of interest: actually doing things with a database.

This section discusses three commands that you can use to locate, extract, or delete from a database records that meet your criteria.

Before issuing any of these commands, you must

1. Create your database and tell Quattro Pro where it is, using the Database⇨Query⇨Block command.

2. Set up your criteria table and tell Quattro Pro where it is, using the Database⇨Query⇨Criteria Table command.

3. Set up an output block and tell Quattro Pro where it is, using the Database⇨Query⇨Output Block command. (This step is necessary only if you're extracting records.)

Locating records

If you merely want to take a look at database records that meet your search criteria (and you don't want to copy them somewhere else), use the Database⇨Query⇨Locate command. Quattro Pro uses the information in your criteria table and searches for records that qualify. When it finds one, it highlights the entire record in Text mode (but only the first column in WYSIWYG mode). You can then use the left- and right-arrow keys to move around in this record and even edit contents of the fields if you like.

When you're ready to move on to the next qualifying record, press the down arrow. If you press the up arrow, you go back to the previous qualifying record. In Figure 16-4, Quattro Pro highlights the next entry meeting the search criteria (Business, in this case).

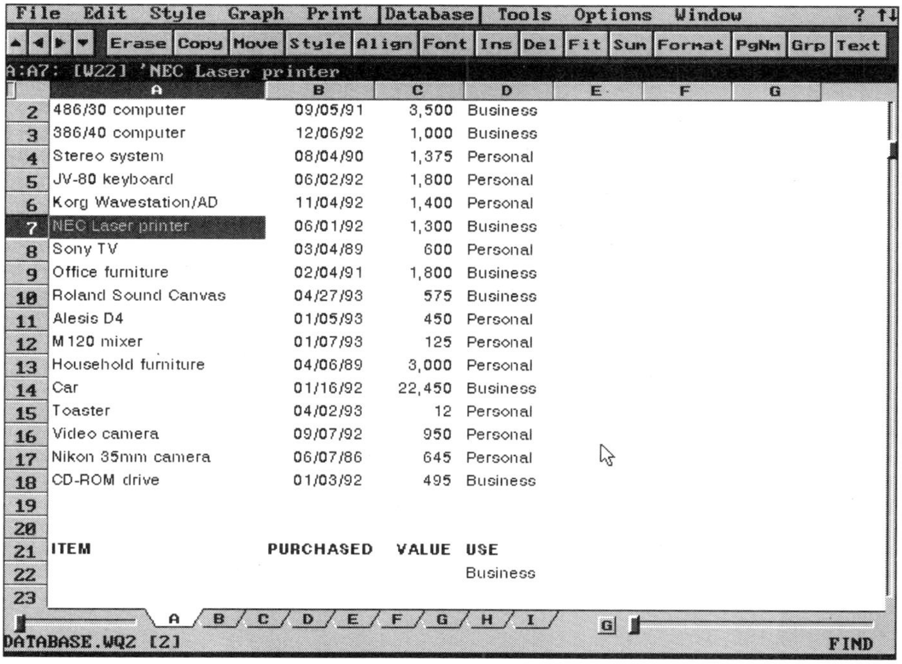

Figure 16-4: Quattro Pro has located and highlighted a record that meets the search criteria.

Extracting records

Often, you want to pull out specific records and put them in another area. For this, use the **Database⇨Query⇨Extract** command.

When you extract database records, they are not removed from the database — they are simply copied to the output range.

If you want to copy records and then delete the original records from the database, use **Database⇨Query⇨Extract** command, followed by **Database⇨Query⇨Delete** command (both with the same criteria table).

Deleting records

If you ever need to do mass deletions from your database, **Database⇨ Query⇨Delete** is the command for you. This is a fast way to get rid of many records in one fell swoop. Say you have a database that keeps track of accounts payable. You can clear out all records that have been paid, simply by setting up the appropriate search criteria in a criteria table and then using **Database⇨Query⇨Delete** to do the deed.

Before you use the **Database⇨Query⇨Delete** command, it's a good idea to keep a copy of your file before you delete the records. That way, you can always go back to it if you discover that you actually need some of that deleted information.

Printing databases

If you want to print your database, you don't have to do anything special. Just use the knowledge you gained from Chapter 10. To print an entire database, specify the database as your print block with the **Print⇨Block** command. Then change any settings and print it.

If you only want to print records that meet certain criteria, use the information in this chapter to extract those records to an output block, and then specify the output block as your print block.

The **Print⇨Headings⇨Top Headings** command is particularly useful when printing databases. This command lets you specify the row that holds your field names as a heading that will print on every page.

Chapter 17
Cool Formulas You Can Use

There once was a man named Nabil
Who thought it a sin to steal.
But he stole all my tricks
To get out of a fix,
Saying "No sense reinventing the wheel."

In This Chapter

▶ Lots of clever formulas that you can use

▶ Demonstrations of how the formulas work

▶ Explanations of the formulas so that you can adapt them to your own use

I've found that people who use spreadsheets tend to want to do the same general sorts of tasks. Many of these procedures are built right into the spreadsheet in the form of menu commands or @functions. But lots of other popular spreadsheet actions require formulas.

Although I can't develop formulas for you, I *can* share with you some formulas that I find useful. Most of these formulas use @functions, so this chapter also demonstrates some realistic uses of these functions. You might find one or two that are just what you need to do get that report out on time. Or seeing a formula here may give you an idea for a similar formula you can create.

In any case, feel free to do what you want with these formulas: Study them diligently or ignore them completely (and anything in between).

Read This First

The formulas in this chapter use names for @function arguments. This means that you cannot simply enter the formulas into a worksheet and expect them to work. You have to make some minor changes to adapt the arguments to your own needs. When you incorporate these formulas into your own worksheets, you must do one of the following:

✔ Substitute the appropriate cell or block reference for the block name I use. For example, the formula @SUM(*expenses*) uses a block named *expenses*. If you want to sum the values in A12..A36, substitute that block reference for *expenses*. Therefore, your adapted formula would be @SUM(A12..A36).

✔ Name cells or blocks on your worksheet to correspond to the range names used in the formulas. Using the previous example, you could simply use the **Edit**⇨**Names**⇨**Create** command to assign the name *expenses* to the block A12..A36.

✔ Use your own block names and make the appropriate changes in the formulas. If your worksheet has nothing to do with tracking expenses, define a name that's appropriate for what you're doing.

To refresh your memory on how to name cells and blocks, see Chapter 7.

Common, Everyday Formulas

The formulas in this section are relatively simple (and perhaps even trivial). But they are all commonly used in spreadsheets.

Calculating a sum

To calculate the sum of a block named *expenses*, use the following formula:

```
@SUM(expenses)
```

Computing an average

To calculate the average (also known as the *arithmetic mean*) of a block named *expenses*, use the following:

```
@AVG(expenses)
```

Calculating a percentage change

If you want to calculate the percentage change between the value in a cell named *old* and the value in a cell named *new*, use the following formula:

```
+(new-old)/old
```

If *old* is greater than *new*, the percentage change value will be positive. Otherwise, the value will be negative.

If there's a chance that *old* will be equal to 0, use the following formula instead:

```
@IF(old=0,@NA,(new-old)/old)
```

This revised formula displays NA rather than ERR, which shows up if you attempt to divide by zero.

Finding the minimum and maximum in a block

To find the largest number in a block named *scores*, use the following formula:

```
@MAX(scores)
```

To find the smallest number in a block named *scores*, use the following formula:

```
@MIN(scores)
```

Calculating a loan payment

This example assumes you have cells named *amount* (which is the loan amount), *term* (which is the length of the loan in months), and *rate* (which is the annual interest rate). The following formula returns the monthly payment amount:

```
@PMT(amount,rate/12,term)
```

Notice that this formula divides the annual interest rate (*rate*) by 12. This is done to get a monthly interest rate. If you were making payments every other month, you would divide rate by 6.

Mathematical Formulas

These formulas have to do with mathematical operations — square roots, cube roots, random numbers, and so on.

Finding a square root

The square root of a number is the number that, when multiplied by itself, gives you the original number. For example, 4 is the square root of 16 since 4×4=16. To calculate the square root of a cell named *value*, use the following formula:

```
@SQRT(value)
```

Finding a cube (or other) root

Besides square roots, there are other roots (carrots, potatoes, and so on). The cube root of a number is the number that, when multiplied by itself twice, results in the original number. For example, 4 is the cube root of 64 because 4×4×4=64. You can also calculate 4th roots, 5th roots, and so on. To get the cube root of a number in a cell named *value*, use the following formula:

```
+value^(1/3)
```

The fourth root is calculated as

```
+value^(1/4)
```

Calculate other roots in a similar manner.

Checking for even or odd

To determine whether the value in a cell named *cointoss* is odd or even, use the following formula:

```
@MOD(cointoss,2)
```

This formula returns 1 if *cointoss* is odd, and 0 if it's even.

For an even fancier formula that returns words rather than numbers, use this:

```
@IF(MOD(cointoss,2)=1,"ODD","EVEN")
```

The @MOD function, by the way, returns the remainder when the first argument is divided by the second argument. So in the first example, the value in *cointoss* is divided by 2, and the @MOD function returns the remainder of this division operation.

Generating a random number

To get a random number between 0 and 1, use the following formula, which displays a new random number every time the worksheet is recalculated or every time you make a change to any cell:

```
@RAND
```

If you need a random integer (whole number) that falls in a specific range, the formula gets a bit trickier. The next formula returns a random integer between two numbers stored in *low* and *high*. For example, if *low* contained 1 and *high* contained 12, the formula would return a random number between (and including) 1 and 12.

```
@INT(@RAND/(1/(high-low+1)))+low
```

Rounding numbers

To round a number (in a cell named *amount*) to the nearest whole number, use the following:

```
@ROUND(amount,0)
```

To round the number to two decimal places, substitute a 2 for the 0 in the formula. In fact, you can round the number off to any number of decimal places by changing the second argument.

The value returned by the @ROUND function is the actual rounded value of its argument. If you merely want to change the number of decimal places displayed in a cell, you can change the numeric formatting with the Style⇨Numeric Format command. In other words, @ROUND affects not only how the value is displayed, but also the value itself.

Finding the number of non-decimal digits

At some point in your life, you may need to know how many digits a number has to the left of the decimal point. If the number is in a cell named *amount,* this formula will tell you:

```
@INT(@LOG(@ABS(amount)))+1
```

If *amount* is zero, this formula returns ERR. You can get around this by making the formula slightly more complicated:

```
@IF(amount=0,0,@INT(@LOG(@ABS(amount)))+1)
```

Label Formulas

As you know, Quattro Pro can deal with text (or labels) as well as numbers. Here are a few formulas that let you manipulate labels.

Adding labels together

When you join two strings together, it's called *concatenation*. Assume the cell named *first* contains the label *Miles* and the cell named *last* contained *Davis*. The following formula concatenates these strings into a single name:

```
+first&" "&last
```

The ampersand is the concatenation operator. Note that I concatenated a space character to separate the two names (otherwise the result would be *MilesDavis*, not *Miles Davis*). Note also that you can concatenate a label with a label (not a label with a value). But see the next example for a way around this.

Adding labels to values

If you want to concatenate a label with a value, you must first convert the value to a label. In this example, the cell named *word* holds the label *AMOUNT:*. The cell named *answer* holds the value 125. The formula below displays the label and the value in a single cell.

```
+word&" "&@STRING(answer,0)
```

@STRING converts a value to a label, and the second argument for the @STRING function is the number of decimal places to be displayed (in this case, none).

The result of this formula is

```
AMOUNT: 125
```

Displaying a label and a value in one cell

The preceding formula effectively displays a label and a value in a single cell. Here's yet another example. Assume you have a block of cells named *scores*. The following formula displays a label and the maximum value in *scores* in one cell:

```
+"Largest:"&@STRING(@MAX(scores),0)
```

The @STRING function converts the value returned by the @MAX function into a label. This label is then concatenated with the string *Largest:*. Pretty neat, eh?

Determining whether a label has certain text

You can use the @FIND function to determine whether a label contains a certain string of letters. Assume a cell named *fullname* has a person's name, and you want to find out if this name has a middle initial. Since a middle initial has a period after it, you can use the following formula to tell you whether the name has a middle initial:

```
@FIND(".",fullname,0)
```

If *fullname* has a period in it, this formula returns a value that represents the position of the period. If it doesn't have a period, the formula returns ERR. The third argument, by the way, means to start looking from position 0 of *fullname* (position 0 corresponds to the first character).

You can make this a bit fancier and avoid the display of ERR by changing it as follows:

```
@IF(@ISERR(@FIND(".",fullname,0)),"NO","YES")
```

Changing a string to upper- and lowercase

If the cell named *fullname* contains a label in uppercase (such as CHICK COREA), you can convert it to proper case (Chick Corea) with the following formula:

```
@PROPER(fullname)
```

Don't forget that there are similar functions to change a string to uppercase (@UPPER) and to lowercase (@LOWER).

Extracting a last name

Sometimes, you may end up with a list of names that you want to sort by last name. If the names are in standard format (that is, first name first, last name last), sorting by last name is pretty much impossible. Therefore, you need to extract the last name for a sort key. If a cell named *fullname* has a label such as Milt Jackson, the following formula picks out the last name (Jackson):

```
@RIGHT(fullname,@FIND(" ",fullname,0))
```

Notice that this formula simply searches for the first blank character and considers that to be the separator between the first and last name. Therefore, this formula will not work if the name has a middle name or initial. If the name is *William B. Smith,* the preceding formula returns *B. Smith.* However, if you want to use a much more complicated formula, the following formula works even if *fullname* includes a middle name or initial (such as *Tom T. Hall*):

```
@RIGHT(fullname,@LENGTH(fullname)-@IF(@ISERR(@FIND
(" ",fullname,@FIND(" ",fullname,0)+1)),@FIND(" ",fullname,0),
@FIND(" ",fullname,@FIND(" ",fullname,0)+1))-1)
```

After creating this formula and copying it so it applies to all of the names in your list, you can then use the **Database**⇨**Sort** command to sort the list, using the column with the formulas as the 1st sort key.

Extracting a first name

Here's a formula that returns the first name from a string, ignoring middle names and middle initials:

```
@LEFT(fullname,@FIND(" ",fullname,0))
```

If you want to extract everything except the last name, use this formula:

```
@LEFT(fullname,@IF(@ISERR(@FIND(" ",fullname,@FIND
(" ",fullname,0)+1)),@FIND("",fullname,0),@FIND
("    ",fullname,@FIND(" ",fullname,0)+1)))
```

Reversing names

Now it's time to take this to the next logical step and combine the two preceding formulas into one. The formula below takes a name such as *Frank Lloyd Wright* and turns it into *Wright, Frank Lloyd:*

```
@RIGHT(name,@LENGTH(name)-@IF(@ISERR(@FIND(" ",name,@FIND
(" ",name,0)+1)),@FIND(" ",name,0),@FIND(" ",name,@FIND
(" ",name,0)+1))-1)&", "&@LEFT(name,@IF(@ISERR(@FIND
(" ",name,@FIND(" ",name,0)+1)), @FIND
(" ",name,0),@FIND(" ",name,@FIND(" ",name,0)+1)))
```

Therefore, this single formula (when copied to apply to every name in a list) can completely convert a list of names into a more useful format.

If you can enter this formula without making a mistake, congratulations.

Date Formulas

Here are a few formulas that deal with dates.

The date and time @functions get their information from your computer's clock. If you rely on any of these functions for serious work, make sure that the date and time are set properly in your computer. Procedures for setting computer clocks vary, so consult your system manual for instructions.

Finding out what day it is

If you would like your worksheet to display the current date, enter the following formula into any cell:

```
@TODAY
```

This formula returns a date serial number, so you need to use the **Style⇨Numeric Format⇨Date** command to format it as a date (you may also have to make the column wider so that the date will show up).

Determining the day of the week

The following formula returns the current day of the week:

```
@CHOOSE(@MOD(@TODAY,7),"Sat","Sun","Mon","Tue","Wed","Thu","Fri")
```

You can replace @TODAY with a reference to a cell that has a date serial number in it to get the day of the week for any date.

Determining the last day of the month

In business situations, it's often necessary to know the last day of the month. The following formula returns the last day of the current month:

```
@DATE(@YEAR(@TODAY),@MONTH(@TODAY)+1,1)-1
```

To figure out the last day of the month for any date serial number, for both occurrences of @TODAY, substitute a reference to a cell that has a date.

Miscellaneous Formulas

Here are a few more miscellaneous formulas for your dining and dancing pleasure.

Looking up a corresponding value

Many spreadsheets need to look up a value in a table, based on another value. Examples include parts lists and income tax tables (you need to look up the tax rate from a table, and the tax rate is based on a person's taxable income).

Figure 17-1 shows an example of a small lookup table. In this worksheet, the user can enter a part number into cell B3 (which is named *partnum*). The formulas in cells B4 and B5 return the corresponding price and discount. The lookup table is in D2..F11 and has the name *partlist*. The values in the first column of any lookup table must be in ascending order.

The formula in cell B4, which displays the price, is

```
@VLOOKUP(partnum,partlist,1)
```

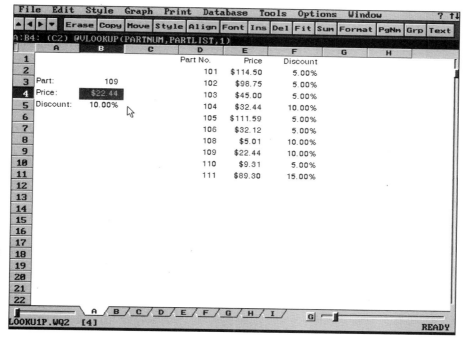

Figure 17-1:
Looking up
a value in
a table.

The formula in cell B5, which displays the discount, is

```
@VLOOKUP(partnum,partlist,2)
```

The @VLOOKUP function looks for the first argument (here, *partnum*) in the first column of the block specified by the second argument (here, *partlist*). It then returns the value in the column represented by the third argument (0 corresponds to the first column in the table, 1 is the second column, and 2 is the third column, and so on). If the formula doesn't find an exact match, it simply uses the first row that's not greater than what it's looking for. In some cases this is okay, but in others it's a problem.

Looking up an exact corresponding value

The following formulas solve the problem I discussed in the preceding section. This time, the formula makes sure that the part number actually exists by using an @IF function. If the part number doesn't exist, the formula returns the string "Not found."

The following formula substitutes for the formula in cell B4 of the preceding example:

```
@IF(partnum=@VLOOKUP(partnum,partlist,0),@VLOOKUP(partnum,
partlist,1),"Not found")
```

The following formula substitutes for the formula in cell B5 in the preceding example:

```
@IF(partnum=@VLOOKUP(partnum,partlist,0),@VLOOKUP(partnum,
partlist,2),"Not found")
```

Making underlines that match a label's width

If you would like to create a row with underline characters (hyphens) that match the contents of the cell directly above, use the following formula. Here, *above* refers to the cell directly above the cell that contains the formula.

```
@REPEAT("-",@LENGTH(above))
```

Although Quattro Pro's Style⇨Line Drawing command is usually a better way to go, using hyphens to underscore words is useful if you plan to print your worksheet in Draft mode (without fancy formatting) or output it to a text file that will be read by some other program.

Chapter 18
Enough about Macros to Get By

Melissa was always judicious,
But her typing was quite repetitious.
She made a macro one day
And had more time to play
And all the while felt surreptitious.

In This Chapter

▶ An introduction to macros

▶ How to create simple macros — and why you might want to do so

▶ How to use macros that other people created

▶ Examples that help clarify this topic

▶ Even more about macros that you can probably safely ignore

Somewhere along the line, you may have heard that computers are supposed to make your life easier and save time. When it comes to spreadsheets, the one feature most often cited as a time-saver is the macro feature. Learning about macros is not essential to using Quattro Pro. In fact, most spreadsheet users wouldn't know a macro from a mango. But you owe it to yourself to at least learn what macros can do so that you'll know what you're missing out on.

What Is a Macro?

Imagine that you have a spreadsheet set up, and you need to enter the name of your company in a bunch of places throughout the worksheet. You can type the company name each time you need it, or you can enter the company once and then copy it to the other locations. Another way is to create a macro to type the company name for you automatically upon command.

If your company's name is *Superior Widgets Corporation of America,* you can assign these letters to a key combination such as Alt-S. Then whenever you press Alt-S, Quattro Pro spits out this text instantly (and, as a bonus, always spells it correctly).

And — believe it or not — it gets even better. You can also create macros that execute a series of commands. Suppose that you like to apply specific formatting such as bold, red text, and a border. You can assign all of these commands to a key combination such as Alt-F. Then pressing Alt-F executes these commands in the blink of an eye.

So there you have it. A macro is simply a shortcut way of typing text, numbers, or even commands. The only hitch is that you have to create the macro before you use it.

More about Macros

Before you get too far into this, there are a few things you should know about Quattro Pro macros:

- ✔ A macro can play back predefined keystrokes.

- ✔ Playing back the predefined keystrokes is called *running the macro* or *executing the macro.* You do this by pressing a key combination that you specify.

- ✔ The key combination must consist of the Alt key plus a letter key.

- ✔ You have to assign a name to every macro. The name consists of a backslash, plus the key that you press to run it. For example, you execute the macro named \A by pressing Alt-A.

- ✔ You usually store your macros in the worksheet that you plan to use them with. Actually, macros are simply labels — labels that have a special meaning to Quattro Pro.

- ✔ You must create the macro before you can use it, and there are two ways to create a macro: manually and by recording your keystrokes.

- ✔ You can use a macro as many times as you want, and the macro always does exactly the same thing.

Why "macro"?

Contrary to popular belief, *macro* does *not* stand from Messy And Confusing Repeatable Operation. Actually, I don't know why they use this term. The dictionary tells me that *macro* means large and is the opposite of *micro.* My guess is that they call these things macros because you can perform a large operation by making a small effort. If anybody knows the real answer, please let me in on it.

Your First Macro

Ready to give it a try? You'll create a macro that types your name into a cell and then moves the cell pointer to the cell directly below. You'll assign the macro to the Alt-N key combination. When you're finished, you'll be able to go to any cell in the worksheet and press Alt-N to have Quattro Pro enter the text you specified and move the cell pointer down to the cell below.

Creating the macro

1. Start with a blank worksheet.

2. Move the cell pointer to cell B1, and type your name in the cell followed by a tilde (~). For example, if your name is John Doe, type **John Doe~**.

3. Move the cell pointer to cell B2 and type **{DOWN}**.

4. Move the cell pointer to cell A1 and type **'\n** (a single quote, a backslash, and the letter *n*).

5. With the cell pointer in cell A1, select **Edit⇨Names⇨Labels⇨Right** and press Enter.

   This step assigns the name \n to cell B1.

That's it. Your worksheet should look like Figure 18-1 (although the name in cell B1 will be different). This macro consists of two labels, and it's named \n.

Running the macro

You can now play the macro in one of two ways. You can use the macro's name (Alt-N in this example), or you can use the **Tools⇨Macro⇨Execute** command.

With the macro name

1. Move the cell pointer to any blank cell in the worksheet.

2. Press Alt-N.

The macro types your name and then moves the cell pointer down one cell. You can move all over the worksheet and press Alt-N as much as you want. You'll see your name show up each time you execute this macro.

If the macro doesn't do what it's supposed to do, the source of the problem is probably with the name. Cell B1 must be named \n. You used the **Edit⇨Names⇨Labels⇨Right** command to do this. Make sure the cell pointer is in cell A1 when you issue this command.

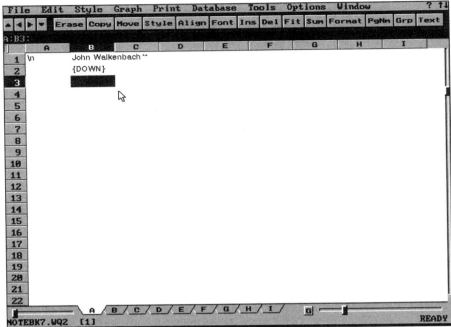

Figure 18-1:
A simple
macro that
types your
name.

With the Tools⇨Macro⇨Execute command

Earlier in this chapter, I told you that all macros must have a name. I lied. Although it makes them easier to work with, macros don't need to have a name. You can run a macro that doesn't have a name by using the Tools⇨**Macro**⇨Execute menu command. After you issue this command, Quattro Pro responds with the message Enter block of macros to execute. Simply enter or point to the first cell of the macro, and Quattro Pro executes the commands.

Modifying the macro

Now, modify the macro so that it adds the first line of your address:

1. Move to cell B3 (the cell directly below the end of the existing macro) and enter the first line of your address. You're adding on to the existing macro to make it type an address.

   Since addresses always start with numbers, make sure you start your address with a label prefix such as a single quote ('). Put a tilde {~} after the address to represent pressing Enter.

2. Move to the cell below and type {UP}. This macro command tells Quattro Pro to move the cell pointer up. Therefore, when you execute the macro, the cell pointer returns to the spot where you started.

How it works

This simple two-cell macro does two things: it types your name, and it moves the cell pointer down one cell. When you press Alt-N, Quattro Pro goes through the following thought process:

1. Hmmm. This user just pressed an Alt-N.

2. Is there a macro named \n? If no, I'll just beep.

3. Hey, there *is* a macro named \n. That means I'll have to execute it.

4. The first cell in the macro is just a bunch of letters. I'll just stick them in the cell where the cell pointer is. There's a tilde at the end of the letters, so I'll press Enter.

5. There's another cell below, so I'll take a look at it.

6. This cell has a command which tells me to move the cell pointer down. Okay.

7. Since there's nothing below this macro command, my job's over for now.

You probably notice a few things about this two-cell macro. The tilde character after your name represents the Enter key. When Quattro Pro encounters a tilde, it's just like you pressed Enter. The {DOWN} part of the macro is responsible for moving the cell pointer. {DOWN} is a macro command. Quattro Pro has quite a few macro commands, which are always enclosed in curly brackets. If this command were not in brackets, Quattro Pro would simply type the letters *D, O, W,* and *N*. As you might expect, you can use other commands such as {UP}, {LEFT}, and {RIGHT} to move the cell pointer around.

This modified macro types your name, moves down, types your address, and then moves up a cell. Move to a blank cell and press Alt-N. Quattro Pro starts to execute the macro but stops and gives you the error message shown in Figure 18-2. In other words, there's an error in the macro.

What's the problem? When Quattro Pro gets to the address portion of the macro, it tries to enter the address into the cell but can't because it thinks you're trying to enter an invalid number. The first quote only tells Quattro Pro that it's a label; you still need to enter a second quote, which is actually entered when the macro is played back. The solution, then, is to add *another* label prefix to the macro in cell B3 so that the address starts with *two* single quotes.

Notice that you don't have to rename this macro if you make any changes. The original name (\n) still applies to the first cell of the macro.

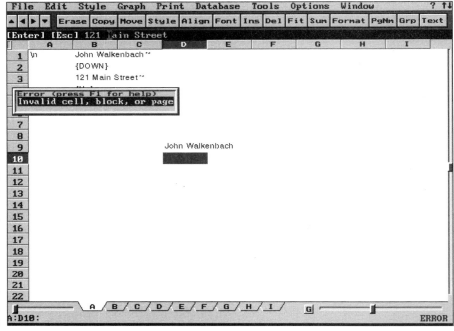

Figure 18-2:
A Quattro Pro error message telling you there's a problem with your macro.

Some macro rules

Now that you've had a little experience creating a macro, you're ready for some rules of the game:

- A macro consists simply of labels made up of text and special macro commands enclosed in brackets.

- A macro is stored in one or more cells in a single column.

- You can edit the text that makes up a macro command just like you would edit any other cell.

- Quattro Pro plays back the labels and executes the commands in order, starting at the top and working down the column until it hits a blank cell.

- The first cell of a macro must have a name that starts with a backslash and has one additional character. This additional character is used with the Alt key to execute the macro.

- You can put any number of macro commands in one cell (but you make it easier on yourself if you use only one command per cell).

- You can enter macros directly, or you can use the macro recorder to record your keystrokes (explained in the next section).

The Macro Recorder

You don't have to type a macro in, letter by letter. Quattro Pro has a special built-in feature that's capable of storing the keystrokes you make and creating a macro out of them. This works much like a tape recorder: turn recording mode on, do your thing, turn recording mode off, and then play it back as many times as you want. Cool, eh?

Recording a macro

Ready to record a macro? Ready or not, that's what this section does. At the risk of being bored to tears, you'll record the same macro you created earlier.

Use the keyboard, not the mouse, when you record the macro. Otherwise, Quattro Pro won't pick up all of your actions and the macro won't work correctly.

Start with a blank worksheet (not necessary, but it makes it easier for me to describe), and then do the following:

1. Move the cell pointer to cell A1.

2. Select the **Tools**⇨**Macro**⇨**Record** command to turn on the macro recorder. From this point on, all of your keystrokes will be recorded.

3. Enter your name in cell A1 and press Enter.

4. Move down to cell A2 and enter your address (start it with one single quote character to make it a label).

5. Move the cell pointer back up to cell A1.

6. Select the **Tools**⇨**Macro**⇨**Record** command to turn off the macro recorder.

7. Move to cell E1 — this is where you'll put the recorded macro.

8. Select the **Tools**⇨**Macro**⇨**Paste** command to place the recorded information into the worksheet.

9. Quattro Pro asks you for a name for the macro. Type **\n** and press Enter.

10. Now you see a message in the input line that says Enter macro block to paste. Quattro Pro wants to know where it should paste this macro and suggests the current cell (E1). Press Enter to accept this.

11. Quattro Pro dumps the macro into the worksheet beginning in cell E1.

    The macro should look just like the one you entered manually in the previous exercise. Notice that Quattro Pro is smart enough to start the address cell with *two* label prefixes (avoiding the problem you encountered previously).

This macro will be named \n, but Quattro Pro doesn't put the range name to the left of the first macro cell. You can do that yourself, if you like, to remind you how to execute this masterpiece.

Try the macro out by moving to a blank cell in the worksheet and pressing Alt-N. If it doesn't work, check your work and try again.

A useful macro that you don't have to be a rocket scientist to create

So far, the macros you've developed have been pretty wimpy and not really all that useful. Now you'll record a macro that actually does something constructive.

The macro you create will format the current cell with a currency numeric format, including two decimal places, and then draw lines around the cell. For

example, the macro will convert the value in cell A2 in the worksheet shown in Figure 18-3 so that it looks like the value in cell C2 — all with a single keystroke.

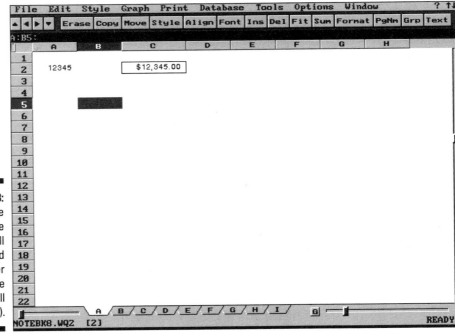

Figure 18-3: Before running the macro (cell A2) and after running the macro (cell C2).

Record this macro, using the keyboard rather than the mouse.

You'll record the macro that does this formatting. For simplicity, start with a blank worksheet.

1. Type **12345** in cell B3 and press Enter. This is just a value to give us something to start with. Keep the cell pointer in this cell.

2. Select the **Tools**⇨**Macro**⇨**Record** command to turn on the macro recorder.

3. Issue the **Style**⇨**Numeric Format**⇨**Currency** command and press Enter to accept the suggestion of two decimal places.

4. Press Enter again to specify the single-cell block for the formatting.

   Notice that the column is too narrow to display this value.

5. Use the **Style**⇨**Column Width** command, and press the right-arrow key five times to make the column wide enough to handle large values. Press Enter.

6. Issue the **Style**⇨**Line Drawing** command and press Enter to accept the single cell that Quattro Pro suggests.

7. Press A to select **All** from the Placement menu and press S to select **Single** from the Line Types menu. Then choose **Q**uit to get rid of this menu.

8. Turn off the macro recorder by selecting **Tools**⇨**Macro**⇨**Record**.

9. Move to an out-of-the-way cell such as E4. This will be the first cell of the pasted macro.

10. Select **Tools**⇨**Macro**⇨**Paste**.

11. Type **\F** for the macro name, accept the suggest block, and press Enter.

If you did everything right, your worksheet should look something like Figure 18-4. Now, try out your macro.

Move to a blank cell such as B6 and enter a value (**7843.4**, for example). Press Alt-F; Quattro Pro executes the macro. In a flash, the number is formatted, the column widened, and a line drawn around the cell. You've just executed three commands with a single key combination.

Figure 18-4:
A more
complex
macro that
adds
formatting.

Recording modes

Actually, Quattro Pro has two different macro recording modes. By default, it records macros in the Logical mode. In Logical recording mode, menu commands that you issue are translated to macro commands. For example, the Style⇨Numeric Format command is translated into the {/ Block;Format} macro command.

The other macro recording mode is Keystroke mode. In this mode, every keystroke you make is recorded verbatim. You can't use your mouse if you're recording in Keystroke mode.

Changing modes

You can change the macro recording mode by selecting the Tools⇨Macro⇨Macro Recording command and then selecting either **Logical** or **K**eystroke. Figure 18-5 shows the previous macro recorded in Keystroke mode.

Why the macro looks strange

The macro you recorded in the previous example looks pretty strange, don't you think? Some parts of it don't look anything like the keys you pressed when you recorded it. Rather, it has commands such as {/ Block;Format} and {/ Column;Width}.

Here's what's happening. As you were recording that macro, Quattro Pro was interpreting your actions and converting your keystrokes into special macro commands. Not all keystrokes were converted, however; some of them were recorded exactly. For example, the "asq" at the end of the macro shown in Figure 18-4 represents the keystrokes you made in the Line Drawing menus.

Why two modes?

In the old days, spreadsheet macros were always recorded in Keystroke mode. This presented a problem, however, if the spreadsheet company made any changes to their menus — which they almost always do. If you get a later version of the spreadsheet program, there's no guarantee that a macro you recorded with the earlier version will work with the new version. Using the Logical recording mode takes care of this problem.

So what's a poor spreadsheet user to do? My advice is to forget all about Keystroke mode and stick with Logical mode.

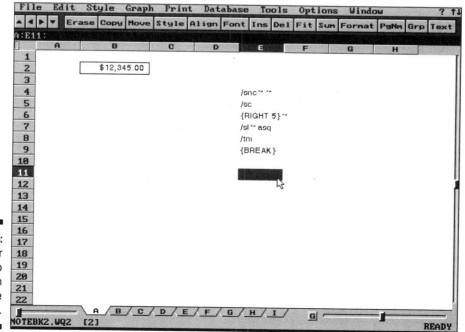

Figure 18-5:
A familiar
macro
recorded in
Keystroke
mode.

Macro debugging

Quattro Pro not only lets you create macros, but it also helps you correct them when they are wrong. If you stick with simple macros, you can usually quickly identify any errors in the macro and correct them. But for more complex macros, finding errors is more difficult. For hard-core macro freaks, Quattro Pro offers several debugging tools that help you track down errors in your macros.

You can enter Debug mode by selecting **Tools**⇨**Macro**⇨**Debugger** and selecting **Yes**. (You also can press Shift-F2 to toggle in and out of Debug mode.) In Debug mode, you can run macros in slow motion (step-by-step) and do several other things to let you know what's going on.

When you run a macro in Debug mode, a special window appears that shows the macro. Press the spacebar to move through the macro one command at a time, which is also useful when you need to figure out what somebody else's macro is doing. Simply enter Debug mode and step through the macro. Soon, you'll have a pretty good idea of what the macro is doing — or be convinced that the person who developed the macro knows even less about Quattro Pro than you do.

Check out the on-line help for more information about the debugger.

Using Other People's Macros

You may, at some point in your career, receive a worksheet from somebody who actually knows how to write a macro. This worksheet may have one or more macros on it, and you've been told that these macros make the spreadsheet do something useful. In fact, this scenario isn't all that unusual. Some people take great pride in developing macros that do useful things.

If you're lucky, the worksheet will have instructions that tell you what to do. For example, it may say something like "To print this worksheet, press Alt-P" or "Press Alt-U to update the monthly sales figures."

The person who created such a worksheet was simply trying to make things easier for you or anyone else who uses the spreadsheet. The macros may do quite a bit behind the scenes — more than you care to do or know how to do. In this case, running a macro is much like issuing a command.

You don't have to know what the macro is doing in order to use it. Just press the appropriate key combination and sit back and relax while Quattro Pro follows the orders in the macro.

Macro Mania

If you're hungry for more examples, read on. These examples demonstrate more uses for macros. If you like what you see, re-create the macro on your worksheet and give it a name.

Alignment macros

Figure 18-6 shows three simple macros that make it easy for you to align values or labels in cells. Pressing Alt-L aligns the entry to the left, Alt-R to the right, and Alt-C centers it.

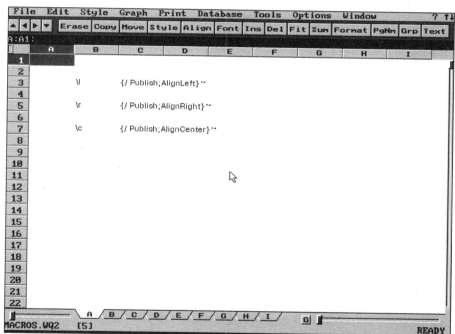

Figure 18-6:
Three
simple
alignment
macros.

An automatic month labels macro

This macro, shown in Figure 18-7, is useful for budgeters who need to put month names in their worksheet. The macro types, aligns, and modifies each month name.

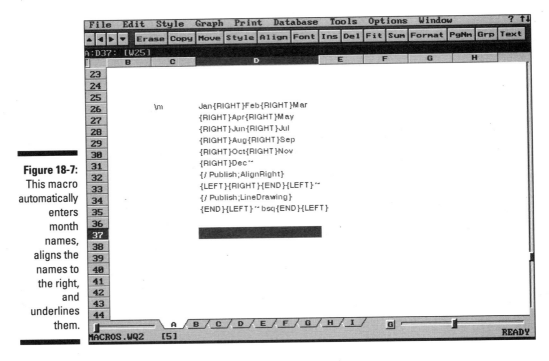

File Edit Style Graph Print Database Tools Options Window ? ↑↓

Erase Copy Move Style Align Font Ins Del Fit Sum Format PgNm Grp Text

A:D37: [W25]

\m	Jan{RIGHT}Feb{RIGHT}Mar		
	{RIGHT}Apr{RIGHT}May		
	{RIGHT}Jun{RIGHT}Jul		
	{RIGHT}Aug{RIGHT}Sep		
	{RIGHT}Oct{RIGHT}Nov		
	{RIGHT}Dec"'		
	{/ Publish;AlignRight}		
	{LEFT}{RIGHT}{END}{LEFT}"'		
	{/ Publish;LineDrawing}		
	{END}{LEFT}"'bsq{END}{LEFT}		

Figure 18-7:
This macro
automatically
enters
month
names,
aligns the
names to
the right,
and
underlines
them.

A B C D E F G H I G

MACROS.WQ2 [5]   READY

An AutoSum macro

Figure 18-8 shows a macro that's useful for people who tend to create a lot of
@SUM formulas to add up columns of numbers. Before you start this macro,
move the cell pointer to the blank cell directly below the column of numbers
you want to add up. Press Alt-S, and the macro goes to work.

Note: This macro will only work when Quattro Pro is in READY mode.

This macro starts by entering a double underline (using the equal sign) in the
current cell; then it uses pointing and anchoring keys to create the @SUM
formula in the cell below the underline.

Advanced Macro Stuff

Writing macros can be very complicated. Actually, you can do a *lot* with
macros, and this chapter just barely scratches the surface. For those who just
can't get enough, I wrap up this chapter with even more mundane macro
minutiae.

Running 1-2-3 macros

Quattro Pro can easily load worksheets prepared in Lotus 1-2-3, and 1-2-3 handles macros in much the same way as Quattro Pro. But since the 1-2-3 menus are different, Quattro Pro cannot run 1-2-3 macros.

Macro libraries

Normally, a macro only works in the worksheet where it is stored. This makes sense because macros usually perform a task specific to a single worksheet. Sometimes, however, you may create macros that would be useful in all of your worksheets — a macro to type your company's name, for example.

Quattro Pro lets you designate a worksheet as a macro library. This means that macros stored in such a worksheet can be executed from within any other worksheet — even if you don't have a library card. The macro library, of course, has to be open before you can use the macros (it can't just be in a file on your disk). To avoid conflicts with macros that have the same name, it's a good idea to only have one macro library open at a time.

To designate a worksheet as a macro library file, select the Tools⇨Macro⇨ Library command and specify **Yes**.

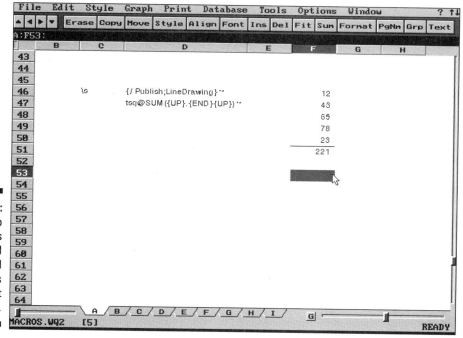

Figure 18-8:
A macro that creates an @SUM formula and underlines the last entry.

After-the-fact macros

You probably don't realize it, but Quattro Pro is constantly keeping track of every keystroke you make and every command you issue — spying on you as you go about your business. It stores the keystrokes in a special area called a *transcript.* You can use this transcript to your advantage.

Suppose that you complete a complex procedure and discover that you need to repeat exactly the same commands somewhere else in the worksheet. Well, you *could* have created a macro, but now it's too late — or is it?

Select the **Tools**⇨**Macro**⇨**Transcript** command, and Quattro Pro displays a window like the one shown in Figure 18-9. This transcript window holds your

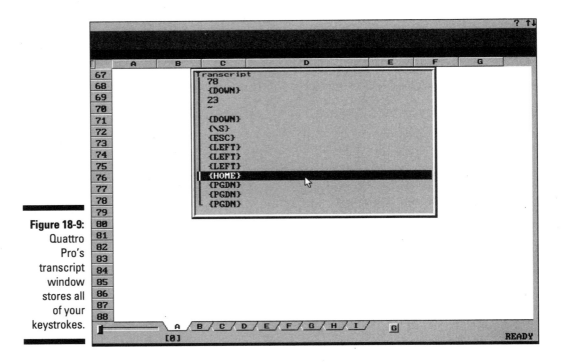

Figure 18-9:
Quattro
Pro's
transcript
window
stores all
of your
keystrokes.

most recent keystrokes and commands stored in the normal macro format. Press / to display the special transcript menu. This lets you copy a block of the commands into your worksheet to turn them into a macro. Or you can simply tell Quattro Pro where to start executing the commands. Refer to the on-line help for more information on this nifty feature.

> ***Note***: Although the transcript records commands you issue with a mouse, it doesn't record other mouse actions such as scrolling and selecting cells and blocks.

Chapter 19
How Do I...

There once was a man named Ross
Who was confused by Quattro and DOS,
So he consulted this book,
Explored every cranny and nook,
And now he knows more than his boss.

In This Chapter

▶ A quick reference that tells you how to perform common — and some not so common — Quattro Pro operations

▶ Things that aren't covered in other chapters

Here's where you go when you need to do something in Quattro Pro, but you can't quite remember how to do it. Besides steering you to the right menu command, I also tell you what you need to look out for, and I even list the shortcut keys you can use.

The chapter is arranged somewhat logically, grouped by classifications such as Editing, Formatting, Graphing, and so on. And, of course, don't overlook the catch-all Miscellaneous section at the end.

Editing

These procedures involve modifications you make to a worksheet. For additional details on these procedures, see Chapter 8.

Changing the contents of a cell

If you have something in a cell and you want to put something else in the cell, you can just enter the new value, label, or formula, and it will replace what's already there.

If you just need to make a small change, you're probably better off editing the cell. Move the cell pointer to the cell you want to edit and press F2. Use the left-arrow and right-arrow keys to move the insertion point to the part of the cell you want to change. You can use Del to delete the next character and Backspace to delete the previous character. To add new characters, just type them — everything will be pushed to the right to accommodate the new text.

Copying a block of cells

Use the Edit⇨Copy command or press the Ctrl-C shortcut. You can copy one cell to another cell, one cell to a block of cells, or a block of cells to another block. When you copy a cell that has a formula containing references to cells or blocks, the references change (unless they are absolute references). This is usually what you want.

Copying between worksheets

Copying a cell or block from one worksheet to another is really no different from copying within a single worksheet — but both worksheets have to be open. Issue the Edit⇨Copy command, and select the cell or block to be copied and press Enter. Then activate the worksheet that you want to copy to by pressing Shift-F6 until the proper worksheet appears. Move the cell pointer to the cell you want to copy the information to and press Enter.

Copying a cell, but not its formats

Use the Edit⇨Copy Special⇨Contents command.

Copying only the formats

Use the Edit⇨Copy Special⇨Formats command.

Moving a block of cells somewhere else

Use the Edit⇨Move command, or press the Ctrl-M shortcut.

Deleting a cell or block

To erase the contents of one cell, move the cell pointer to it and press Del. To erase a block of cells, use the Edit⇨Erase Block command (or press Alt-E).

Reversing the effects of a command

If you do something that screws up your worksheet royally, there's an excellent chance that you can undo it. Simply select the Edit⇨Undo command immediately (or use the Alt-F5 shortcut).

In order for this to work, you must have Undo enabled. To find out whether undo is enabled or disabled (or to change from one to the other), use the Options⇨Other⇨Undo command.

Inserting a new column

Use the Edit⇨Insert⇨Columns command. Expand the highlighting horizontally if you want to insert more than one column.

Inserting a new row

Use the Edit⇨Insert⇨Rows command. Expand the highlighting vertically to insert more than one row.

Entering labels that start with a number

If you want to enter a label that starts with a number (such as *3rd Quarter*), you must precede the label with one of the three label prefixes: '(single quote, for left aligned), " (double quote for right aligned), and ^ (caret, for centered).

If you plan to enter a lot of labels that start with a number, use the Database⇨Data Entry⇨Labels Only command to preformat the block. Then you don't have to bother with label prefixes.

Entering dates

To enter a date, use the @DATE function, and then use **Style**⇨**Numeric Format** command (or press Ctrl-F) to format the cell so that it appears as a date. For example, to enter December 3, 1976, use this formula: @DATE(76,12,3). If the cell fills with asterisks, you have to make the column wider so that the date fits.

If you're entering a bunch of dates, a better way is to preformat the block for dates. Use the **Database**⇨**Data Entry**⇨**Dates Only** command and specify the block that you'll be putting dates into. Then you can enter dates directly. For example, you can enter **7/4/94**, and Quattro will interpret it as a date — otherwise, it thinks you're entering a formula that divides 7 by 4 and then divides the result by 94.

Sorting a block

To sort a block of data, use the **Database**⇨**Sort** command. Make sure that you highlight the entire block. You can specify up to five sort keys if you want to perform a sort within a sort.

Converting formulas to values

If you have one or more formulas that never change (that is, *always* return the same answer), you can convert the formulas to values by using the **Edit**⇨**Values** command. Converting formulas to values makes your worksheet less complicated and makes it recalculate faster. Just be absolutely sure that you only convert formulas that always return the same answer; otherwise, you could cause yourself some problems.

You can also convert a formula to a value before it even goes into a cell. Enter the formula in the input bar, but press F9 before you press Enter. The formula disappears, and in its place is its result. Press Enter to store the result in the cell.

Converting vertical data into horizontal data (and vice versa)

If you enter a bunch of data vertically (down a column) and you discover that you should have entered it horizontally (across a row), you don't have to reenter it. Rather, go for the **Edit**⇨**Transpose** command. This command copies the source block to a different block and changes the orientation in the process. You can then go back and delete the source block. Be careful, however, because this command copies the result of formulas, not the formulas themselves. If you have any formulas in the source block, only their values get transposed.

Searching and replacing

Most word processing users are familiar with the concepts of searching and replacing. Quattro Pro has a similar feature. Rather than pound on the keyboard trying to find something that may be hundreds of rows and columns away, use the Edit⇨Search & Replace command. This command also lets you replace a particular text string with something else — either globally or selectively in a block.

Formatting

The procedures in this section involve changing how things look on your worksheet. See Chapters 5 and 8 for more details.

Changing the way numbers display

Use the Format⇨Numeric Format command (or press Ctrl-F) and choose a numeric format from the list. You can also control how many decimal places are displayed. Remember that this command only changes the way numbers appear — it has no effect on the actual value that is stored and used by formulas.

For some worksheets, you might like all numbers that you enter to look different than the standard General format. For example, you might want everything to have the currency format with two decimal places. You can change the default numeric format with the Options⇨Formats⇨Numeric Format command. Be aware, however, that changing the global numeric format does not affect cells that you already formatted.

Making lines and boxes

Use the Style⇨Line Drawing command to make lines and boxes.

If you want to underline text in a cell (not underline only the cell), use the Style⇨Font command and select Underlined. This command makes the underlining extend across the entire cell contents — even if the contents spill over to the next cell.

Changing fonts and font sizes

Use the Style⇨Font command.

Changing column widths

Select the Style⇨Column Width command (or press Ctrl-W) and enter a column width or use the arrow keys to adjust the column width. If you need to change the widths of several adjacent columns, use the Style⇨Block Size⇨Set Width command.

If you would like *all* of the columns in your worksheet to be a different width, use the Options⇨Formats⇨Global Width command. Note, however, that changing the global column width does not affect column widths that you already modified.

Changing label and number alignment

Use the Style⇨Alignment command (or press Ctrl-A) to change label and number alignment.

Shading cells

Use the Style⇨Shading command and choose either Gray or Black.

Graphing

This section deals with — you guessed it — commands you can use with graphs. Chapter 13 tells you more about graphing.

Making a graph

The easiest way to create a graph is to select **Graph**⇨**Fast Graph** command (or press Ctrl-G), and then select the block that contains the data to be graphed. The only time you can't use this command is if your data series are not all in a block of contiguous cells.

Changing the graph type

Select **Graph**⇨**Graph Type**, and then choose the desired graph.

Adding things to a graph

You can customize a graph by adding text, arrows, clip art, and other things by using the graph annotator. First, create the graph as usual. Then select the **Graph**⇨**Annotate** command.

Working with more than one graph

If your worksheet has more than one graph, you must give names to the graphs. Use the **Graph**⇨**Name**⇨**Create** command.

Printing

Care to guess the topic of this section? If you need a hint, check out Chapter 10 — where you'll learn even more.

Printing a worksheet

First, tell Quattro Pro what block you want to print by using the **Print**⇨**Block** command (you have to do this even if you want to print everything). Make sure the correct print destination is set using the **Print**⇨**Destination** command. Then use the **Print**⇨**Spreadsheet Print** command to send the job to the printer.

Adding a header or a footer

Use the **Print**⇨**Layout** command and enter the text and alignment codes you want for the header and/or footer in the appropriate fields.

Printing page numbers

You can put page numbers either in a header or a footer. Select **Print**⇨**Layout** and move to the Header text or Footer text field. Enter a pound sign (#) to represent page numbers. You can precede the pound sign with other text, *Page #*, for example. To center the page number, use |#, and to right justify the page number, use ||#.

Squeezing to fit on a page

Select the **Print**⇨**Print to Fit** command. If you want to adjust everything manually, use the **Print**⇨**Layout** command, and adjust the % Scaling factor (less than 100 for smaller, greater than 100 for larger).

Previewing your work

To get a sneak on-screen preview of how your work will look when it's printed, use the **Print**⇨**Destination**⇨**Screen Preview** command, followed by the **Print**⇨**Spreadsheet Print** command.

Printing graphs

Create your graph as usual. Select **Print**⇨**Graph Print**. If you have more than one graph defined, select the **Name** option to choose the graph. Then select **Go** to print the graph. If you prefer, you can preview your graph first by selecting **Destination**⇨**Screen Preview**.

Files and Worksheet Windows

The following procedures cover files and windows that contain worksheets. You can refer to Chapter 9 for more information on these topics.

Opening a file

Use the File⇨**Open** command to open a file that's on a disk. If you want to
replace the worksheet you're working on with another one, use File⇨**Retrieve**
instead.

Saving a file

Use the File⇨**Save** command (or press Ctrl-S) to save your work. If you want to
give the file a different name or save it to a different disk or directory, use
File⇨Save **As**.

Activating a particular worksheet

If you have more than one worksheet open, you can activate the one you want
to work with by choosing the Window⇨**Pick** command (or press Alt-0 [zero]).
Since each worksheet window is assigned a number, a faster way is to press
Alt-1 for the first window, Alt-2 for the second one, and so on.

Seeing more than one worksheet

If you have more than one worksheet loaded, you can view them all at once in
two different styles. The Window⇨**Tile** command arranges all of the worksheet
windows in a tiled pattern on your screen. The Window⇨**Stack** command
(available only in Text mode) stacks the windows neatly, one behind another. If
you want to get back to a full-screen view, activate the worksheet window you
want, and then choose Window⇨**Zoom** (or press Alt-F6).

Moving a window

You must be in Text mode to move a window.

The easiest way to move a worksheet window to another location on your
screen is to use a mouse. Simply click on a border, and then drag the window
where you want it.

If you don't have a mouse, select Window⇨**Move/Size**, and then use the arrow
keys to move the window around. Press Enter when you get the window to the
desired location.

Resizing a window

You must be in Text mode to resize windows.

The easiest way to change the size of a worksheet window is to use a mouse. Simply click on the small rectangle at the lower right corner of the window and drag the mouse until the window is the size you want.

If you don't have a mouse, select Window⇨Move/Size, and then press Shift and use the arrow keys to resize it. Press Enter when the window is the desired size.

To make a window fill the whole screen, select Window⇨Zoom. You can also use this same command to turn a full-screen window into a smaller window.

Splitting a window

Every worksheet window can be split into two panes — either horizontally or vertically. Splitting windows comes in handy when you want to look at two parts of a worksheet that are not near each other.

To split a window vertically, move the cell pointer to the cell where you want to split the window. Then select Window⇨Options⇨Vertical. Use F6 to jump between the panes. To get rid of the split, choose Window⇨Options⇨Clear.

To split a window horizontally, move the cell pointer to the cell where you want to split the window. Then select Window⇨Options⇨Horizontal. Use F6 to jump between the panes. To get rid of the split, choose Window⇨Options⇨Clear.

When a worksheet window is split vertically or horizontally, you can choose whether or not to synchronize the scrolling in the two panes. Do this with the Window⇨Options⇨Synch or the Window⇨Options⇨Unsync command.

Deleting a file from disk

To erase a file from a disk, select the File⇨Utilities⇨File Manager command to bring up a File Manager Window. Locate the file you want to erase and select it by pressing Shift-F7 (you can select multiple files, if you like). Then choose the File⇨Erase command to erase it or them.

Making a copy of a file

Select the File⇨Utilities⇨File Manager command to bring up a File Manager Window. Locate the file you want to copy and select it by pressing Shift-F7 (you can select more than one). Then choose the File⇨Copy command to copy the file. Next, specify the disk or directory that you want to copy the file(s) to and select the Edit⇨Paste command.

Miscellaneous

I couldn't find a place to put this stuff, so I created a catch-all category.

Exiting temporarily to DOS

If you ever need to perform a quick task in DOS (such as erase some files), you don't have to exit Quattro Pro. Although you can use Quattro Pro's File Manager for many routine DOS tasks, some people find it easier to use DOS commands directly.

To temporarily exit to DOS, select File⇨Utilities⇨DOS Shell. You see the standard DOS prompt, and you can do most things you normally do in DOS. When you're finished, type **EXIT** at the DOS prompt; you return to Quattro Pro exactly where you left off.

Finding a circular reference

If you have a formula that refers to itself (either directly or indirectly), Quattro Pro displays CIRC in the status line. Normally, this is a sign that something is wrong with one or more of your formulas. To find out which cell is causing the problem, select Tools⇨Audit⇨Circular. This command brings you into a different screen that shows the cells involved in the circular reference. Usually, you can locate the problem cell and fix the formula.

Changing screen colors

There's no need to settle for the boring default screen colors. Use the Options⇨Colors command to change the colors to reflect your own tastes. You'll find that you can change just about everything on the Quattro Pro screen. If you want your color choices to be in effect the next time you use Quattro Pro, make sure you use the **O**ptions⇨**U**pdate command before you quit.

Changing the clock display

If you don't like to be reminded how slowly time passes when you're at work, you can get rid of the clock display at the bottom of the screen. Use the **O**ptions⇨**O**ther⇨**C**lock⇨**N**one command.

Stopping the infernal beeping

If the guy in the next cubicle is complaining about all the beeping coming out of your area, you can turn off Quattro Pro's beep with the **O**ptions⇨**O**ther⇨**S**tartup⇨**B**eep command. Disabling the beep is also handy if you don't want your office-mates to know how many errors you make.

Getting a bird's-eye view

If you have lots of stuff in a worksheet, you can get a quick overview of how your worksheet's laid out by using the **W**indow⇨**O**ptions⇨**M**ap View command. This displays *n* for numeric entries, *l* for labels, + for formulas, *g* for inserted graphs, - (hyphen) for link formulas, and *c* for circular references.

The best way to use this command is to split the window into two panes, and then enter map view in one of the panes. Make sure that the scrolling for the two windows is synchronized. That way, you can see the map in one pane and the cell contents in the other.

Leaving Quattro Pro

You can get out of Quattro Pro by using the **F**ile⇨**E**xit command (or by pressing Alt-X). If you have any unsaved work, Quattro Pro lets you know.

Part V:

Mini-Chapters
with Maxi-Info

In This Part...

For reasons that are mainly historical, all of the books in this ... *For Dummies* series have chapters with lists in them. Since I'm a sucker for tradition, I went along with this and prepared several top-10 lists. You'll find lists of tips, shortcuts, the 10 commandments of Quatto Pro, and a list of common error messages (and instructions on what to do when you see them).

Chapter 20
10 Good Habits You Should Acquire

I once knew a woman named Carter
Who longed to work smarter not harder.
So she pasted an ad
"Quattro Tips to be had —
Paying a dollar and quarter!"

• •

Following are 10 habits that all beginning Quattro Pro users should try to form:

Use the SpeedBars and Shortcut Keys

I've found that many people completely ignore all of the ease-of-use features that spreadsheet designers work so hard to include (and their ad agencies charge so much to promote). Using the menu system for simple things is not only slower, it makes it easier to make mistakes. But don't forget, you need to have a mouse in order to use the SpeedBars.

Don't Save Your Worksheet Files to a Floppy Disk

Always use your hard disk as your primary file storage place. File saves and retrieves are much faster, and hard disks are less likely to go bad than floppies. However, you *should* use floppies to store backup copies of all of your important files.

Take Advantage of the Multi-Page Notebooks

If you have experience using a non 3-D product such as earlier versions of Quattro Pro or Lotus 1-2-3, you may tend to ignore the extra worksheet pages (old habits are difficult to change). However, using these is a great way to organize your work, and jumping to a particular part of your worksheet is as easy as clicking a tab.

Use Cell and Block Names Whenever Possible

If you have some cells or blocks that are used a lot in formulas, you should take a few minutes and give the cells or blocks names. That way, you can use the name (rather than an obscure address) in formulas, making the formulas easier to read and understand. A side benefit is that you can use the F5 (Goto) key to quickly jump to a named cell or block.

Work with More Than One Worksheet at a Time

When you need to access or look at another worksheet file, there's no need to close your current worksheet. Just use File⇨Open (rather than File⇨Retrieve) to open another worksheet while your current worksheet stays active. But if you're getting short on memory, close down all worksheets that you don't really need.

Take Advantage of Quattro Pro's On-Line Help

Great as this book is, it doesn't tell you *everything* about Quattro Pro. If you get stuck, your first line of attack should be to press F1 and see what the on-line help has to say. Often, you can solve your problem by going no further than that.

Don't Be Afraid to Try New Things

As you know, there are dozens of weird commands lurking within the bowels of the Quattro Pro menu system. Don't be afraid to try them out to see what happens. But be on the safe side and have a non-important worksheet open when you do so. Also, make sure you have Undo enabled just in case the command does something drastic.

Don't Waste Time Printing

All too often, people print draft after draft of their worksheets, making only minor changes in between printing. A better approach is to use Print Preview. This feature shows you exactly how your printed output will look, and you can zoom in to examine parts more closely.

Don't Go Overboard with Fancy Formatting

I know that it's very tempting to spend hours trying to get your worksheet to look perfect. It's actually kind of fun to experiment with fonts, type sizes, shading, borders, and the like. But every thing you do is probably not worthy of this much attention. Unless you have lots of time on your hands, it's better to focus on content rather than appearance.

Don't Be Afraid of Macros

Once you get comfortable using the basic features of Quattro Pro, you might want to explore the world of macros. Even a rudimentary knowledge of macros can save you lots of time when you're doing repetitive tasks.

Chapter 21
Top 10 (or so) Shortcuts

A man who was known as Bob
Created spreadsheet files for the mob.
He did it the long way,
Which was also the wrong way.
Ignoring shortcuts cost him his job.

Here, in one handy list, are all of the shortcut keys that every Quattro Pro user should be familiar with.

Even a 5-year old can tell that there are more than 10 shortcuts listed here, but I needed to make the chapter title correspond with the section. By the way, I left off some of the best shortcuts of all — those found on the SpeedBars. I'm assuming you know about these (or you have enough common sense to refer to Chapter 14, where they are listed for you).

Shortcut	Purpose
Ctrl-A	Aligns labels or values in a cell
Ctrl-C	Starts the process of copying a cell or block
Ctrl-D	The easy way to put a date into a cell
Ctrl-E	Erases a block (Del does the same for a cell)
Ctrl-F	Lets you change the way a number appears (its numerical format)
Ctrl-G	The express route to creating a graph when the data is in a block of contiguous cells
Ctrl-I	Lets you insert one or more new rows or columns
Ctrl-M	Gets you started on your way to moving a cell or block
Ctrl-N	Repeats a forward search that you specified previously
Ctrl-P	Repeats a backward search that you specified previously
Ctrl-R	Lets you move or resize a worksheet window
Ctrl-S	Saves the worksheet you're working on
Ctrl-T	Arranges all worksheet windows like floor tiles
Ctrl-W	Lets you adjust a column's width
Ctrl-X	The fast way to get out of Quattro Pro and move on to something more exciting

Shortcut	Purpose
Alt-0	Lets you pick a worksheet to activate (relevant only when more than one worksheet is loaded into memory)
F1	Accesses some friendly on-line help
F2	Lets you start editing the contents of the current cell
F4	When you edit a cell reference, cycles among all the possible relative/absolute combinations
F5	Lets you select a cell or named block to jump to
F6	Moves you to the other pane when the worksheet is split in two
F9	Forces the worksheet to recalculate itself (relevant only if recalculation is set to manual); when you're editing a cell, converts a formula into its value
F10	Displays the current graph (assuming a graph has been created)

Chapter 22
The 10 Commandments of Quattro Pro

There was a man with a long white beard
Who was generally quite revered.
He said "I have ten rules to adhere to,
Please keep them quite near you"
And everyone thought he was weird.

Here, direct from Mount Sinai, are the 10 Commandments of Quattro Pro.

1. Thou shalt always make a backup copy of every important file and storeth this file in a safe place.

2. Thou shalt use the display mode (Text or WYSIWYG) appropriate to thy computer and needs.

3. Thou shalt obey thy program's error messages.

4. Thou shalt check thy work carefully before making decisions based on a Quattro Pro worksheet.

5. Thou shalt honor thy SpeedBar and shortcut keys.

6. Thou shalt not steal the program from others.

7. Thou shalt save thy file to disk before doing anything drastic.

8. Thou shalt keep Undo turned on (memory permitting) and forget not to use it.

9. Thou shalt seek help from thy local wise man (or wise woman) when necessary.

10. Thou shalt not be afraid to experiment with thine own spreadsheet, and thou shalt never experiment with another's work.

Chapter 23
Top 10 (or so) Error Messages

There was an old hippie named Reed
Who spent most of his time smoking weed.
When he messed up his work
Quattro called him a jerk
After showing messages he never did heed.

It doesn't take a beginning user long before he or she is confronted with an error message from Quattro Pro. Usually, these messages take the form of a red pop-up window (assuming you have a color monitor) that's accompanied by a beep. Often, the error is obvious, but sometimes you may have no idea what's causing the problem.

This chapter has a list of the most common error messages you're likely to encounter. Actually, I left out some of the common ones that are very obvious. For example, the error message *Missing right parenthesis* is pretty self-explanatory. And yes, I realize that there are more than 10 error messages listed here.

Whenever you get an error message, you can press F1 to get an explanation of what the message means.

File not found

This message means that Quattro Pro could not locate the file name you entered manually. The file must be in the current directory. The best way to avoid this is to point to the filename with the arrow keys or mouse after selecting the File⇨Open or File⇨Retrieve command.

Incomplete formula

This one's easy. You probably ended a formula with a plus sign, minus sign, or some other arithmetic operator.

Invalid cell, block, or page

This message means that your formula refers to something that doesn't exist. The most likely cause is a typo — you may have misspelled a block name or entered a cell address incorrectly. Look in the input line. Quattro Pro puts the insertion point at the place where it found the error. You'll also get this error message if you begin a label with a number and forget to insert a label prefix character (', ", or ^).

Invalid character in file name

You specified a filename, either when trying to load a file or save a file, that Quattro Pro does not like. Remember, a filename cannot contain any spaces, asterisks, or question marks.

Missing arguments

You see this message if you enter an @function in a formula and do not provide enough arguments. Quattro Pro is very picky about this, so double-check the syntax of the @function and fix your mistake.

No block defined

This one shows up most often when you try to print your worksheet without using the **Print**⇨**Block** command to tell Quattro Pro what you want to print. It also appears when you use other commands for which you need to specify a block first.

Not enough memory for [action]

The thing you're trying to do takes more memory than you have available. Free up some memory by closing any worksheets that you don't need. Also, you might want to have someone check your system configuration to make sure that you have as much free memory available as possible.

Out of memory

This is another version of the previous error. This message occurs when you're in the middle of something — usually trying to copy a very large block. See the suggestions listed in the preceding.

Printer I/O error

The most likely cause for this is that your printer is not turned on or it's not set to "on-line." Check out your printer and try again.

Undo is disabled. cannot undo

This means that you tried to correct a mistake by invoking Undo, but you did not have Undo turned on. You can enable Undo with the Options⇨Other⇨Undo⇨Enable command. To turn it on permanently, use the Options⇨Update command to save your configuration choices (in this case, enabling Undo).

Unknown @function

The most likely cause for this is a typo. Check the spelling of the @function and try again.

Appendix A
Installing Quattro Pro

Before you can use Quattro Pro — or any software for that matter — you must install the software on your computer. When you install software, you simply copy files from floppy disks to your hard disk in such a way that the program works when you execute the program. Most software (including Quattro Pro) includes a special Install program that does this for you automatically.

If you're lucky, Quattro Pro is already installed on the computer that you'll be using. (In most large companies, there are whole departments full of nerds who specialize in these types of tasks.) In smaller companies, you're often on your own. But you can usually find some sort of computer guru who will be happy to help you out (and at the same time demonstrate just how smart he or she is).

If You Have to Install Quattro Pro Yourself

If you're sitting at your computer and holding a shrink-wrapped box that contains Quattro Pro, you're probably going to have to install the sucker yourself. If you've never done such a thing before, don't be afraid to ask for help from someone more experienced. However, installing Quattro Pro is not a difficult process if you can follow simple instructions and know how to insert a floppy disk into a disk drive. Obviously, if Quattro Pro is already installed, you can skip this appendix (unless you thrive on redundancy).

Pre-Flight Checkout

Checking out a few details before you install any software is usually a good idea:

  ✔ **Make sure you have the right equipment**. Quattro Pro works on just about any PC as long as it has a hard disk. Most computers nowadays have a hard disk, but if you're unfortunate enough to be stuck with a system that has only floppy drives, you can't use Quattro Pro until you invest in a hard drive or buy a new computer.

✔ **Make sure you have the right size disks.** Some software packages include both 5 ¹/₄- and 3 ¹/₂-inch disks. Others have only one size or the other. Make sure that you have a disk drive that can handle the disks in your Quattro Pro box. If not, call borland, and they'll send you the right disks. Or you can get someone with both size floppy drives to copy the disks to the format that your system can use.

✔ **Make sure that you have enough room on your hard disk to hold the program and its files**. The amount of space you need varies with different versions of Quattro Pro. Check the box to see how much disk space you need. You'll need about 6MB of free space on your hard disk to install Quattro Pro Version 5. If you don't have enough room on your hard disk, you'll have to delete some files to make room.

If you don't know what you're doing, I strongly suggest that you seek assistance before you start deleting files. Otherwise, you may delete files your system needs to work properly.

Installing Quattro Pro

To install Quattro Pro, follow these steps:

1. Turn on your computer and make sure you're at the DOS prompt, which looks like

```
C:>
```

2. Tear the shrink wrap off the Quattro Pro box and dig around until you find the diskettes. Tear the shrink wrap off the diskettes (software companies just love shrink wrap) and find the disk labeled Disk 1.

3. Insert Disk 1 in your disk drive.

4. Type **a:install** if you're installing the program from drive A. Type **b:install** if you're using drive B.

5. Follow the instructions on the screen. You'll need to specify which drive you're installing from and which drive and directory your installing to. In most cases, you can just accept the defaults proposed by the Install program.

   Quattro Pro tells you when you need to insert the other disks. You'll also have to answer a few questions about your equipment and enter the serial number (which is printed on the first disk).

   If you find all of this confusing, refer to the Quattro Pro manual. It'll tell you everything that you need to know (and more).

How much disk space is left?

To see how much disk space you have, type **CHKDSK** at the DOS C:> prompt. You will see something like the following (but the numbers will be different):

```
C:\>chkdsk
Volume DriveC  created Nov 21, 1991 2:57p
33454080 bytes total disk space
   57344 bytes in 5 hidden files
   61440 bytes in 20 directories
29855744 bytes in 702 user files
    2048 bytes in bad sectors
 3463168 bytes available on disk

  651264 bytes total memory
  515456 bytes free
```

The line you're interested in is the one that says *bytes available on disk.* In the example shown, the computer has 3,463,168 bytes available (almost 3 ½MB). The system in this example has plenty of space for Quattro Pro.

With Quattro Pro installed, you're now ready to tackle the rest of this book. Chapter 1 is a good place to start.

Appendix B
Don't Read This: It's Just a Function Reference

My editor calls me and rages
"Write more words to earn all your wages!"
So out of sheer deference
I made up this reference
To fill up some more of these pages.

In This Appendix

▶ A list of all the @functions available in Quattro Pro, categorized by my arbitrary classification system

▶ A brief description of what each function does

This appendix has a complete list of the @functions (and their arguments) and a short description of what the @function displays or returns when it's evaluated. If you find one that looks like it may do the trick, check it out in the on-line help system for more information about its arguments and maybe even an example.

Most people can get by just fine using only a handful of Quattro Pro @functions. But you never know when someone might ask you to calculate the hypotenuse of a right triangle, and you'll need a special @function. At the very least, skimming through this stuff will give you a feel for Quattro Pro's potential.

The categories I use are based on "normal" usage of Quattro Pro. A function that's listed in the Virtually Useless category is usually not used by normal users — but it may be absolutely essential for someone else. So don't take these categories too seriously. I also grouped functions that are useful for particular users together (that is, trig functions and financial functions) and made no attempt to classify these in terms of usefulness.

Very Useful Functions

@ABS (x)

Returns the absolute value of *x*. If *x* is negative, the result is positive.

@AVG (list)

Returns the average (or arithmetic mean) of *list*.

@COUNT (list)

Returns the number of nonblank cells in *list*.

@DATE (year, month, day)

Returns a date, in the form of a serial number for *year, month*, and *day*.

@FIND (substring, string, startpos)

Returns the character position of the first occurrence of *substring* in *string*, beginning at position *startpos*. The first character is considered position 0.

@HLOOKUP (x, block, row)

Returns the contents of the cell *row* number of rows beneath *x* in *block*.

@IF (cond, trueexp, falseexp)

Returns *trueexp* if *cond* is true, *falseexp* if *cond* is false.

@INT (x)

Returns the integer (that is, whole number) portion of *x*.

@LEFT (*string,num*)

Returns the first *num* characters in *string*.

@LENGTH (*string*)

Returns the number of characters in *string* (including blanks).

@LOWER (*string*)

Returns *string*, converted to all lowercase letters. Numbers and non-alphabetical characters are not affected.

@MAX (*list*)

Returns the maximum value in *list*.

@MID (*string,startpos,num*)

Returns *num* characters from *string*, beginning with the character in *startpos*. The first position in the string is considered position 0.

@MIN (*list*)

Returns the minimum value in *list*.

@MOD (*x,y*)

Returns the remainder when x is divided by y.

@NOW

Returns a serial number that represents the date and time when the worksheet was last calculated.

@PROPER (string)

Returns *string*, converted so that the first character in each word is uppercase and the other letters are lowercase. Numbers and non-alphabetical characters are not affected.

@RAND

Returns a random number between 0 and 1 (inclusive).

@RIGHT (string,num)

Returns the last *num* characters in *string*.

@ROUND (x,num)

Returns *x*, rounded to the number of digits specified with *num*.

@SQRT (x)

Returns the square root of *x*.

@STRING (x,num)

Returns the numeric value of *x* as a string, with *num* decimal places.

@SUM (list)

Returns the sum of the values in *list*.

@SUMPRODUCT (block1,block2)

Returns the sum of the products of corresponding values in *block1* and *block2*.

@TODAY

Returns the serial number that represents the current date.

@UPPER (string)

Returns *string*, converted to all uppercase letters. Numbers and non-alphabetical characters are not affected.

@VLOOKUP (x, block, column)

Returns the contents of the cell *column* number of columns to the right of *x* in *block*.

Semi-Useful Functions

@CHAR (code)

Returns the character that corresponds to ASCII code number *code*.

@CHOOSE (number, list)

Returns the value in *list* in the position of *number*.

@CLEAN (string)

Returns only the printable characters in *string*. All of the strange characters are eliminated.

@CODE (string)

Returns the ASCII code for the first character in *string*.

@COLS (block)

Returns the number of columns in *block*.

@DATEVALUE (datestring)

Returns a date serial number resulting from *datestring* (a string that looks like a date).

@DAY (serialnumber)

Returns the day of the month from a date *serialnumber*.

@ERR

Returns the value ERR.

@EXACT (string 1, string2)

Returns 1 (or true) if *string1* is identical to *string2*. Otherwise, returns 0 (or false).

@EXP (x)

Returns the mathematical constant *e* raised to the *x*th power.

@FALSE

Returns the logical value 0.

@HOUR (serialnumber)

Returns the hour of the day from a date *serialnumber*.

@INDEX (block,column,row)

Returns the contents of the cell located at the specified *column* and *row* in *block*.

@ISERR (x)

Returns 1 (or true) if *x* is ERR. Otherwise, returns 0 (or false).

@ISNA (x)

Returns 1 (or true) if *x* is NA. Otherwise, returns 0 (or false).

@ISNUMBER (x)

Returns 1 (or true) if *x* is a numeric value. Otherwise, returns 0 (or false).

@ISSTRING (x)

Returns 1 (or true) if *x* is a string. Otherwise, returns 0 (or false).

@MINUTE (serialnumber)

Returns the minute of the hour from a date *serialnumber*.

@MONTH (serialnumber)

Returns the month of the year from a date *serialnumber*.

@N (block)

Returns the numeric value of the upper left cell in *block*. Returns 0 if it's a label or blank.

@NA

Returns the value NA.

@REPEAT (string,num)

Returns *string*, repeated *num* times.

@REPLACE (string,startpos,num,newstring)

Removes *num* characters from *string*, beginning with *startpos*, and inserts *newstring* in its place. The first character is considered position 0.

@ROWS (block)

Returns the number of rows in *block*.

@S (block)

Returns the string value of the upper left cell in *block*. Empty string if it's a value.

@SECOND (serialnumber)

Returns the second of the minute from a date *serialnumber*.

@TIME (hr,min,sec)

Returns a time serial number.

@TIMEVALUE (timestring)

Returns a time serial number resulting from *timestring* (a string that looks like a time).

The 5th Wave

By Rich Tennant

Re·al Pro·gram·mers

Real Programmers either smoke two packs of cigarettes a day, or they don't smoke at all.

@TRIM (string)

Returns *string*, but without any leading, trailing, or consecutive spaces.

@TRUE

Returns the logical value 1.

@VALUE (string)

Returns the numeric value of *string* (which looks like a value).

@YEAR (serialnumber)

Returns the year from a date serial number.

Virtually Worthless Functions

@@ (cell)

Returns the contents of the cell specified by the cell address stored in *cell* (an indirect reference).

@CELL (attribute, block)

Returns the specified *attribute* of *block*. See the on-line help for a list of attributes.

@CELLINDEX (attribute, block, column, row)

Returns the specified *attribute* of the cell in the *column* and *row* offset of *block*. See the on-line help for a list of attributes.

@CELLPOINTER (attribute)

Returns the specified *attribute* of the current cell.

@CURVALUE (generalaction, specificaction)

Returns the current value of the specified menu command.

@FILEEXISTS (filename)

Returns 1 (or true) if *filename* is found on disk. Otherwise, returns 0 (or false).

@HEXTONUM (string)

Returns the decimal value of *string* (which looks like a hexadecimal number).

@ISAAF (addin, function)

Returns 1 (or true) if *addin* is loaded and *function* is a defined @function. Otherwise, returns 0 (or false).

@ISAPP (addin)

Returns 1 (or true) if *addin* is loaded. Otherwise, returns 0 (or false).

@LN (x)

Returns the log (base *e*) of *x*.

@LOG (x)

Returns the log (base 10) of *x*.

@MEMAVAIL

Returns the amount of conventional memory available when the worksheet was last calculated.

@MEMEMSAVAIL

Returns the amount of expanded (EMS) memory available when the worksheet was last calculated.

@NUMTOHEX (x)

Returns the hexadecimal value of *x*.

@SHEETS (block)

Returns the number of pages in *block*. (This function is not available in Version 4.)

@STD (list)

Returns the population standard deviation of the non-blank values in *list*.

@STDS (list)

Returns the sample standard deviation of the non-blank values in *list*.

@VAR (list)

Returns the population variance of the non-blank values in *list*.

@VARS (list)

Returns the sample variance of the non-blank values in *list*.

@VERSION

Returns the version number of Quattro Pro.

Functions for Financial Types

@CTERM (rate, futurevalue, presentvalue)

Returns the number of compounding periods for a loan.

@DDB (cost,salvage,life,period)

Returns Double-declining depreciation allowance.

@FV (payment,rate,periods)

Returns the future value of an annuity.

@FVAL (rate,periods,payment)

Returns the future value of an annuity. This is an improved version of @FV.

@IPAYMT (rate,period,periods,presentvalue)

Returns the portion of a loan payment that goes towards interest.

@IRATE (periods,payment,presentvalue)

Returns the periodic interest rate for a loan. This is an improved version of @RATE.

@IRR (guess,block)

Returns the Internal rate of return for values stored in *block*. *guess* is an initial guess.

@NPER (rate,payment,presentvalue)

Returns the number of periods for a loan.

@NPV (rate,block)

Returns Net present value.

@PAYMT (*rate,periods,presentvalue*)

Returns the payment amount for a loan. This is an improved version of @PMT.

@PMT (*presentvalue,rate,periods*)

Returns the payment amount for a loan.

@PPAYMT (*rate,period,periods,presentvalue*)

Returns the portion of a loan payment that goes towards principal.

@PV (*payment,rate,periods*)

Returns the present value of an annuity.

@PVAL (*rate,periods,payment*)

Returns the present value of an annuity.

@RATE (*futurevalue,presentvalue,periods*)

Returns the periodic interest rate.

@SLN (*cost,salvage,life*)

Returns the straight-line depreciation allowance.

@SYD (*cost,salvage,life,period*)

Returns the sum-of-the-years-digits depreciation allowance.

@TERM (payment,rate,futurevalue)

Returns the number of payment periods of an investment.

Functions for Database Mavens

@DAVG (block,column,criteria)

Returns the average of the values in *column* of *block* that meet criteria stored in *criteria*.

@DCOUNT (block,column,criteria)

Returns the number of values in *column* of *block* that meet criteria stored in *criteria*.

@DMAX (block,column,criteria)

The maximum of the values in *column* of *block* that meet criteria stored in *criteria*.

@DMIN (block,column,criteria)

The minimum of the values in *column* of *block* that meet criteria stored in *criteria*.

@DSTD (block,column,criteria)

The population standard deviation of the values in *column* of *block* that meet criteria stored in *criteria*.

@DSTDS (block,column,criteria)

Returns the sample standard deviation of the values in *column* of *block* that meet criteria stored in *criteria*.

@DSUM (block,column,criteria)

Returns the sum of the values in *column* of *block* that meet criteria stored in *criteria*.

@DVAR (block,column,criteria)

Returns the variance of the values in *column* of *block* that meet criteria stored in *criteria*.

@DVARS (block,column,criteria)

Returns the sample variance of the values in *column* of *block* that meet criteria stored in *criteria*.

Functions for Triangle Freaks

@ACOS (x)

Returns the arccosine of x.

@ASIN (x)

Returns the arcsine of x.

@ATAN (x)

Returns the two-quadrant arctangent of x.

@ATAN2 (x,y)

Returns the four-quadrant arccosine of y/x.

@COS (x)

Returns the cosine of x.

@DEGREES (x)

Returns the number of degrees in x radians.

@PI

Returns the value of pi.

@RADIANS (x)

Returns the number of radians in x degrees.

@SIN (x)

Returns the sine of x.

@TAN (x)

Returns the tangent of angle x.

Appendix C
How to Act Like You Know All about Computers

There once was a girl named Yvette
Who tried to impress everybody she met
She learned high-tech words
And then spoke to some nerds
Who knew that Yvette was all wet.

. . . .

In This Appendix

▶ The ultimate faker's guide to computers and software

▶ A crash course in some of the hottest topics computer people talk about

▶ Lots of words that you may hear if you hang around with PC-types

▶ Things you can say to make people think you know what you're talking about

. . . .

Let's face it, computers are here to stay. By reading this book, you've at least demonstrated that you're willing to take a few baby steps to jump on this technological bandwagon. On the other hand, you're probably not willing to spend all your free time reading thick computer magazines, pushing a shopping cart through computer superstores, running up your phone bill by connecting to the on-line services, and attending user group meetings populated with geekoids. In other words, you're quite willing to participate in the computer revolution, but you prefer to hang out on the sidelines.

You'll find lots of computer information here, and most of it is not essential to using your computer to run Quattro Pro. The goal is to give you a semi-firm foundation in computers and computer-speak so that when you hear people talking about computers, at least a few of the words will sound familiar.

This information is valid as of 1993. But things change rapidly, so if you're reading this book in 1997, it should be good for a few nostalgic laughs.

Disclaimer: This chapter contains dozens of ready-made quotes that you can use at the next cocktail party you attend. The author is not responsible for any embarrassment or ridicule you might suffer as a result of doing so. If, after using one of these quotes, someone asks you to explain what you mean, my suggestion is to excuse yourself and go to the bathroom until that person leaves the party.

Computers

Okay, the basics: A computer is the hardware thingamajig that you use to run software. The computer you use can only be used by one person at a time, so it's called a personal computer, or PC. Your computer probably has three main pieces: the computer unit itself (which contains lots of other parts), a display monitor (the thing that looks like a T.V. screen), and a keyboard (the thing that looks like a typewriter). There may be some other things attached, called peripherals (described later).

Parts of a computer

Here's where I go into more detail about the parts of a computer. Read it carefully; it will be on the final exam.

If you ever find yourself with nothing to do on a rainy afternoon, you might want to open up your computer and take a look inside. It's usually just a matter of removing a few screws and sliding the metal case off. Check your computer manual — it always tells you how to open the thing (but rarely tells you how to put it back together). Besides a surprising amount of dust and maybe even some cobwebs, you'll find lots of interesting things inside.

Power supply

The big squarish-looking thing with a fan is the power supply. This plugs into the wall and supplies power to everything inside. The hum that you hear when you turn on the computer is the sound of the fan. If it weren't for the fan, your PC would be completely quiet (except when you access a disk or make an error in Quattro Pro).

Motherboard

At the bottom of the inside of your computer is a printed circuit board with a bunch of electronic-looking gizmos sticking out. This is the motherboard, and it contains all the circuitry that makes a computer a computer.

Good computers always cost $3,300

In my lifetime, I've purchased four computers for my personal use: An original model IBM PC, an 80286 AT clone, a 386/25 clone, and a 486/33 clone. Interestingly, each one set me back about $3,300. The point of all this is that technology continues to march forward, but the price/performance ratio for the consumer continues to improve. I can't wait to see what my $3,300 gets me in 1998.

Your computer's central processor unit (CPU) is located on the motherboard. It essentially determines how fast and powerful your computer is. The CPU in your computer is probably made by Intel and is probably labeled 80286, 80386, or 80486. The motherboard also contains chips that hold your computer's memory. Also on the motherboard are a number of slots. Some of these slots have expansion cards inserted in them.

Math coprocessor

Some computers (notably 80286s and 80386s) have a chip on their motherboard known as a math coprocessor. This chip speeds up mathematical operations quite a bit and can make spreadsheets like Quattro Pro recalculate results lightning fast (reducing your coffee break time considerably). If your computer is an 80486, a math coprocessor is built right in to the CPU. If you find yourself waiting for large spreadsheets to recalculate, you might consider popping one of these puppies into your PC.

Expansion cards

Your computer probably has several expansion cards. These cards stick out of the back of your computer and often have jacks into which you plug wires and cords. Some expansion cards are necessary for the computer to operate (for example, a video card), and some give it added powers (such as a sound card). You probably have at least one expansion card that supplies your system with serial and parallel ports to connect a modem, printer, or some other device.

Ports

Computers communicate with external devices (such as printers, modems, and mice) by using ports. There are two types of ports: serial and parallel. A *serial port* sends and receives information in a single stream of bits. These ports are sometimes known as COM ports. Modems, mice, and some printers used serial ports.

A *parallel port* sends and receives information in a bunch of different streams (in parallel). Parallel ports communicate faster than serial ports. Printers use parallel ports.

Memory

Every computer has memory, which usually ranges from 640 kilobytes, up to 8 or more megabytes. 640 Kilobytes of memory is roughly equivalent to 640,000 characters. Eight megabytes works out to about 8 million characters. The more memory you have, the better off you'll be.

There are three types of memory:

- ✔ **Conventional memory**. Normal memory, also known as the lower 640K.

- ✔ **Extended memory**. Memory above 640K, used by Windows and some non-Windows programs.

- ✔ **Expanded memory**. Special memory above 640K used by some non-Windows programs such as Quattro Pro.

Disks

Every computer has at least one disk drive. Most computers have two, and many computers have three. There are two types of disks: hard disks and floppy disks. Both types store information as a series of magnetic impulses.

A hard disk is fixed inside your computer, and you normally can't remove it — although there *is* such a thing as a removable hard disk. Hard disks store a large amount of information, and they transfer the information very quickly. Hard disks come in a variety of sizes. The smallest is usually about 40MB, and you can get them up to a gigabyte or more (but these are outrageously expensive and more storage than the average person needs). Your hard disk is usually known as drive C. You can have more than one hard disk in a PC, and a single hard disk can be partitioned so that it appears to be more than one disk.

Floppy disks are removable and come in two sizes: 3 ½ inch and 5 ¼ inch. Contrary to popular belief, 3 ½ inch disks are not floppy; rather they have

---

Of Ks, megs, and gigabytes

You can't be around computers for long without being exposed to some new measurement units. Computer memory and disk storage come in different capacities. Here's the lowdown on all this:

- ✔ **Bit.** The smallest unit, either on or off

- ✔ **Byte.** Eight bits

- ✔ **Kilobyte.** 1,000 bytes (abbreviated as K)

- ✔ **Megabyte.** A million bytes, or 1,000K (abbreviated as MB)

- ✔ **Gigabyte.** A billion bytes, or 1,000MB (abbreviated as Gbyte)

sturdy plastic cases. The disk inside, however, is quite floppy. Floppy disks come in different capacities. 3 ½ inch floppies can store either 740K or 1.44K. 5 ¼ inch floppies can store either 360K or 1.2K. Your first floppy disk drive is known as drive A. If you have another floppy drive, it's called drive B.

Monitor

Your monitor displays information that your software wants you to see. There are many types and sizes of monitors, and they vary in resolution — which is how many pixels they have. The more pixels, the higher the resolution, and the higher the resolution, the better the picture. Your monitor works in conjunction with your video card, and the combination of these two determine exactly how the information looks. The standard monitor in use today is VGA (640 pixels wide by 400 pixels high), although SuperVGA (800 x 600) is also quite common.

Keyboard

Your keyboard is the main way that you give information to your software. There are a number of different keyboard layouts available, and most people don't really give much thought to it. Keyboards also feel different; some people prefer "clicky" keys, while others like a more mushy feel.

Categories of computers

PCs and PC/XTs

The original IBM PC first came out in 1982. Not too long after, the PC/XT came out. It was essentially the same, except it had a small hard disk. These computers are based on the 8088 microchip and are very slow by today's standards. They are okay for simple word processing and minor league spreadsheets, but that's about it.

ATs (80286s)

I remember when I saw my first AT. I couldn't believe how fast the sucker was — but then I was used to the original model PC. There are still lots of computers around that use an 80286 chip, but they're rapidly being retired in favor of 386 and 486 machines. As Microsoft Windows continues to gain popularity, 286 machines will become even more rare.

80386s

These computers were once the envy of nearly everyone who knew anything about PCs. Nowadays they're pretty common and are considered standard fare. They differ from 286s in that they can do 32-bit operations, rather than 16-bit operations. They come in different speeds, which is expressed in megahertz

(MHz). Typically, 386s come in 16, 20, 25, and 40 MHz models. So you might, for example, have a 386/25 system that uses an 80386 chip running at 25 MHz. Some 386 systems have an SX after the numbers (for example, a 386SX/20). These are usually a bit slower than the non-SX versions.

80486s

As I write this, 486s are the fastest PCs available. They come in a variety of processor speeds, ranging from 25 MHz to 66 MHz. For example, your system might be a 486/33, which means it has an 80486 CPU that runs at 33 MHz. If you're buying a new computer, go for a 486.

Pentium

As I was writing this, systems based on Intel's Pentium chip were just being announced. Pentium is actually the successor to the 80486 and could have been called the 80586. In any case, computers based on these new chips will be *very* fast and will start out being *very* expensive.

Notebook computers

Notebook computers come with all different types of processors. What sets them apart from standard desktop computers is their diminutive size — not much larger than a notebook. Notebooks usually run on batteries, and people on planes like to show them off. Notebooks have gotten very powerful over the years, and some are real screamers — but they're much more expensive than equally powerful desktop models.

Things you can say about computers

✔ "I ran into some poor guy today who was actually trying to run Windows on a 386SX with only 2 meg of RAM." (People in the know *never* say "megabyte" when "meg" will do.)

✔ "You need to reconfigure extended memory as expanded memory. I'd get myself a good memory manager if I were you."

✔ "Computer parts are commodities. If you know what you're doing, you can buy the parts and put together a computer much cheaper than buying one already made."

✔ "One of my favorite pastimes is to go into a computer store and intimidate the clerks."

✔ "What to do with your old XT? Well, I need a door stop for my office. I'll give you five bucks."

The age-old question: Mac or PC?

When people start thinking about buying a computer for home, someone will invariably suggest that they get a Macintosh. Somebody else will claim that a PC clone is the way to go. In fact, people argue for hours over the relative merits of these two types of machines, and — like religion and politics — nobody ever changes his mind. What's the difference, and does it matter?

A Macintosh (or Mac) is known for its ease of use. It's a completely graphical computer; it shows different type fonts and sizes and uses lots of pictures and icons. A PC that runs Microsoft Windows can do all of this. Macs tend to cost more than PCs. PCs are common in most businesses. Macs are common among graphic artists and musicians. That's about it. So stop your arguing.

> ✔ "Memory's cheap. If you're running Windows, there's no reason to have less than 8 meg of RAM."

> ✔ "My new system has a 2-meg SVGA card with maximum display of 1280x1024, capable of 65,536 colors. My 17-inch monitor has .28 dot pitch with a horizontal frequency of 30 to 65 KHz. What've you got?"

> ✔ "You want my recommendation? Don't buy a system with a hard drive less than 300 meg."

Computer Peripherals

Computer peripherals are things that are attached to the computer and aren't absolutely essential to the computer's basic operation. For example, a modem (not essential) is a peripheral, but a display screen (essential) is not. To some people, peripherals are toys; to others, they're confusing pieces of junk that never work right.

Following is a description of some of the more popular peripheral devices.

Modems

The most common way to make your computer communicate with other computers is to use a modem. A modem connects your PC to normal phone lines and (if you're lucky) makes a connection with another computer that has a modem. If you want to do things like call computer bulletin board systems, connect to on-line services such as CompuServe or Prodigy, or send and receive faxes, you need a modem.

Originally modems were 300 baud, which means they sent and received about 300 characters per second. The next step up was 1,200 baud, and this was followed by 2,400 baud. Currently modems that operate at 9,600 or even 14,400 baud are common and reasonably priced.

Printers

Most computers have a printer attached. Go back to Chapter 10 for information on printers.

Scanners

Did you ever wonder how people get those fancy (and sometimes titillating) high-resolution pictures into a computer? The ones that look almost as good as photographs? Chances are they used a scanner. This peripheral device can convert an image on paper into a series of bits and bytes that can be displayed on your computer. Some scanners are even capable of reading text and dumping it into your word processor. These type of scanners are known as OCR, or optical character recognition.

Pointing devices

You may have found that moving the cursor around on your screen can take some time. The solution is to use a pointing device that's mapped to the screen. A mouse is a common example. There are lots of variations on mice — the most popular is a trackball, which is part of some keyboards.

Sound cards

In its unadulterated state, a computer sounds pretty shabby. Computer manufacturers used to think people were satisfied with a simple beep now and then when they made a mistake. Several years ago, game freaks discovered something called a sound card. A sound card, which is inserted into a slot on your motherboard, is capable of generating much better sound (assuming the software you use knows how to use it). You can hook a sound card to headphones or your home stereo system.

Sound cards have proliferated in the past year, and dozens are available. The sound quality ranges from acceptable to awesome (and you generally get what you pay for).

Storage

Besides standard magnetic disks, computers can store information on other types of media. Examples include tape, CD-ROM, and magneto-optical disks.

The disadvantage to tape is that it's not direct access. Just as you do with an audio cassette, you have to rewind or fast forward a tape to get to the information you need. Computer people don't like to wait, so tape is used mainly to make a backup copy of important information — something that you hope you'll never need to retrieve.

CD-ROM (for Compact Disc Read-Only Memory) is rapidly gaining popularity. This requires a special CD-ROM drive, and it uses CDs that look exactly like the audio CDs you use with your home stereo system. CD-ROMs can hold a massive amount of information — the equivalent of about 300,000 typewritten pages (three stories tall). Unlike disks, however, you cannot write information to them. Once you buy one, you cannot change anything in it. CD-ROM is also *much* slower than normal disks.

Magneto-optical (MO) drives are pretty rare, but I expect them to become more popular. They, like CD-ROMs, use optical technology but do so in conjunction with magnetic technology (hence, the name). The advantage is that the user (you) can read and write information on the removable MO cartridges. MO systems come in a variety of sizes, but the format that will probably prevail is 128M cartridges. Right now, MO drives are expensive, but prices are dropping fast.

Local area networks

Technically, a local area network (LAN) isn't a peripheral, but I couldn't think of anywhere else to discuss it. A LAN is a group of PCs all connected together. Since the PCs are connected by wires, they must all be in the same physical location (hence the term, *local area*).

A LAN has one computer devoted entirely to serving the others. This is known as the *server*. You can store a file on the server, and everyone else on the LAN can get to it. A LAN might also have a computer devoted entirely to printing (a print server). This lets everyone on the LAN share one or more printer. The print server takes care of the details and makes sure no one's print job screws up someone else's.

Things you can say about peripherals

- ✔ "Sure, 300 dpi might be good enough print resolution for most people, but I need 600. I just can't stand those jaggies."

- ✔ "Sound cards used to be used only for games. But now many companies routinely issue purchase orders for them. They think there's a valid business reason for these things."

- ✔ "Today my hard disk crashed when I threw my PC across the room. And I didn't have a backup. I hate when that happens."

- ✔ "If you're buying a new modem, you'd be foolish to get anything but a 14,400 V.32 bis with fax send-and-receive capability."

- ✔ "Which do you prefer, AOL, CIS, or BIX?"

- ✔ "Floppy disk backup? You gotta be kidding. Why not just pop for a 3 ½-inch MO drive and be done with it?"

- ✔ "Double-speed CD-ROM is the only way to go."

- ✔ "When your laser printer's toner cartridge starts to fade, take it out and rock it back and forth. You'll get about 100 more pages."

- ✔ "I spent several hours today trying to configure all my SCSI (pronounce this "skuzzy") devices to work together."

- ✔ "I was in the computer store today and actually overheard some guy asking for a math coprocessor for his 486 machine. Can you believe that?" (Chuckle scornfully.)

Software

Hardware and software go hand in hand. One without the other is completely useless. Your VCR is hardware, videotapes are software. Your CD player is hardware, your CDs are software. Your toaster is hardware, a loaf of bread is software. Get the picture?

The best way to approach software is to understand some of the basic categories. There are no official software categories. I just made these up.

Operating systems

This is basic software that's required for your computer to do anything at all. Without an operating system, you can't run other software. The most popular

The skinny on operating systems

Microsoft, with its MS-DOS, has always held the lion's share of the operating system market. There have been a few imitators — most notably, Digital Research's DR DOS — but the vast majority of PCs run MS-DOS as their operating system.

IBM is attempting to change this with its OS/2 operating system. Although a much more powerful operating system than MS-DOS, OS/2 suffers from the relatively poor reputation IBM has for software development. And Microsoft has an answer to this: Windows NT. Unlike the standard Windows, Windows NT is a complete 32-bit operating system. The ultimate winner in the operating system war remains to be seen (but the smart money is on Microsoft).

By the way, there never was an OS/1. Since IBM introduced its PS/2 computers long before its PS/1 models, perhaps we can look forward to OS/1 in a couple of years.

operating system is MS-DOS, usually known simply as DOS. DOS has gone through a number of versions. You probably use DOS 5 or DOS 6.

Although it's technically not an operating system, some people refer to Microsoft Windows as such. Actually, Windows runs on top of DOS and is better classified as an operating *environment*. However, Windows-NT is a full-blown operating system just like IBM's OS/2 (its main competitor).

Windows vs. non-Windows software

Today, software for PCs comes in two major flavors: software that runs under Microsoft Windows and software that doesn't. Fact is, the vast majority of new software is written for Windows.

So what is Windows? It's an operating environment that runs on top of DOS and provides a graphical user interface. So instead of seeing characters on the screen that are all the same size, Windows displays different fonts and pictures just like they will appear when printed.

Windows also lets you run more than one program at a time so that you can easily switch between a spreadsheet and your favorite game.

Why not use Windows? The main reason for not using Windows is that your computer is not powerful enough to run it. You need at least a 386 system with 2MB of RAM (preferably more). Take my word for it. If you continue to use computers, you'll eventually be using Windows.

Word processing

Most people who use computers are familiar with word processing. It lets your PC function as a super typewriter and lets you write anything from simple memos to massive books. Some popular word processors are Microsoft Word, WordPerfect, and Lotus Ami Pro.

Spreadsheets

If you're reading this book, I hope by now that you have at least some idea what a spreadsheet is. See Chapters 1 thorough 16 for more information. Besides Quattro Pro, popular spreadsheets include Lotus 1-2-3 and Microsoft Excel.

Database

If you have a bunch or organized information that you need to store, update, and/or refer to frequently, chances are you'll keep this information in a database. Database software can deal with huge amounts of data and let you quickly find what you're looking for. Popular database programs include Borland's dBASE, Borland's Paradox, and Microsoft's Access.

Accounting

Although many people use spreadsheets for financial applications, there's another class of software that's much more comprehensive and deals with all aspects of accounting. This software comes in versions for business accounting and home accounting. Examples of home accounting software include Microsoft Money, Managing Your Money, Quicken, and several other packages designed primarily for preparing your income tax returns.

Communications

This class of software requires a modem. It lets you dial up other computers and send information back and forth. If you have the appropriate modem, you can also get software that lets you send and receive faxes.

Desktop publishing

Nowadays, most newsletters, magazines, and books are put together using desktop publishing software. This software is similar to word processing, but it gives you much better control over the layout of your work. Examples include Aldus PageMaker, Ventura Publisher, and QuarkXpress.

Graphics

This is a very broad category. It includes programs that let you display images, draw images, modify images, convert images to and from different file formats, and prepare presentations. Examples include Harvard Graphics, Lotus Freelance Plus, CorelDRAW!, Micrografx Designer, and Microsoft PowerPoint.

CAD

This class of software is used by architects, designers, and others who build and create things. CAD stands for *computer-aided design*. This software has truly changed the way these people work.

Utilities

Utility software is another broad category. These programs let you work with the details of your computer to learn about them, extend the operating system to do things that are normally not possible, and fix problems that come up. Examples of comprehensive utility packages include Norton Utilities and PC Tools. There are thousands of other products that qualify as utilities.

Share and share alike

A lot of people write software, and many of these do it just for the fun of it. Quite a few people write some pretty good programs but have neither the time nor inclination to market them. Often, they designate their creations as *shareware*. You are free to use the shareware, but many authors request that you send some money to them if you use their program a lot.

So where do you get this stuff? Shareware is most often distributed via bulletin boards or on-line services — but several vendors sell it for very nominal charges. You can also get CD-ROMs filled with thousands of shareware and public domain programs. It's a great way to build up your software library. And every once in a while you'll find a gem hidden among the mediocrity.

Education

People often rationalize buying a home computer because of educational software available for the kids. True, you'll find lots of education software — some great, some horrible — for kids of all ages.

CD-ROM is shaping up to be important to educational software. For example, a single CD can hold an entire set of encyclopedias — including the pictures.

Games and recreation

I don't know of a single computer user who doesn't have at least a few games tucked away on his hard drive. And I know of some users who have nothing *but* games. Again, there are thousands of games to choose from — some great, some boring and buggy.

You can choose from hundreds of programs that address your hobby or special interest. For example, there are programs that contain a database of thousands of movies, so you can search by actor, director, year, rating, and so on. And there is music software — programs that let you compose music and control synthesizers through MIDI (a way to connect musical instruments to your computer). The list goes on and on.

Integrated software

Some software attempts to be a jack-of-all-trades and provides lots of different functions in one package. For example, you might have a spreadsheet, word processor, database, and communications package all in one. These integrated software packages are often installed on a computer when you buy it. Examples include Microsoft Works and Lotus Works.

Miscellaneous

There are lots of other software products available that don't fit into any of the categories. For example, your computer might have software that displays a menu of programs that you can run. Many people use project management software that helps them keep track of all the details of complex projects such as building a house.

Things you can say about software

- ✔ "Mark my word. CD-ROM is going to be the standard medium for software distribution within a few years."

- ✔ "Seems like Lotus is finally getting its act together. They realized that all spreadsheet users don't like the thought of using software that's based on 10-year old technology."

- ✔ "Of course, object-oriented programming is the only way to go."

- ✔ If you're into developing spreadsheet apps, Quattro Pro for Windows is the way to go. It's UI Builder is hot, and nothing else even comes close."

- ✔ "Boy, I remember the days when software came on a single floppy disk."

- ✔ "About the only software that's copy-protected these days is games."

- ✔ "Most of the popular music being recorded today uses MIDI and Macintosh computers."

- ✔ "This a.m. I had to convert a dozen PCXs, BMPs, and GIFs into TIFs for my DTP package to work OK. And I had to do it ASAP."

- ✔ "One of the biggest problems is that software companies make it easy to install their hardware, but hardly any of them provide a way to *uninstall* it."

- ✔ "If you're serious about desktop publishing, you'd better get yourself a Mac. That's what most of the publishing houses and printers use."

- ✔ "The OLE implementation in Windows 3.1 is okay, but OLE 2.0 is far superior." (Pronounce OLE as in Frito Lay, but without the "frit" part.)

- ✔ "You program in BASIC? Excuse me, I think I noticed a C programmer over there."

- ✔ "You're running OS/2? You have my deepest sympathy."

- ✔ "Sure, Windows 3.1 doesn't generate UAEs anymore. They just call it General Protection Failures."

The Computer Industry

The computer industry is made up of thousands of companies who are involved in hardware, software, repair, consulting, training, trade shows, publishing, and so on. Like all industries, it can be kind of interesting if you follow along what's happening by reading the industry rags. There are always lawsuits going on, executives are constantly getting fired or quitting, companies announce products years before they are finished, and lots of people try to make sense of it all — or simply sit back and be amused.

Microsoft

This is the biggie. They make MS-DOS, Windows, Excel, Word for Windows, and lots of other software that's very popular. Some people think Microsoft has an unfair advantage since it created DOS and Windows — which everyone needs to use to develop new software. As you might expect, Microsoft gets sued quite frequently. Microsoft's CEO, Bill Gates, is the richest man in the U.S.

IBM

If you've never heard of IBM, you probably just arrived from the planet Zordox. IBM has always been known as *the* computer company. The company started out by making big, expensive mainframes and then developed the IBM PC just for the heck of it. Other companies soon copied IBM's PC. And in practically every case, the clones are much cheaper than real IBMs. As I write this, IBM recently posted an annual loss that exceeds the GNP of many small countries and (for the first time in 50 years) was forced to lay off workers.

Lotus Development

Lotus started out by creating 1-2-3. Although this wasn't the first spreadsheet for PCs, it was great in its time. Lotus made 1-2-3 one of the most successful software products ever. It's no longer the best, but it still sells like crazy. Lotus tends to get involved in lots of lawsuits.

Borland International

Borland makes Quattro Pro, plus several programming languages and database products. The company is one of the industry's favorite success stories. Borland started with virtually nothing and is now one of the top software companies in the world.

WordPerfect Corporation

This started out as a small family-owned business that made a pretty spiffy word processor. The word processor caught on like wildfire, and the company grew at a rapid clip. There's an interesting parallel with Lotus here. WordPerfect, like Lotus, continue to have the top selling product in their class.

Intel

Intel is the company that makes most of the CPUs used in PCs. Consequently, Intel is very successful. Several other companies are trying to get a piece of the action, so lawsuits are pretty common here, too.

Things you can say about the industry

- "Bill Gates has a net worth equivalent to half a million dollars for every day he's been alive."

- "In the final analysis, IBM's MCA bus simply means more expensive add-in cards for end users — assuming they can even find the cards they need."

- "Microsoft may be driving lots of vendors out of business with their pricing strategy, but they sure make some good products."

- "I won't even consider installing OS/2 until IBM puts it on a CD-ROM. I have no interest in shuffling 37 floppies in and out."

- "Advertising toll-free tech support is great. Even if you can get through without a busy signal, have a good book ready to pass the time while you listen to Muzak on hold."

- "Personally, I wouldn't be caught dead at Comdex. It's a zoo."

Now What?

The information in this appendix was presented somewhat tongue-in-cheek, but it is, by and large, true and reasonably accurate.

If you're not the type who goes through life faking it and you really want to learn more about computers, there are plenty of more comprehensive resources. IDG Books has several titles that deal with computers in general terms, and *PC World* is a good source for keeping up with the latest development and getting lots of tips.

If you have a modem, I strongly suggest you join one of the on-line services such as America OnLine, CompuServe, or Prodigy, which are easy to use and have something that will appeal to everyone.

But the best advice is to simply hang in there and don't be afraid to experiment. Everyone makes mistakes, and computers make it all that much easier to make (and correct) mistakes. So if you sometimes feel like you don't know what you're doing, remember that you have plenty of company.

Index

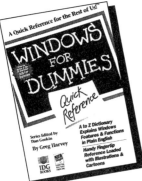

Order Form

Order Center: (800) 762-2974 (8 a.m.-5 p.m., PST, weekdays) or (415) 312-0650

For Fastest Service: Photocopy This Order Form and FAX it to :. (415) 358-1260

Quantity	ISBN	Title	Price	Total

Shipping & Handling Charges

Subtotal	U.S.	Canada & International	International Air Mail
Up to $20.00	Add $3.00	Add $4.00	Add $10.00
$20.01-40.00	$4.00	$5.00	$20.00
$40.01-60.00	$5.00	$6.00	$25.00
$60.01-80.00	$6.00	$8.00	$35.00
Over $80.00	$7.00	$10.00	$50.00

In U.S. and Canada, shipping is UPS ground or equivalent.
For Rush shipping call (800) 762-2974.

Subtotal _____

CA residents add
applicable sales tax _____

IN residents add
5% sales tax _____

Canadian residents
add 7% GST tax _____

Shipping _____

TOTAL _____

Ship to:

Name _____

Company _____

Address _____

City/State/Zip _____

Daytime Phone _____

Payment: ❏ Check to IDG Books (US Funds Only) ❏ Visa ❏ MasterCard ❏ American Express

Card # _____ Exp. _____ Signature _____

Please send this order form to: IDG Books, 155 Bovet Road, Suite 310, San Mateo, CA 94402.
Allow up to 3 weeks for delivery. Thank you!

| BOBFD |

IDG BOOKS WORLDWIDE REGISTRATION CARD

RETURN THIS REGISTRATION CARD FOR FREE CATALOG

Title of this book: Quattro Pro For Dos For Dummies

My overall rating of this book: ❑ Very good [1] ❑ Good [2] ❑ Satisfactory [3] ❑ Fair [4] ❑ Poor [5]

How I first heard about this book:

❑ Found in bookstore; name: [6]

❑ Advertisement: [8]

❑ Word of mouth; heard about book from friend, co-worker, etc.: [10]

❑ Book review: [7]

❑ Catalog: [9]

❑ Other: [11]

What I liked most about this book:

What I would change, add, delete, etc., in future editions of this book:

Other comments:

Number of computer books I purchase in a year: ❑ 1 [12] ❑ 2-5 [13] ❑ 6-10 [14] ❑ More than 10 [15]

I would characterize my computer skills as: ❑ Beginner [16] ❑ Intermediate [17] ❑ Advanced [18] ❑ Professional [19]

I use ❑ DOS [20] ❑ Windows [21] ❑ OS/2 [22] ❑ Unix [23] ❑ Macintosh [24] ❑ Other: [25]_____

(please specify)

I would be interested in new books on the following subjects:

(please check all that apply, and use the spaces provided to identify specific software)

❑ Word processing: [26]

❑ Data bases: [28]

❑ File Utilities: [30]

❑ Networking: [32]

❑ Other: [34]

❑ Spreadsheets: [27]

❑ Desktop publishing: [29]

❑ Money management: [31]

❑ Programming languages: [33]

I use a PC at (please check all that apply): ❑ home [35] ❑ work [36] ❑ school [37] ❑ other: [38] _____

The disks I prefer to use are ❑ 5.25 [39] ❑ 3.5 [40] ❑ other: [41]_____

I have a CD ROM: ❑ yes [42] ❑ no [43]

I plan to buy or upgrade computer hardware this year: ❑ yes [44] ❑ no [45]

I plan to buy or upgrade computer software this year: ❑ yes [46] ❑ no [47]

Name: _____ Business title: [48] _____ Type of Business: [49]

Address (❑ home [50] ❑ work [51] /Company name: _____)

Street/Suite#

City [52] /State [53] /Zipcode [54]: _____ Country [55]

❑ **I liked this book!** You may quote me by name in future IDG Books Worldwide promotional materials.

My daytime phone number is _____

IDG BOOKS

THE WORLD OF COMPUTER KNOWLEDGE